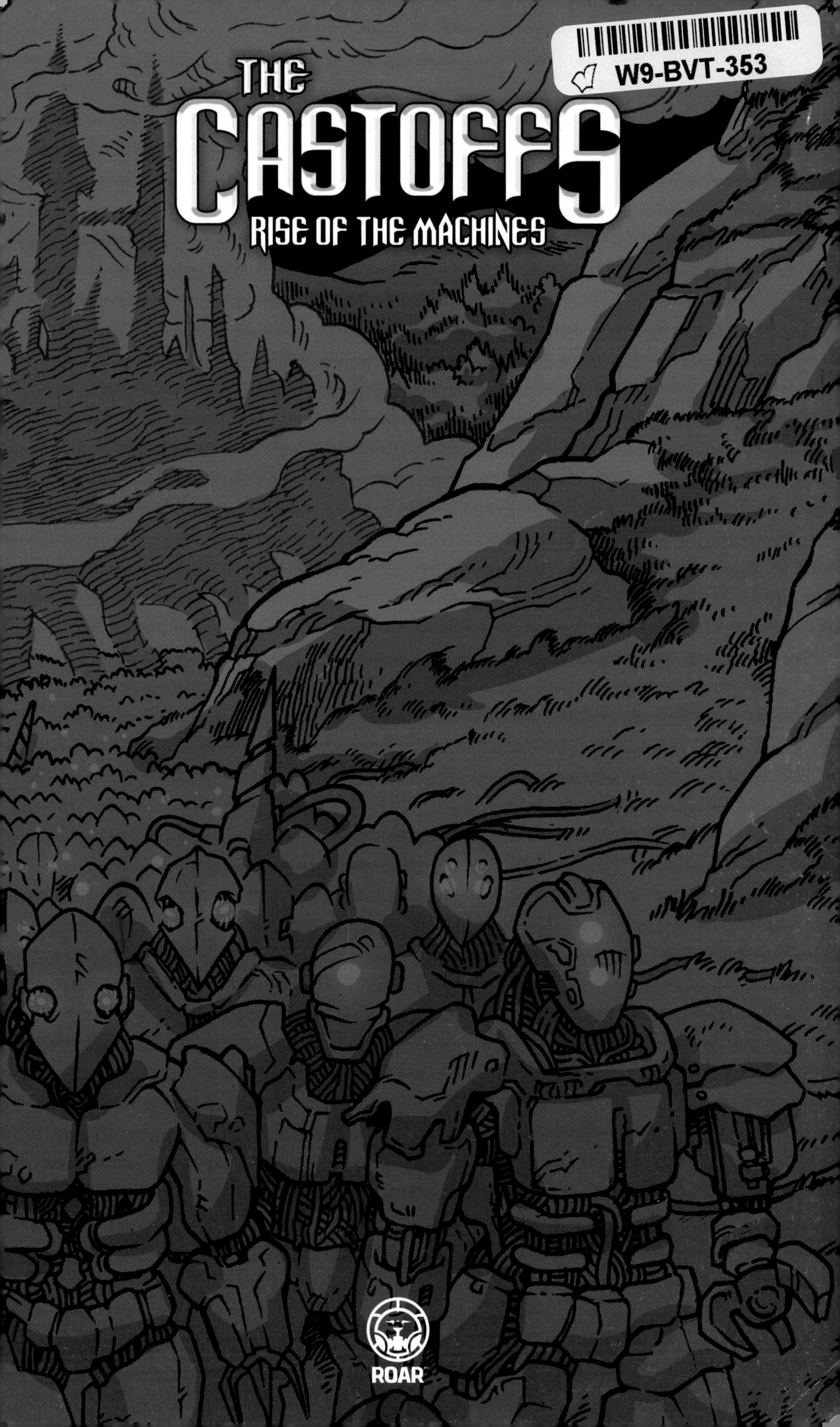
THE
CASTOFFS
RISE OF THE MACHINES
ROAR

THE CASTOFFS

VOLUME 3

RISE OF THE MACHINES

MK REED & BRIAN "SMITTY" SMITH *WRITERS*

WYETH YATES *ARTIST*

KENDRA WELLS *COLORIST*

HAZEL NEWLEVANT
EDITOR

AW'S DC HOPKINS
LETTERER

GRACE BORNHOFT
ASSISTANT EDITOR

ANDWORLD DESIGN
DESIGNER

The Castoffs Vol. 3, published 2018, by The Lion Forge, LLC. Copyright 2017 The Lion Forge, LLC. Portions of this book were previously published in The Castoffs, Vol. 3, Issues 10-14 copyright 2018 The Lion Forge, LLC. All Rights Reserved. ROAR™, LION FORGE™, and the associated distinctive designs, as well as all characters featured in this book and the distinctive names and likenesses thereof, and all related indicia, are trademarks of The Lion Forge, LLC. No similarity between any of the names, characters, persons, and/or institutions in this issue with those of any living or dead person or institution is intended and any such similarity which may exist is purely coincidental. Printed in Korea.

Library of Congress Number: 2017953492
ISBN: 978-1-941302-73-6
10 9 8 7 6 5 4 3 2 1

ROAR™

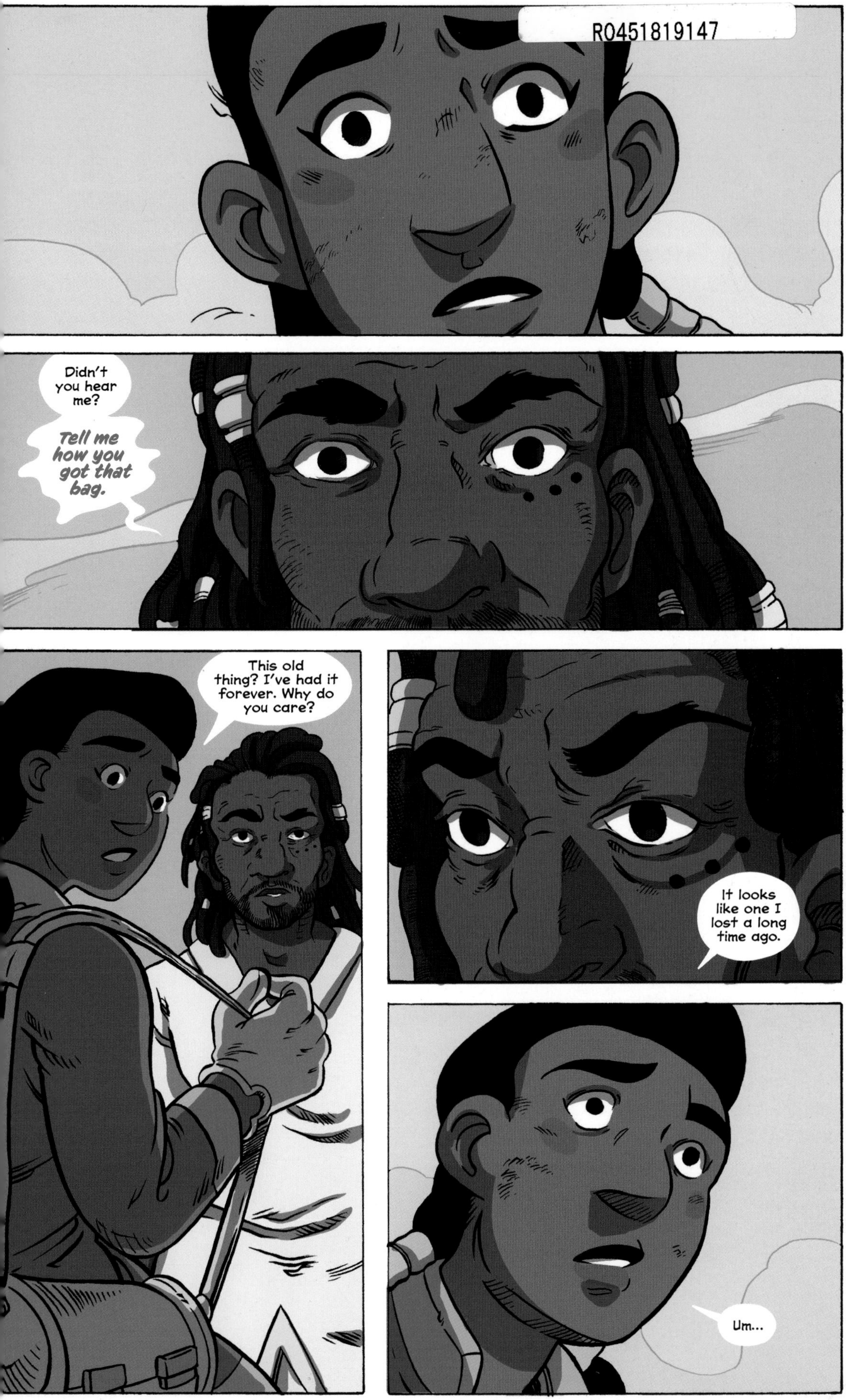

Didn't you hear me?
Tell me how you got that bag.
This old thing? I've had it forever. Why do you care?
It looks like one I lost a long time ago.
Um...

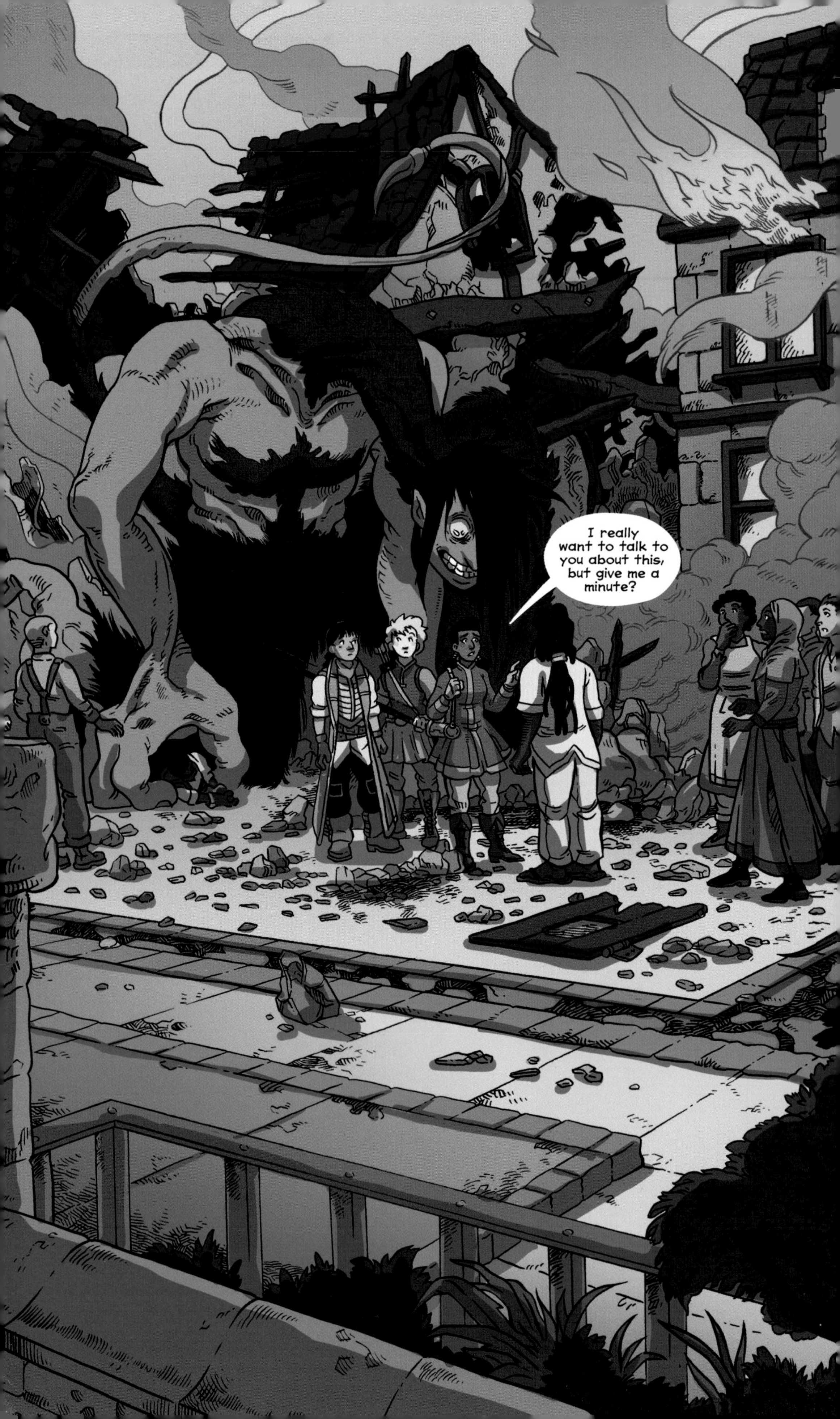
I really want to talk to you about this, but give me a minute?

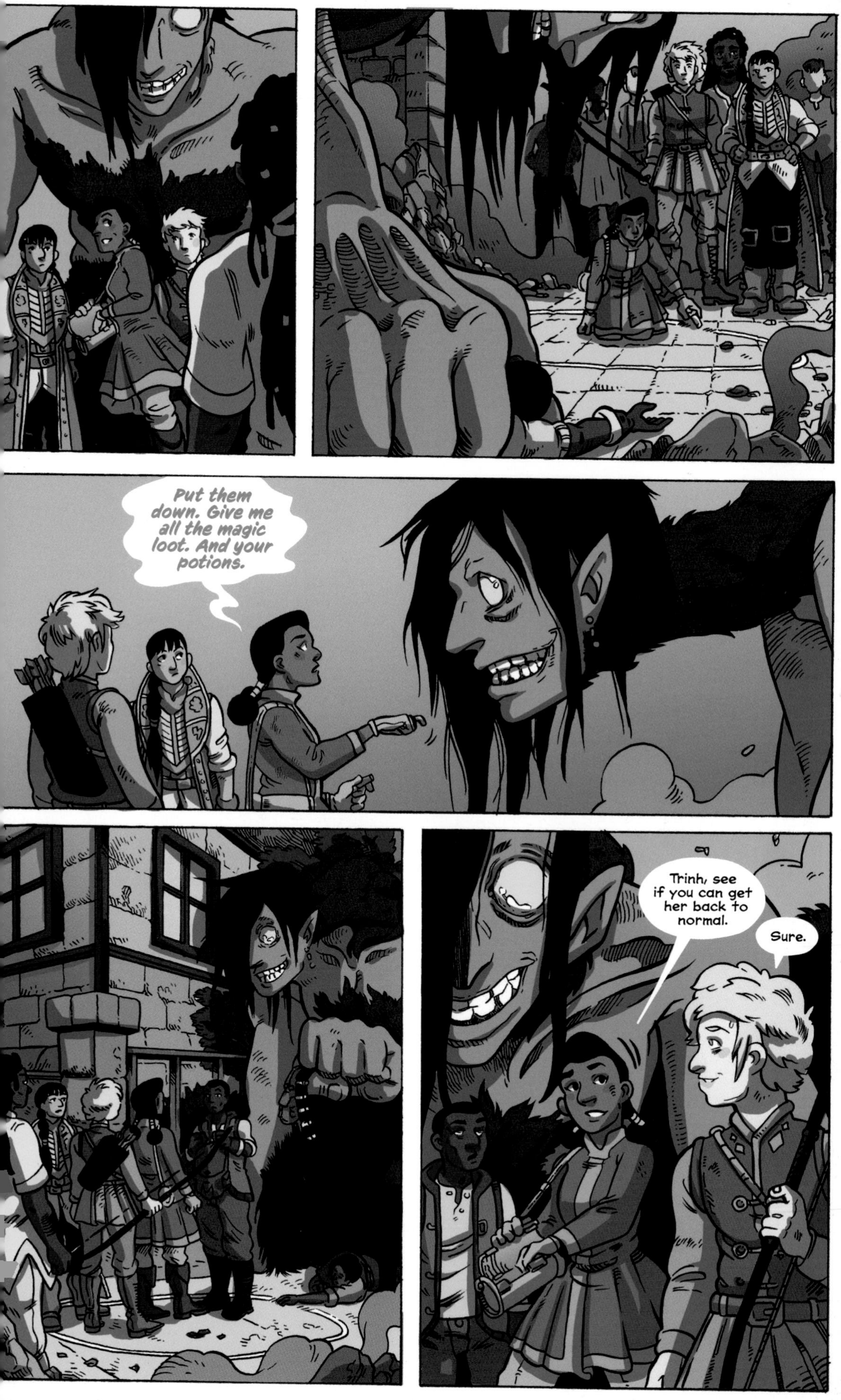
Put them down. Give me all the magic loot. And your potions.
Trinh, see if you can get her back to normal.
Sure.

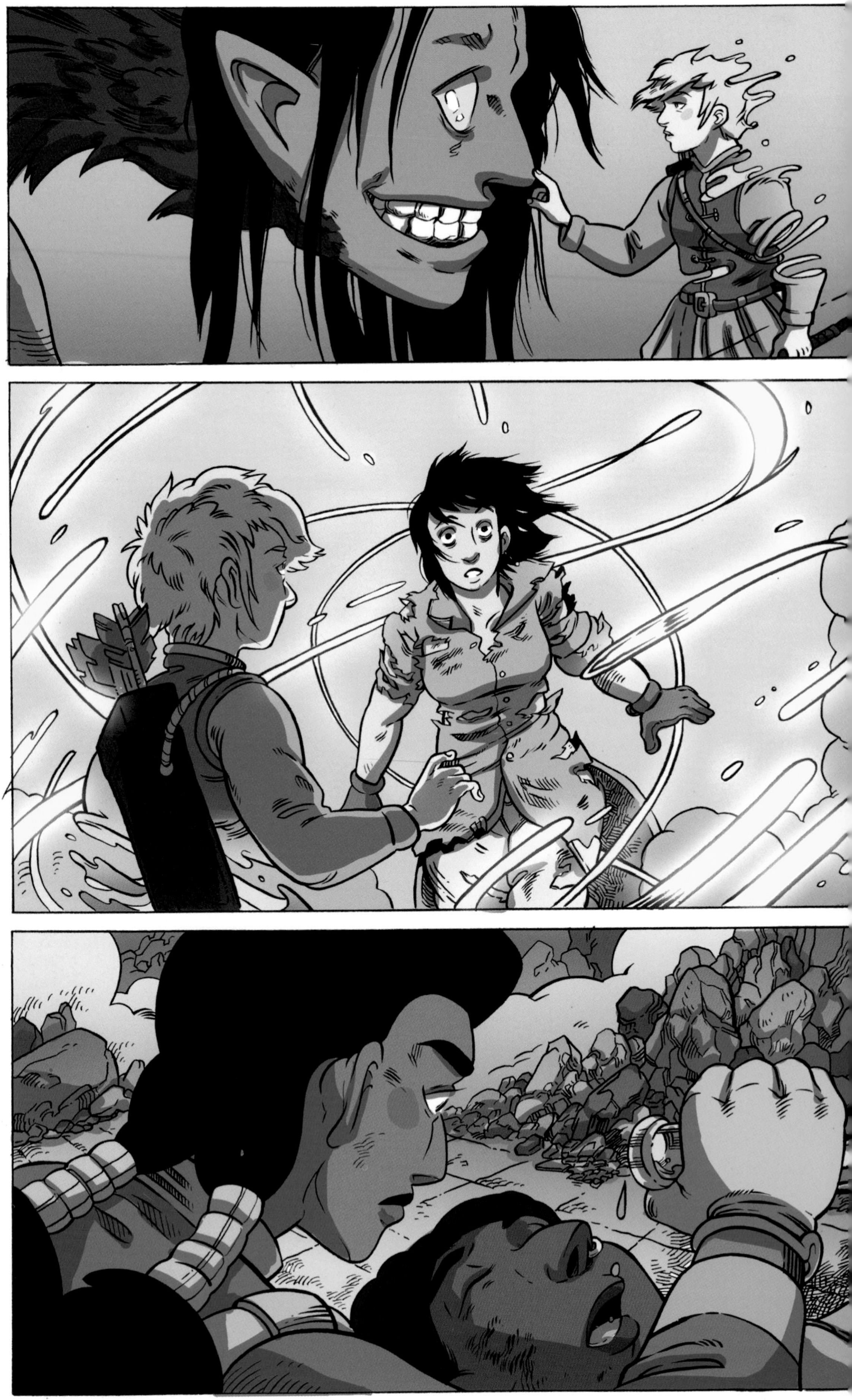

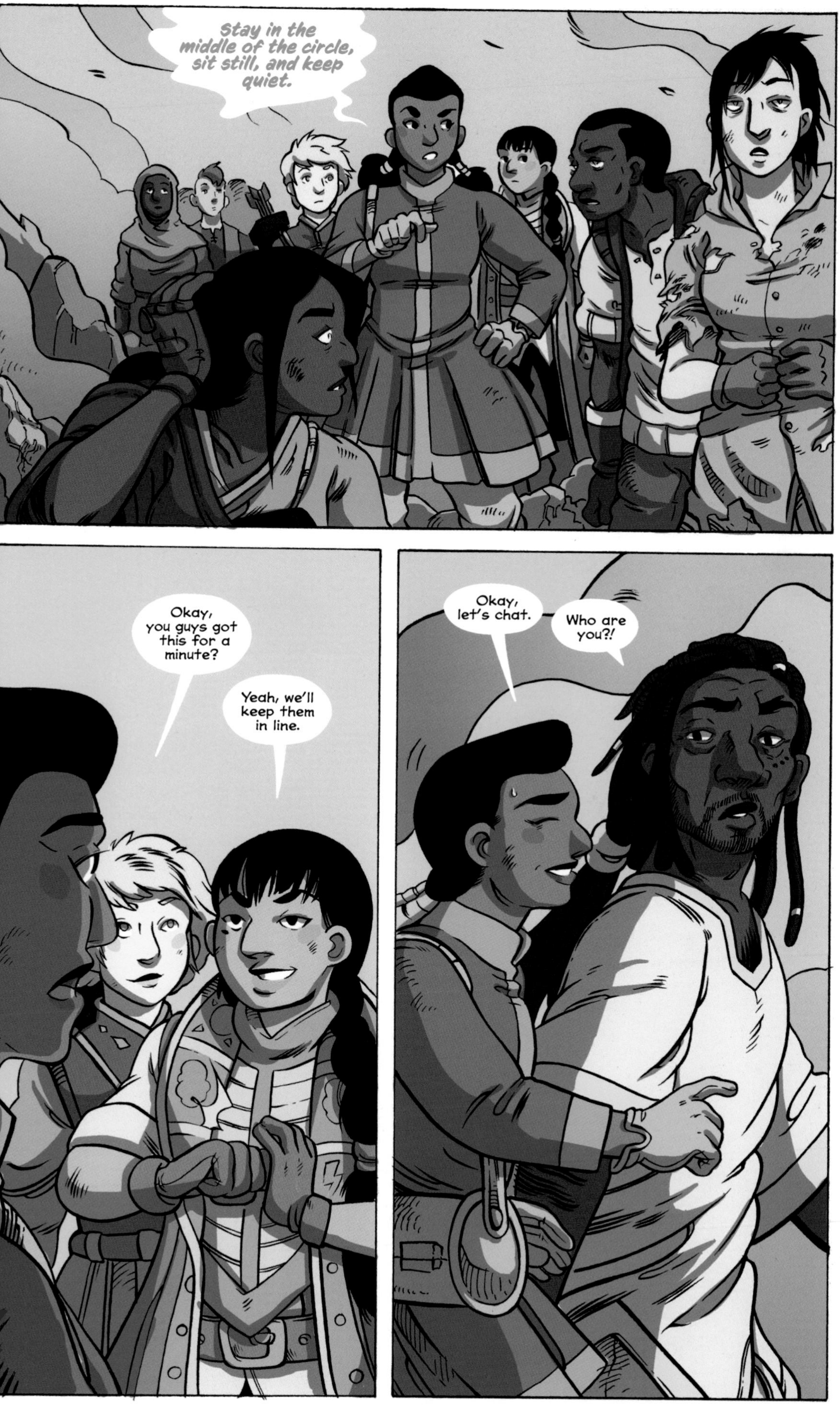
Stay in the middle of the circle, sit still, and keep quiet.
Okay, you guys got this for a minute?
Yeah, we'll keep them in line.
Okay, let's chat.
Who are you?!

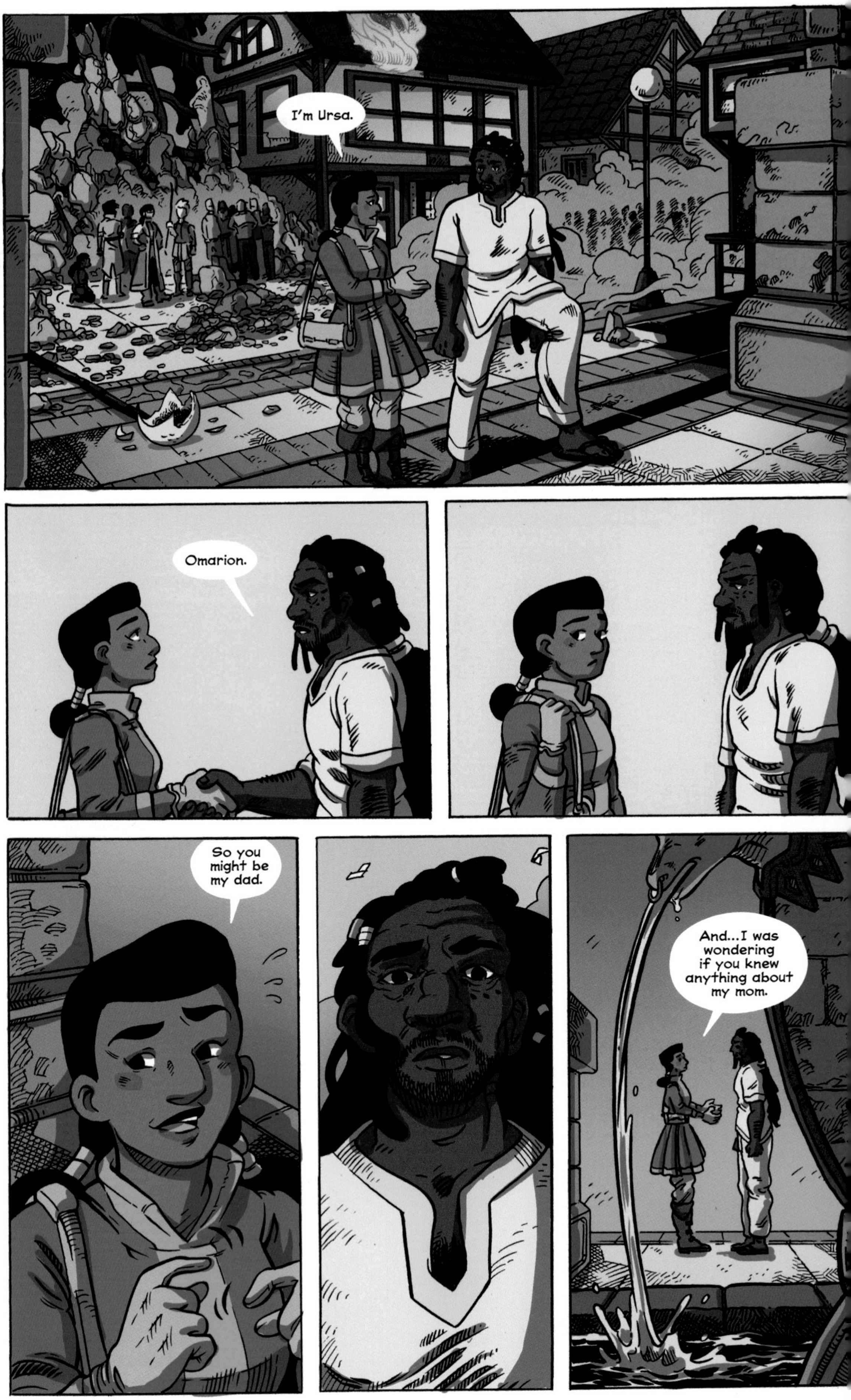
I'm Ursa.
Omarion.
So you might be my dad.
And...I was wondering if you knew anything about my mom.

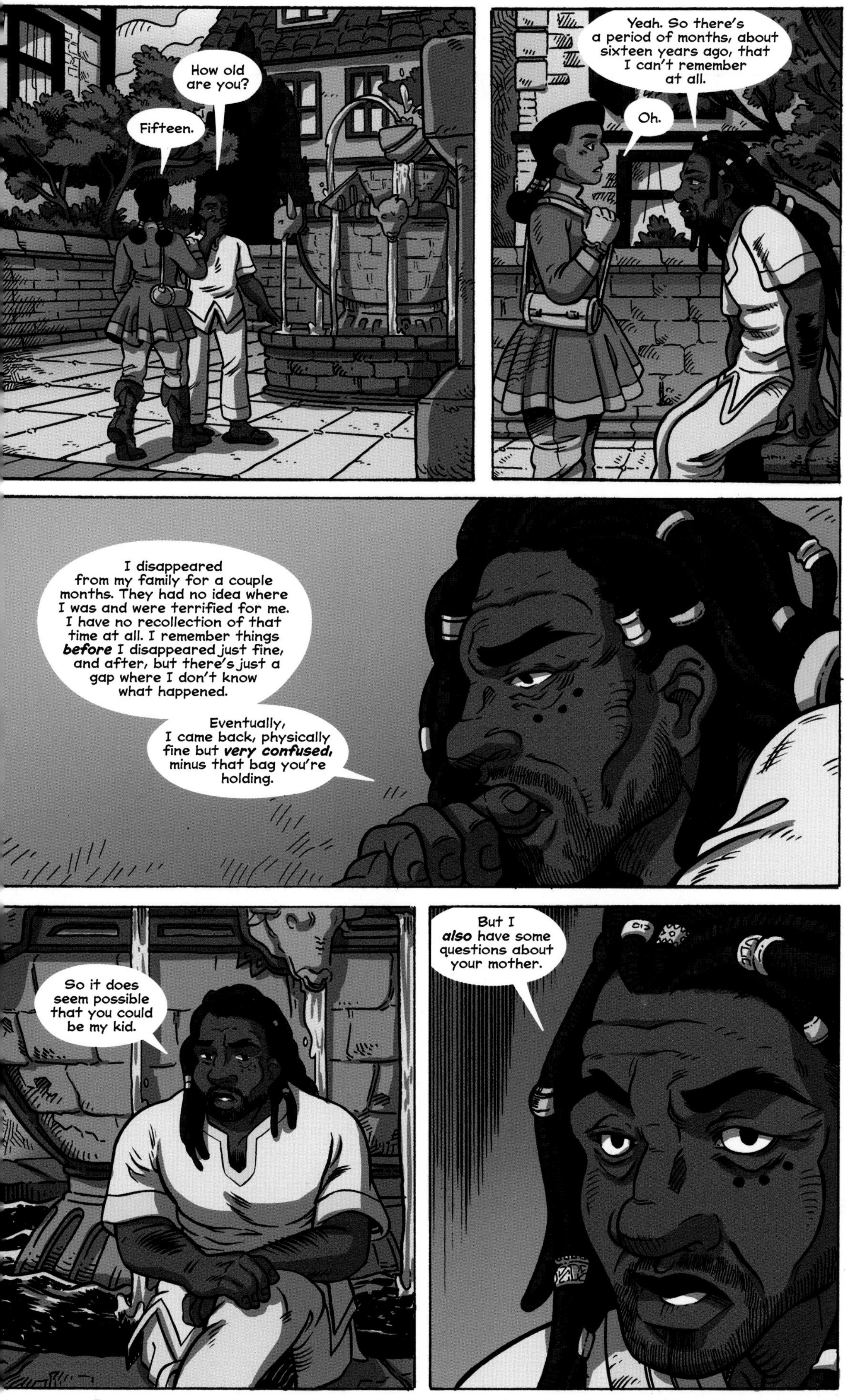
How old are you?
Fifteen.
Yeah. So there's a period of months, about sixteen years ago, that I can't remember at all.
Oh.
I disappeared from my family for a couple months. They had no idea where I was and were terrified for me. I have no recollection of that time at all. I remember things ***before*** I disappeared just fine, and after, but there's just a gap where I don't know what happened.
Eventually, I came back, physically fine but ***very confused,*** minus that bag you're holding.
So it does seem possible that you could be my kid.
But I ***also*** have some questions about your mother.

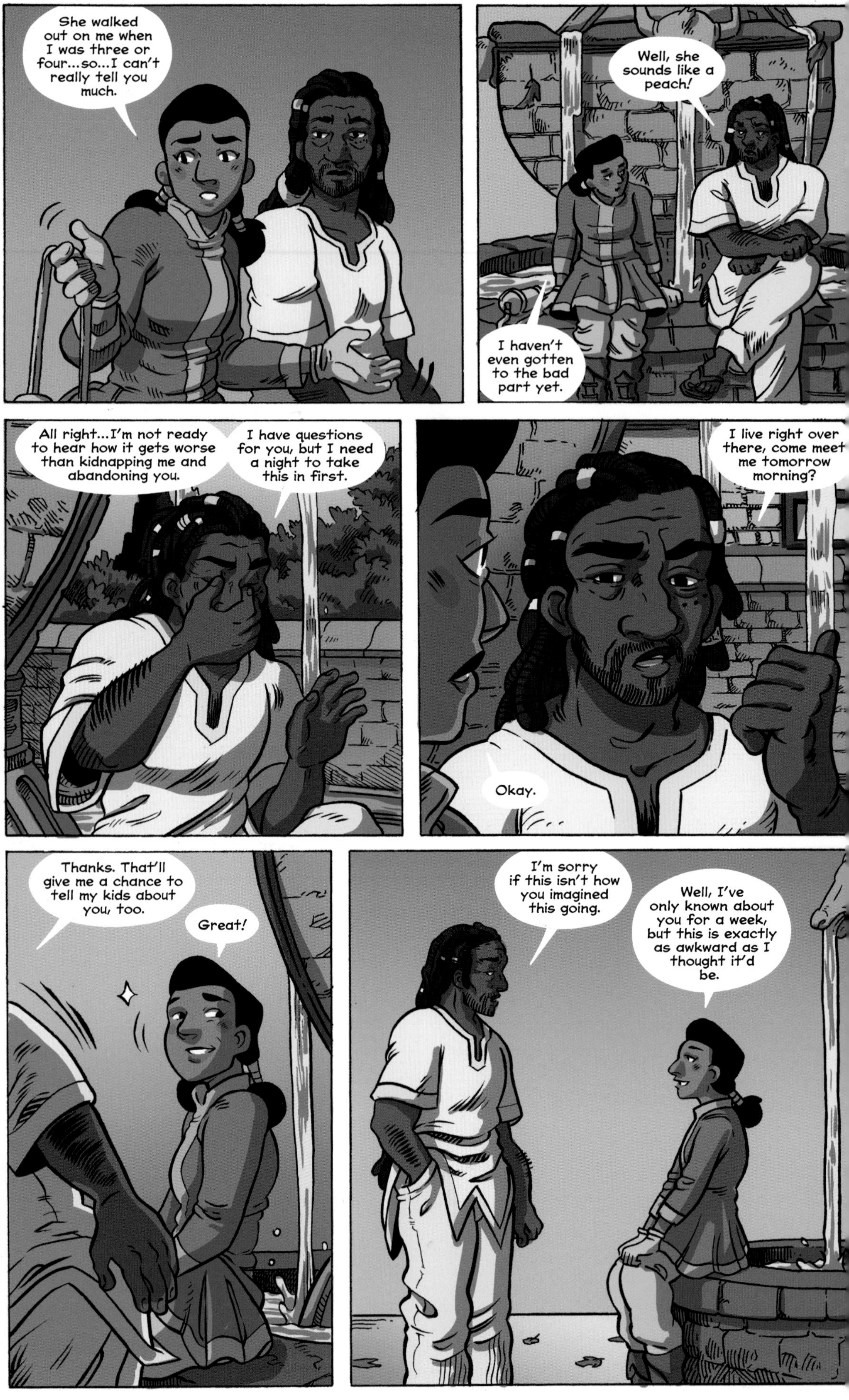

She walked out on me when I was three or four...so...I can't really tell you much.
Well, she sounds like a peach!
I haven't even gotten to the bad part yet.
All right...I'm not ready to hear how it gets worse than kidnapping me and abandoning you.
I have questions for you, but I need a night to take this in first.
I live right over there, come meet me tomorrow morning?
Okay.
Thanks. That'll give me a chance to tell my kids about you, too.
Great!
I'm sorry if this isn't how you imagined this going.
Well, I've only known about you for a week, but this is exactly as awkward as I thought it'd be.

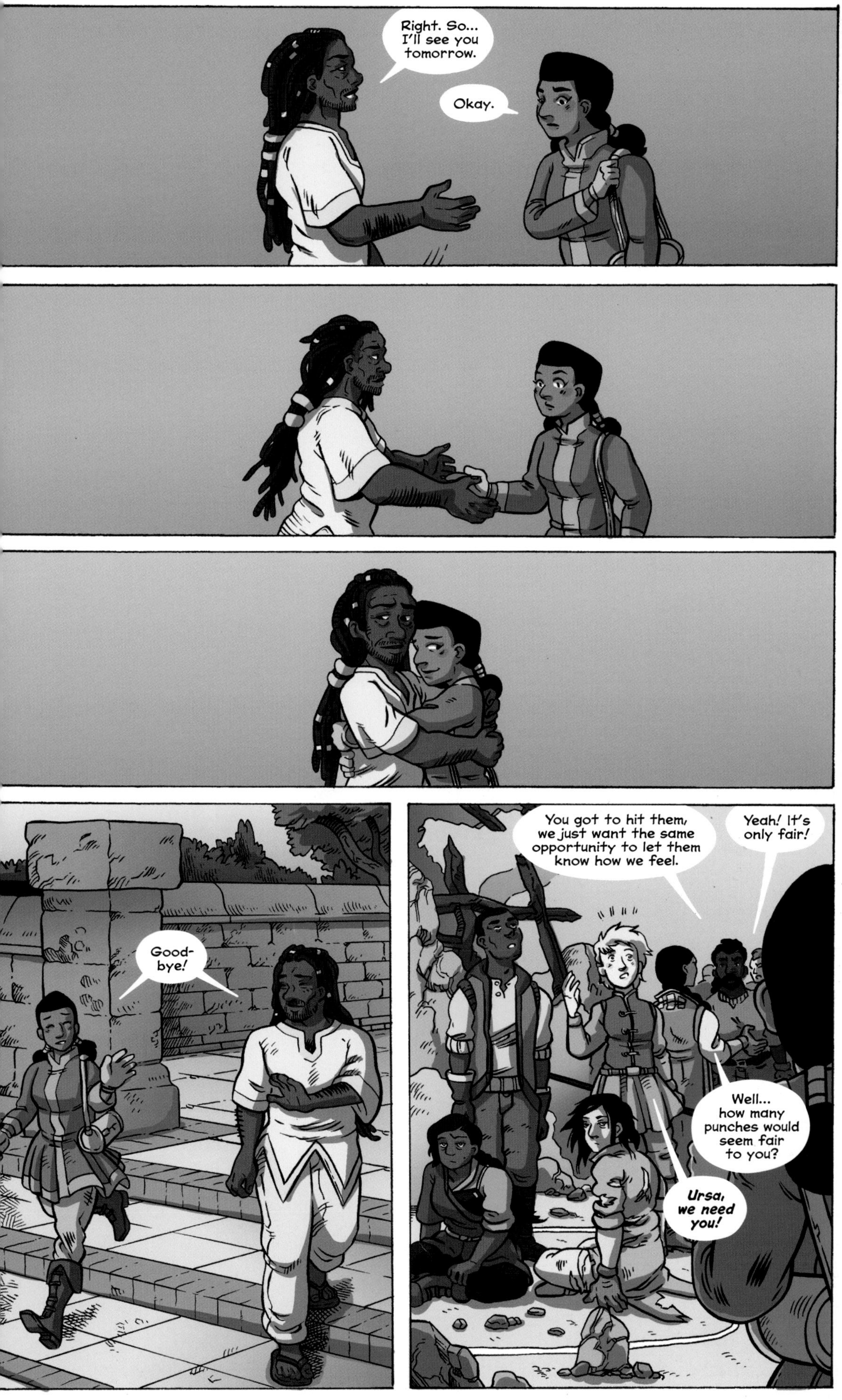
Right. So... I'll see you tomorrow.
Okay.
Good-bye!
You got to hit them, we just want the same opportunity to let them know how we feel.
Yeah! It's only fair!
Well... how many punches would seem fair to you?
Ursa, we need you!

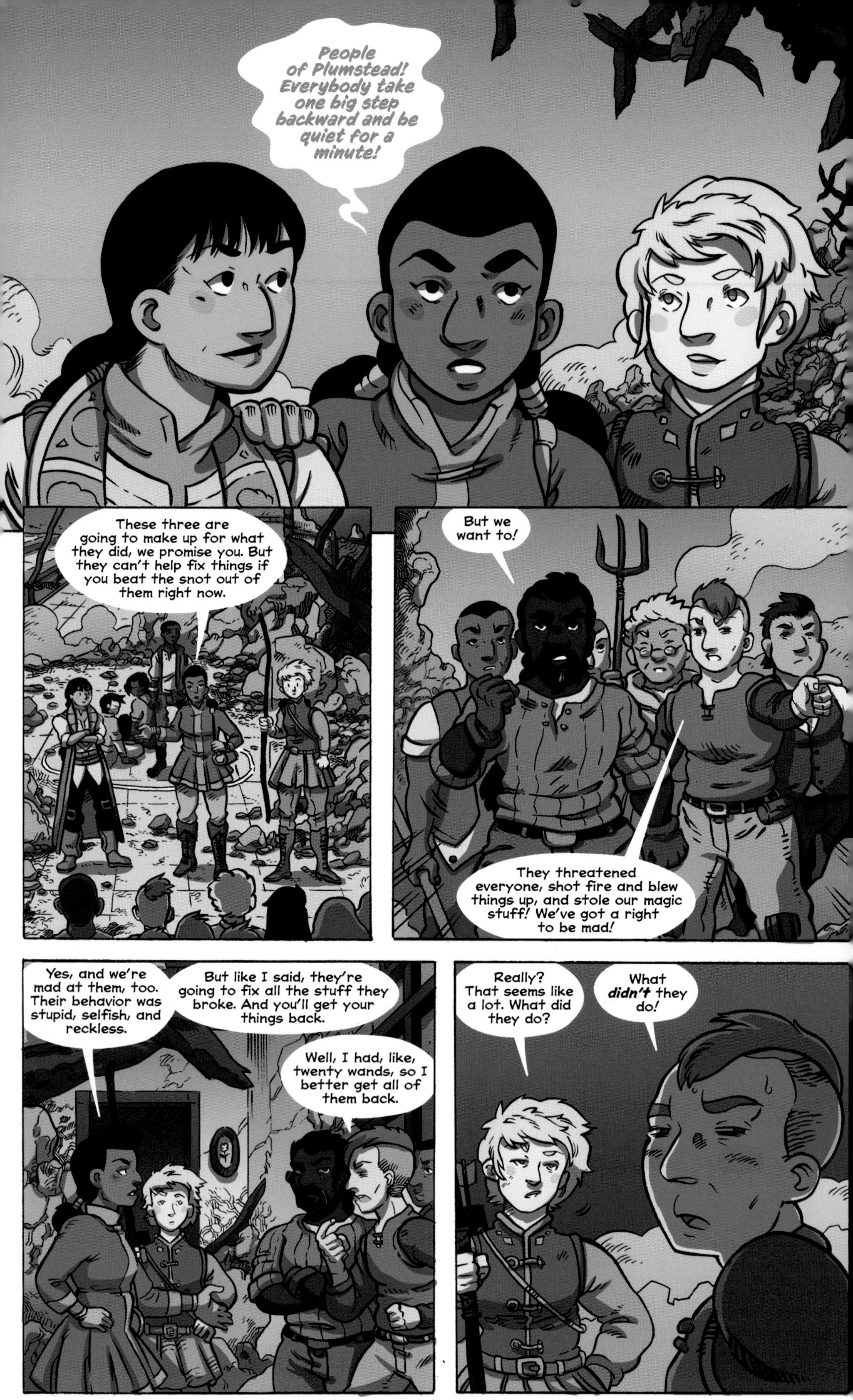
People of Plumstead! Everybody take one big step backward and be quiet for a minute!
These three are going to make up for what they did, we promise you. But they can't help fix things if you beat the snot out of them right now.
But we want to!
They threatened everyone, shot fire and blew things up, and stole our magic stuff! We've got a right to be mad!
Yes, and we're mad at them, too. Their behavior was stupid, selfish, and reckless.
But like I said, they're going to fix all the stuff they broke. And you'll get your things back.
Well, I had, like, twenty wands, so I better get all of them back.
Really? That seems like a lot. What did they do?
What *didn't* they do!

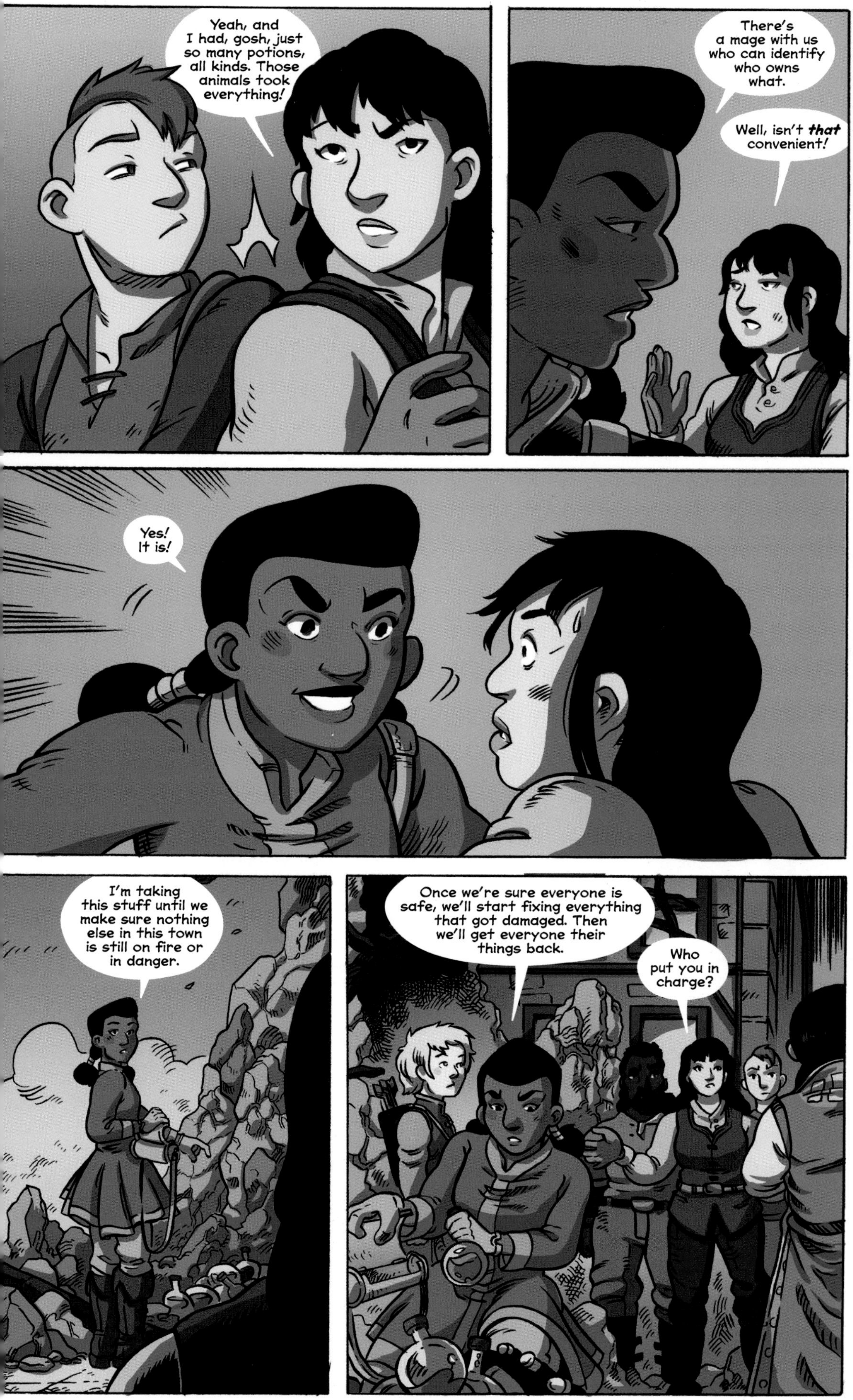
Yeah, and I had, gosh, just so many potions, all kinds. Those animals took everything!
There's a mage with us who can identify who owns what.
Well, isn't *that* convenient!
Yes! It is!
I'm taking this stuff until we make sure nothing else in this town is still on fire or in danger.
Once we're sure everyone is safe, we'll start fixing everything that got damaged. Then we'll get everyone their things back.
Who put you in charge?

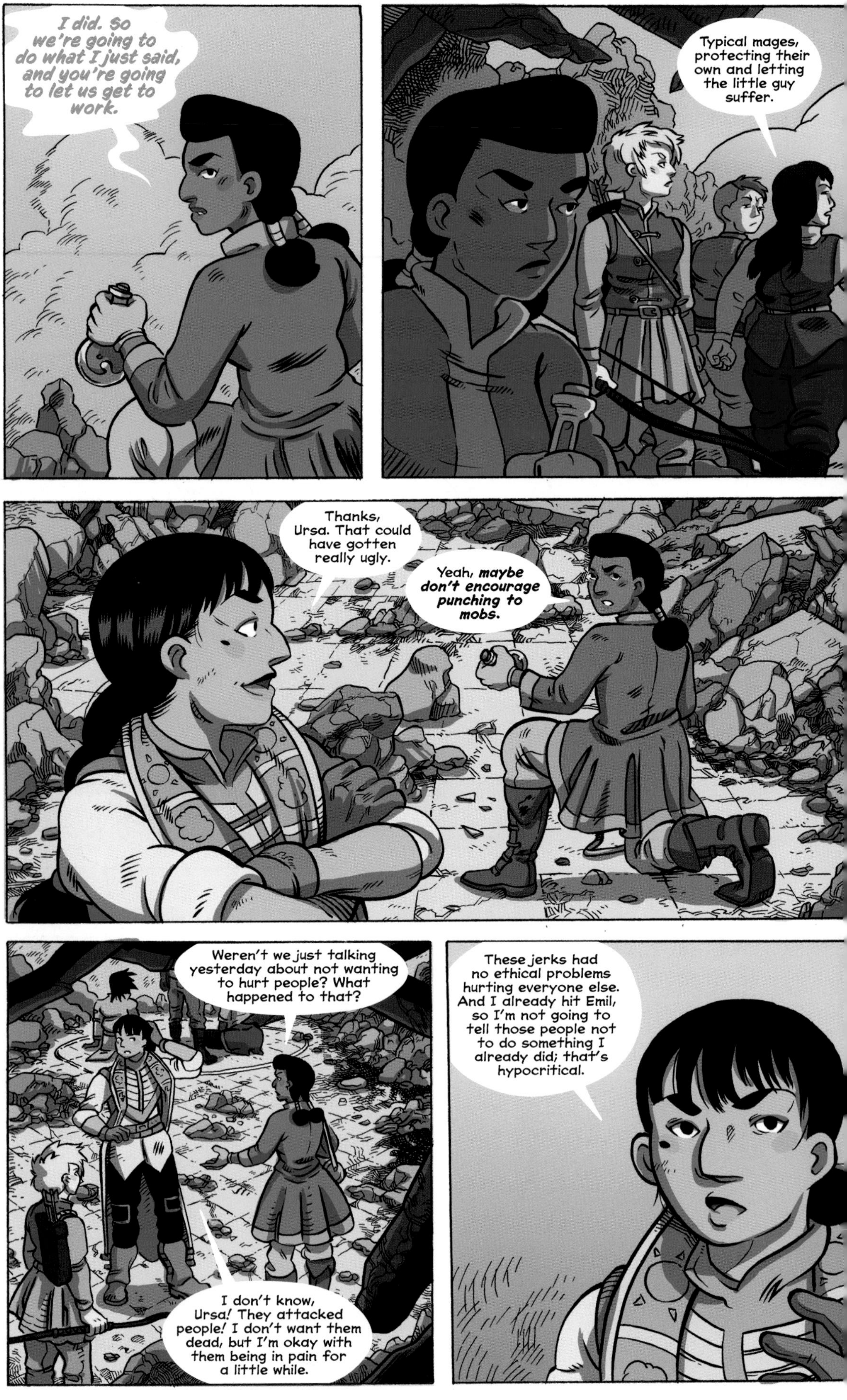
I did. So we're going to do what I just said, and you're going to let us get to work.
Typical mages, protecting their own and letting the little guy suffer.
Thanks, Ursa. That could have gotten really ugly.
Yeah, *maybe don't encourage punching to mobs.*
Weren't we just talking yesterday about not wanting to hurt people? What happened to that?
I don't know, Ursa! They attacked people! I don't want them dead, but I'm okay with them being in pain for a little while.
These jerks had no ethical problems hurting everyone else. And I already hit Emil, so I'm not going to tell those people not to do something I already did; that's hypocritical.

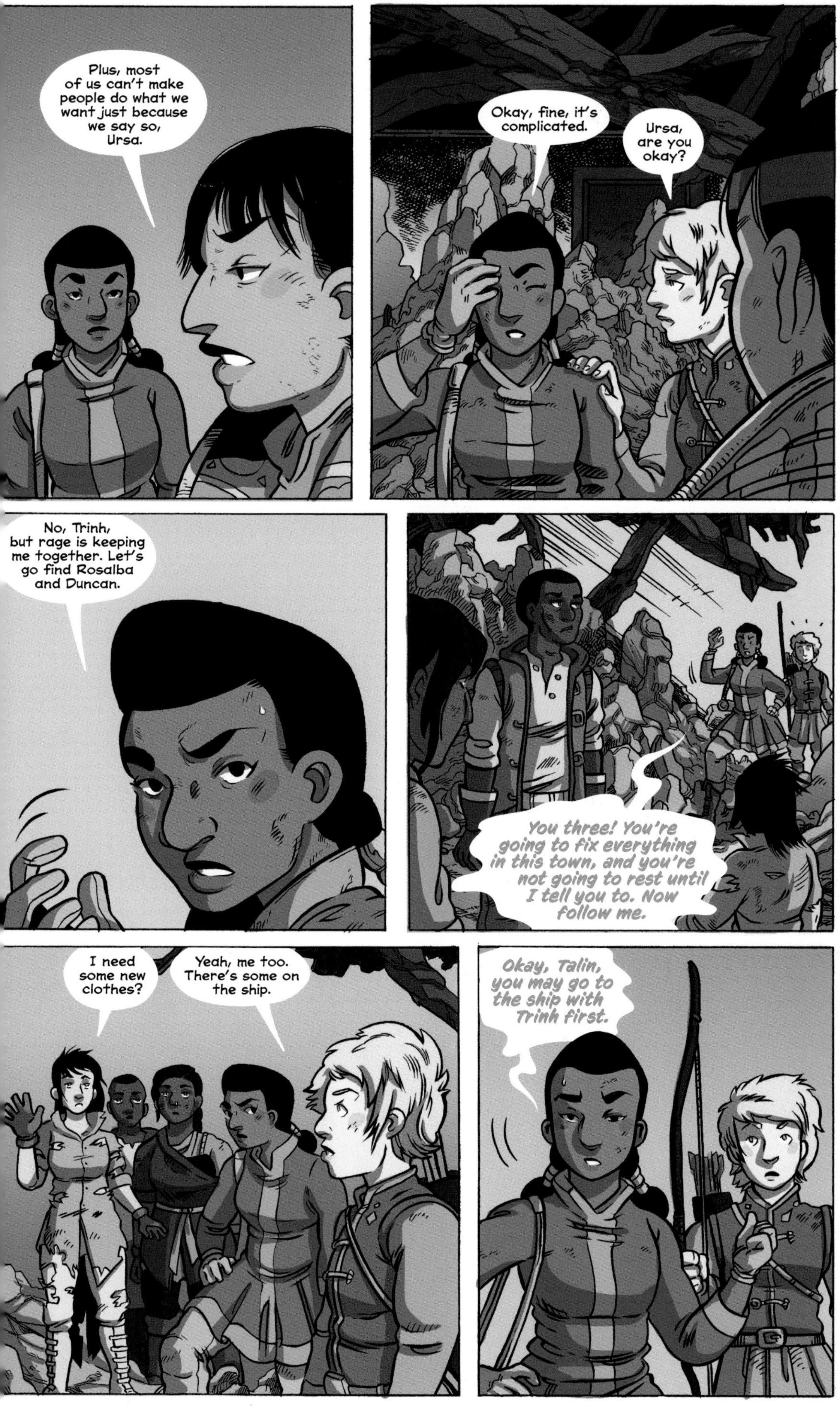
Plus, most of us can't make people do what we want just because we say so, Ursa.
Okay, fine, it's complicated.
Ursa, are you okay?
No, Trinh, but rage is keeping me together. Let's go find Rosalba and Duncan.
You three! You're going to fix everything in this town, and you're not going to rest until I tell you to. Now follow me.
I need some new clothes?
Yeah, me too. There's some on the ship.
Okay, Talin, you may go to the ship with Trinh first.

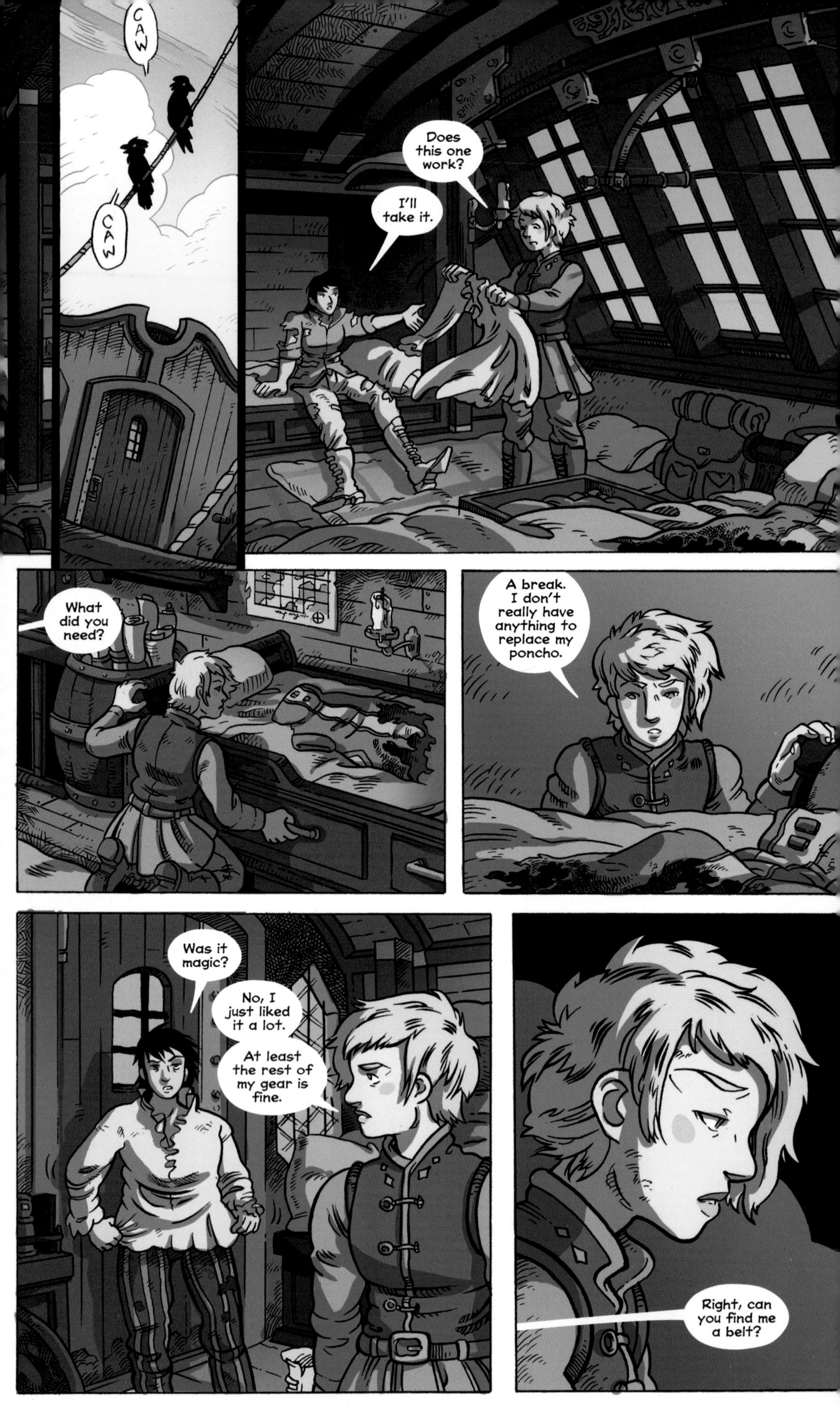
CAW
CAW
Does this one work?
I'll take it.
What did you need?
A break. I don't really have anything to replace my poncho.
Was it magic?
No, I just liked it a lot.
At least the rest of my gear is fine.
Right, can you find me a belt?

Hey, little buddy! Having a good nap?

You missed all the action! But we got it under control.

You're a big, lazy boy, Evil. But I still love you...

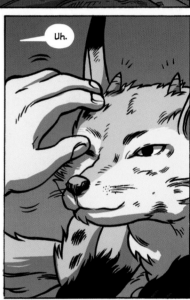

Uh.

Whatever you are.

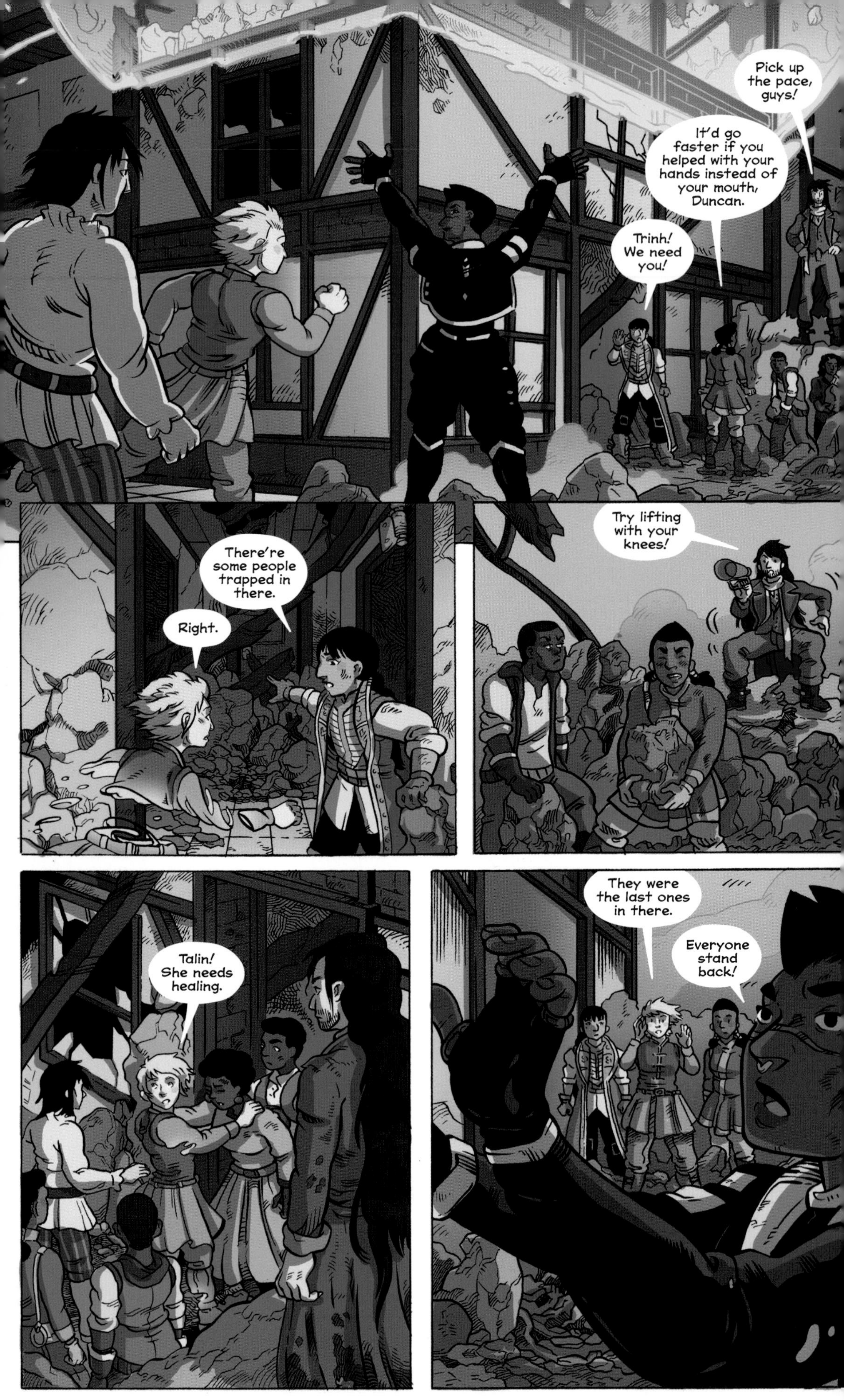
Pick up the pace, guys!
It'd go faster if you helped with your hands instead of your mouth, Duncan.
Trinh! We need you!
There're some people trapped in there.
Right.
Try lifting with your knees!
Talin! She needs healing.
They were the last ones in there.
Everyone stand back!

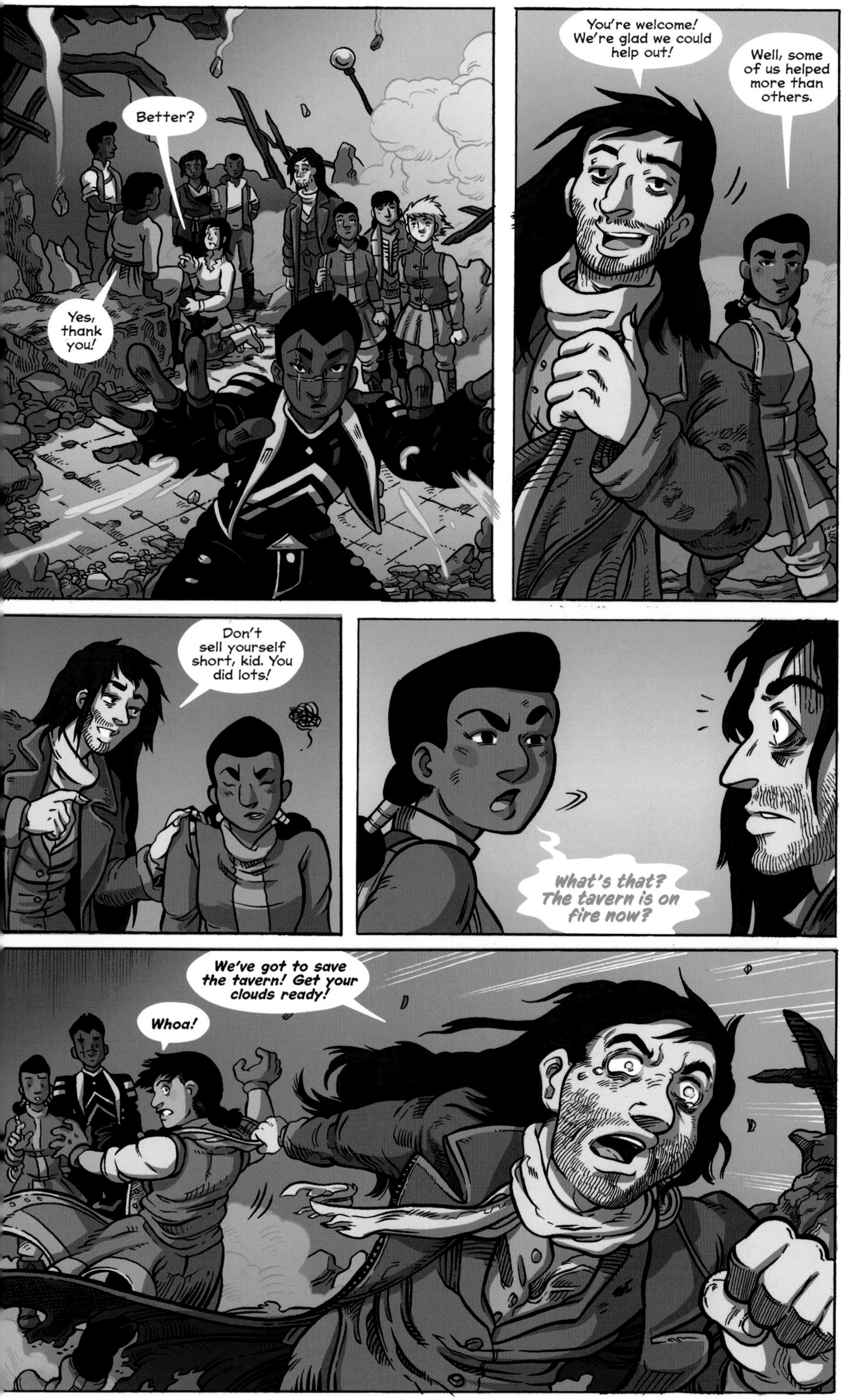
Better?
Yes, thank you!
You're welcome! We're glad we could help out!
Well, some of us helped more than others.
Don't sell yourself short, kid. You did lots!
What's that? The tavern is on fire now?
We've got to save the tavern! Get your clouds ready!
Whoa!

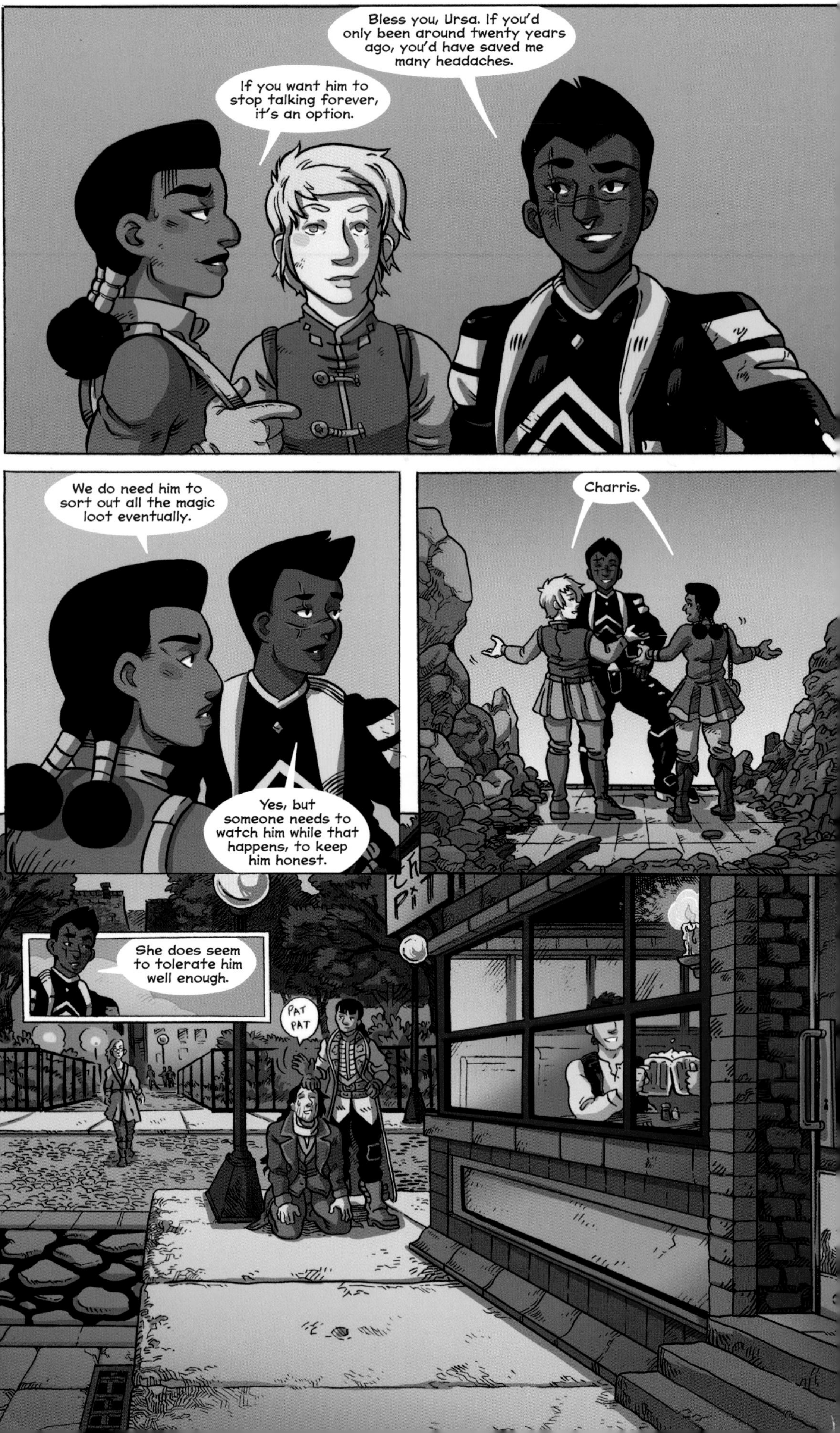
If you want him to stop talking forever, it's an option.
Bless you, Ursa. If you'd only been around twenty years ago, you'd have saved me many headaches.
We do need him to sort out all the magic loot eventually.
Yes, but someone needs to watch him while that happens, to keep him honest.
Charris.
She does seem to tolerate him well enough.
PAT PAT

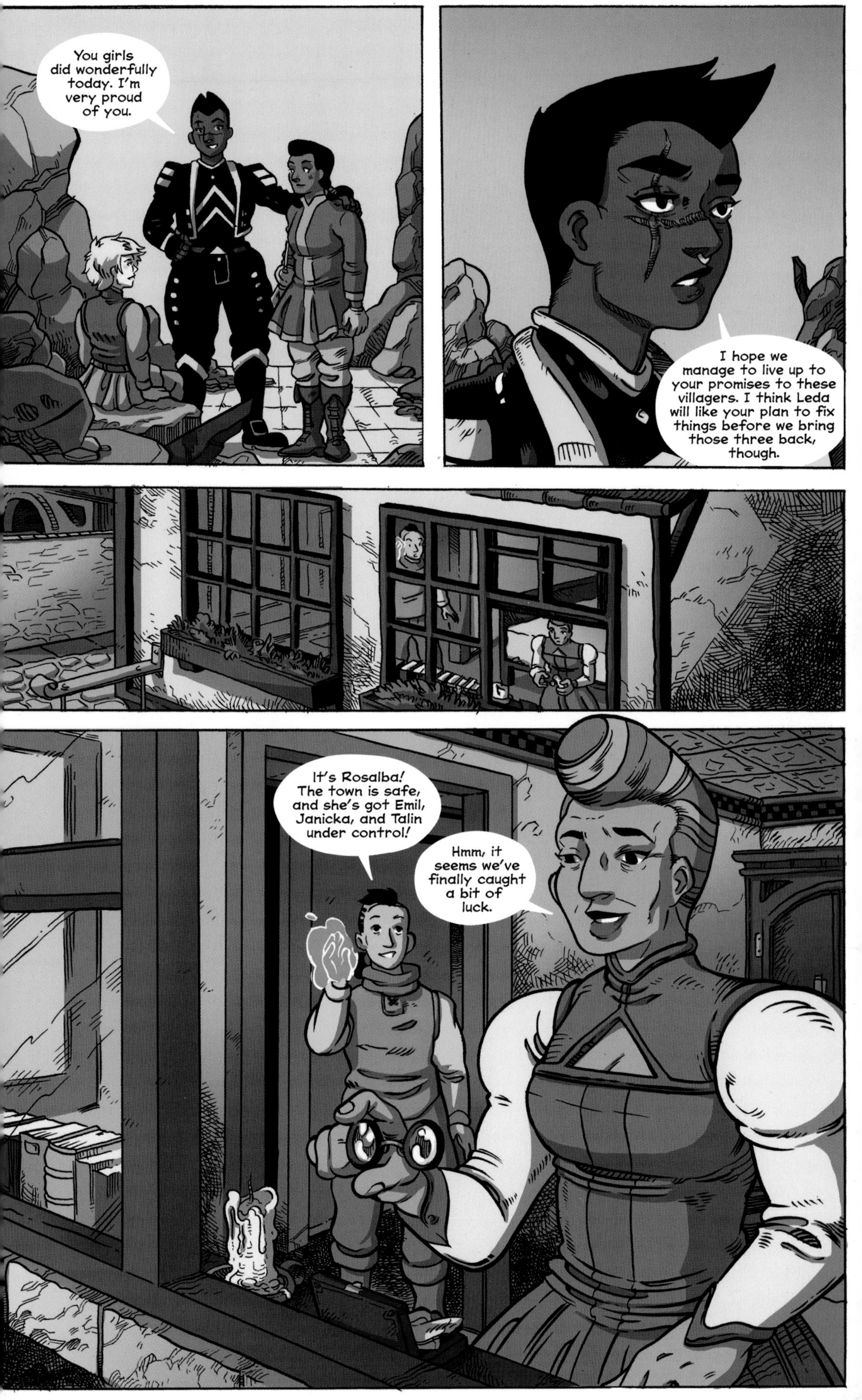
You girls did wonderfully today. I'm very proud of you.
I hope we manage to live up to your promises to these villagers. I think Leda will like your plan to fix things before we bring those three back, though.
It's Rosalba! The town is safe, and she's got Emil, Janicka, and Talin under control!
Hmm, it seems we've finally caught a bit of luck.

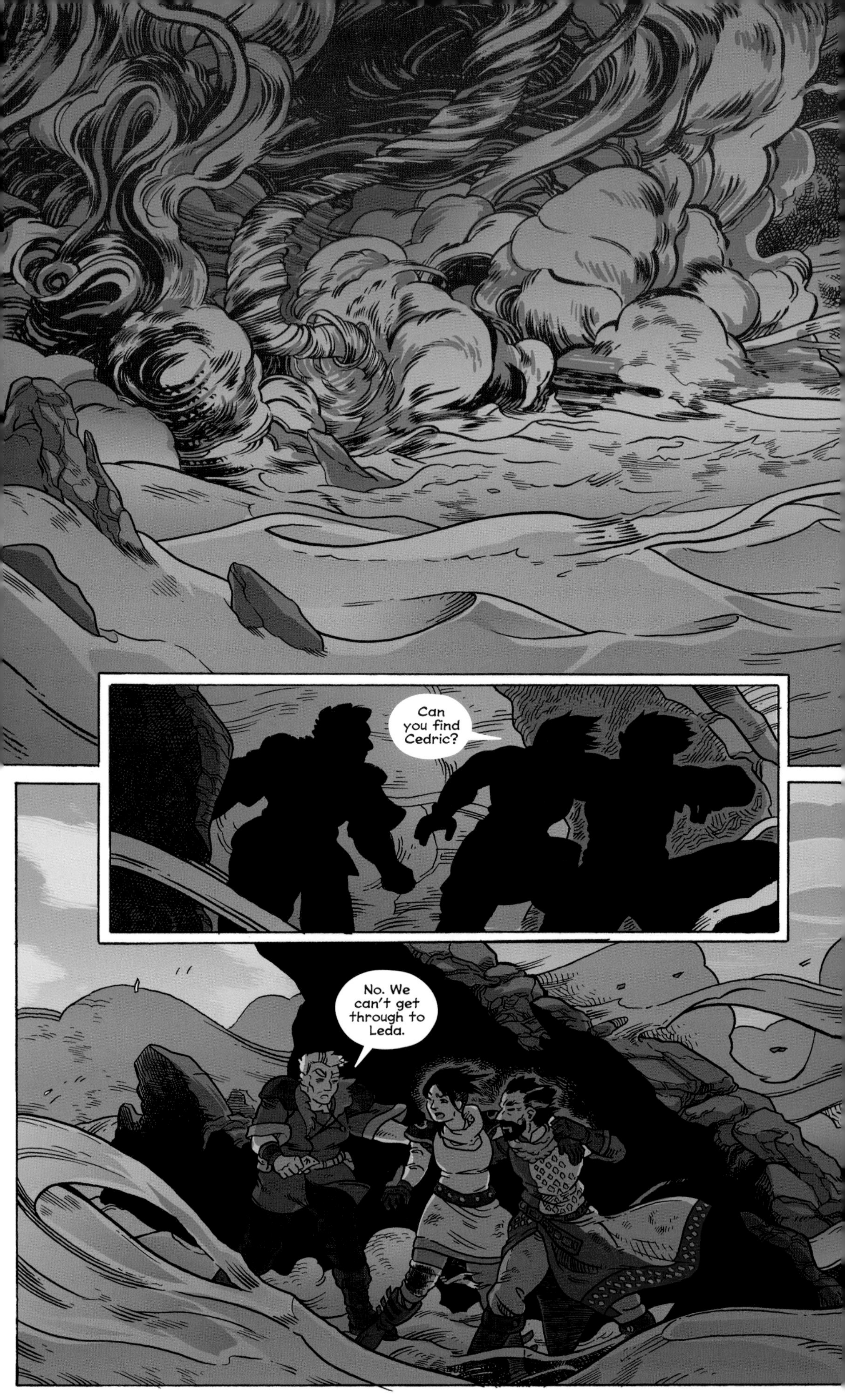
Can you find Cedric?
No. We can't get through to Leda.

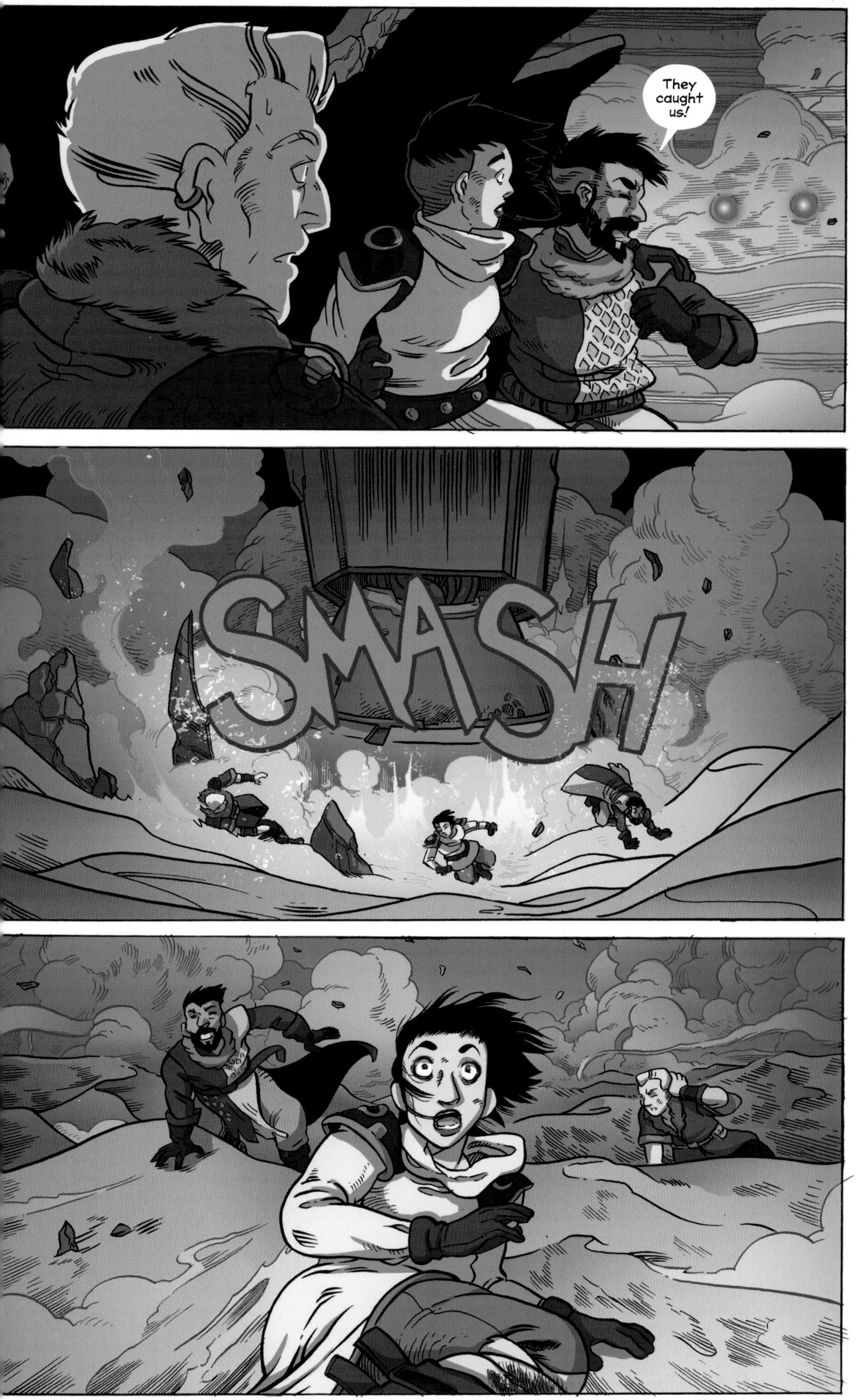
They caught us!
SMASH

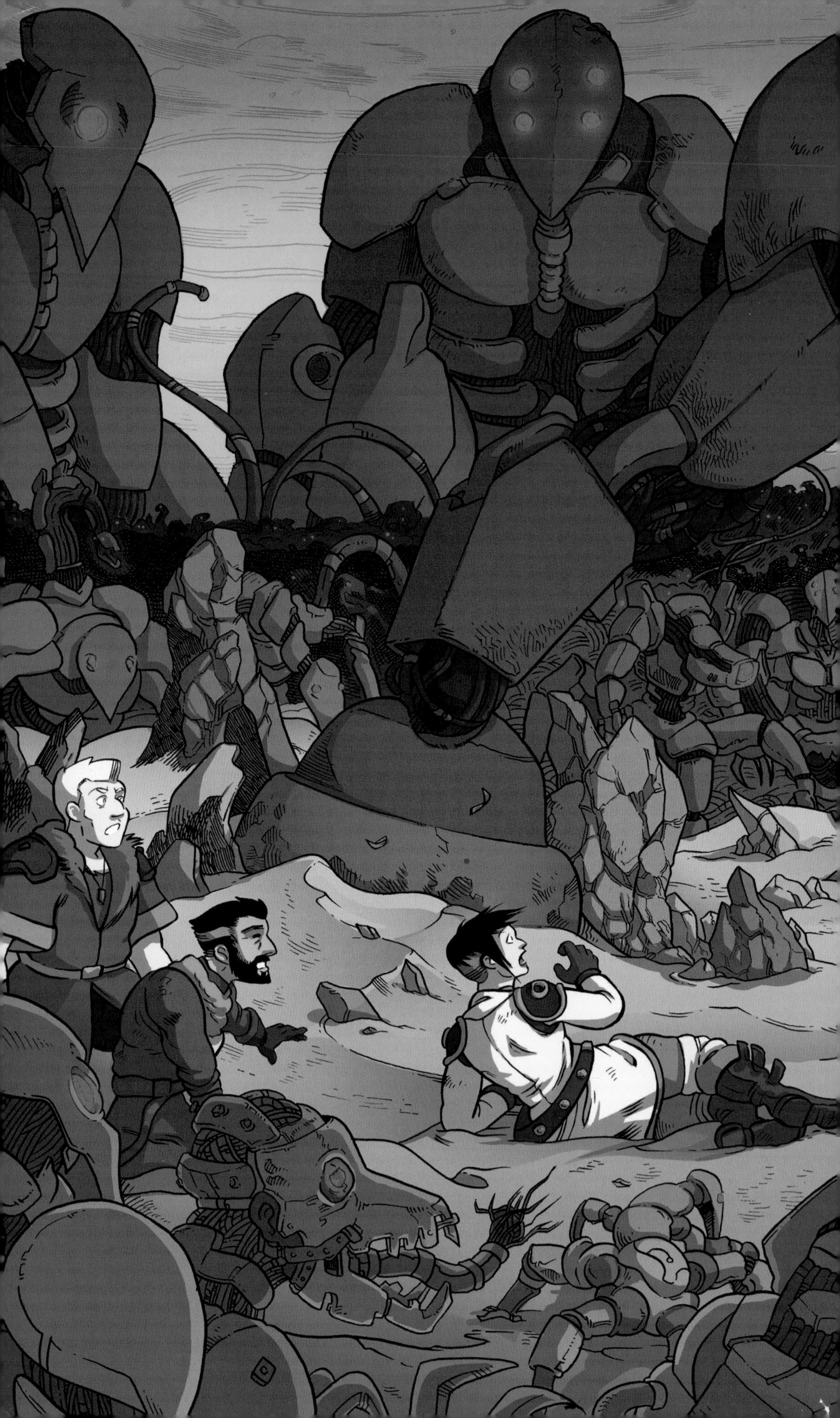

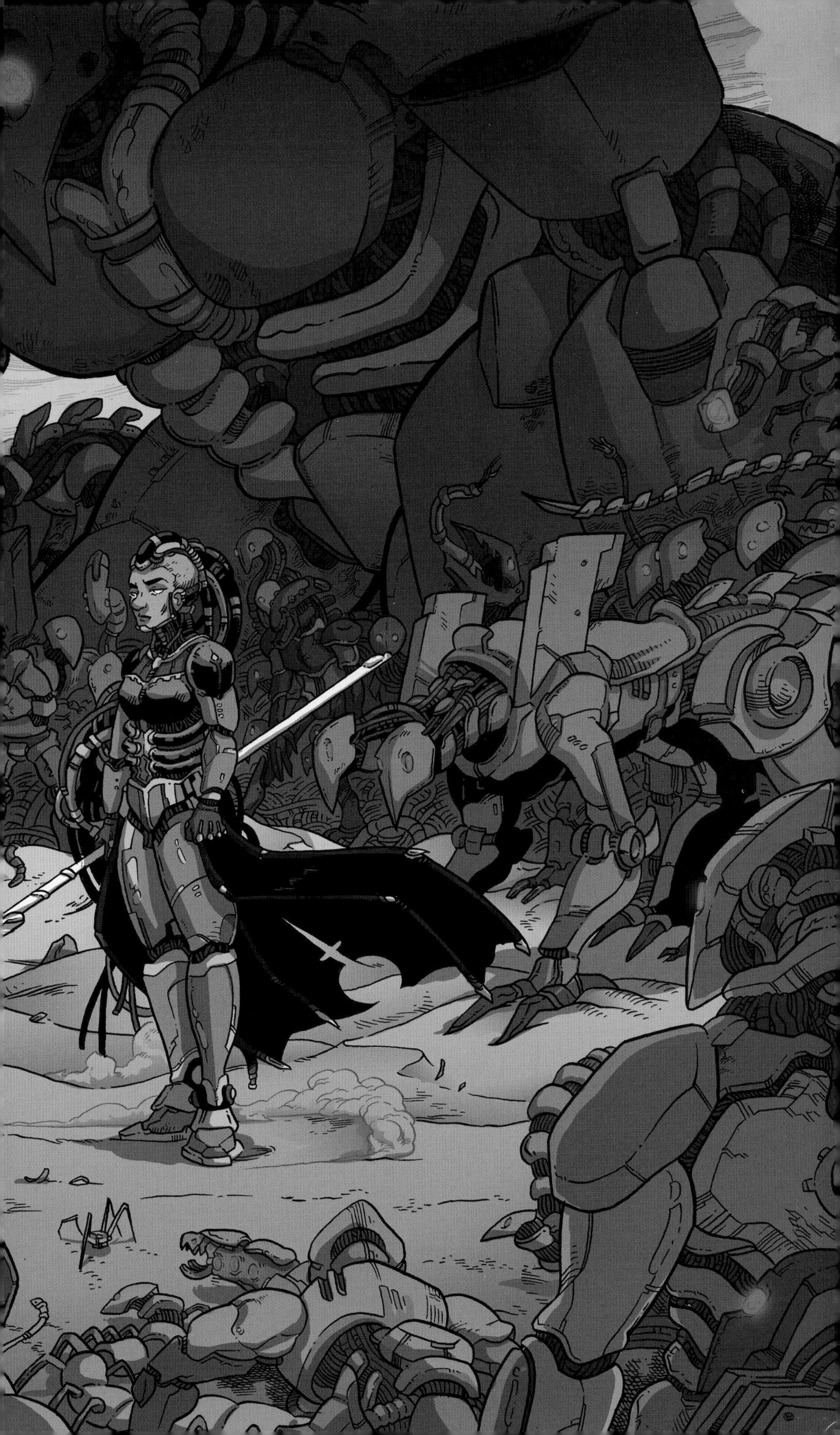

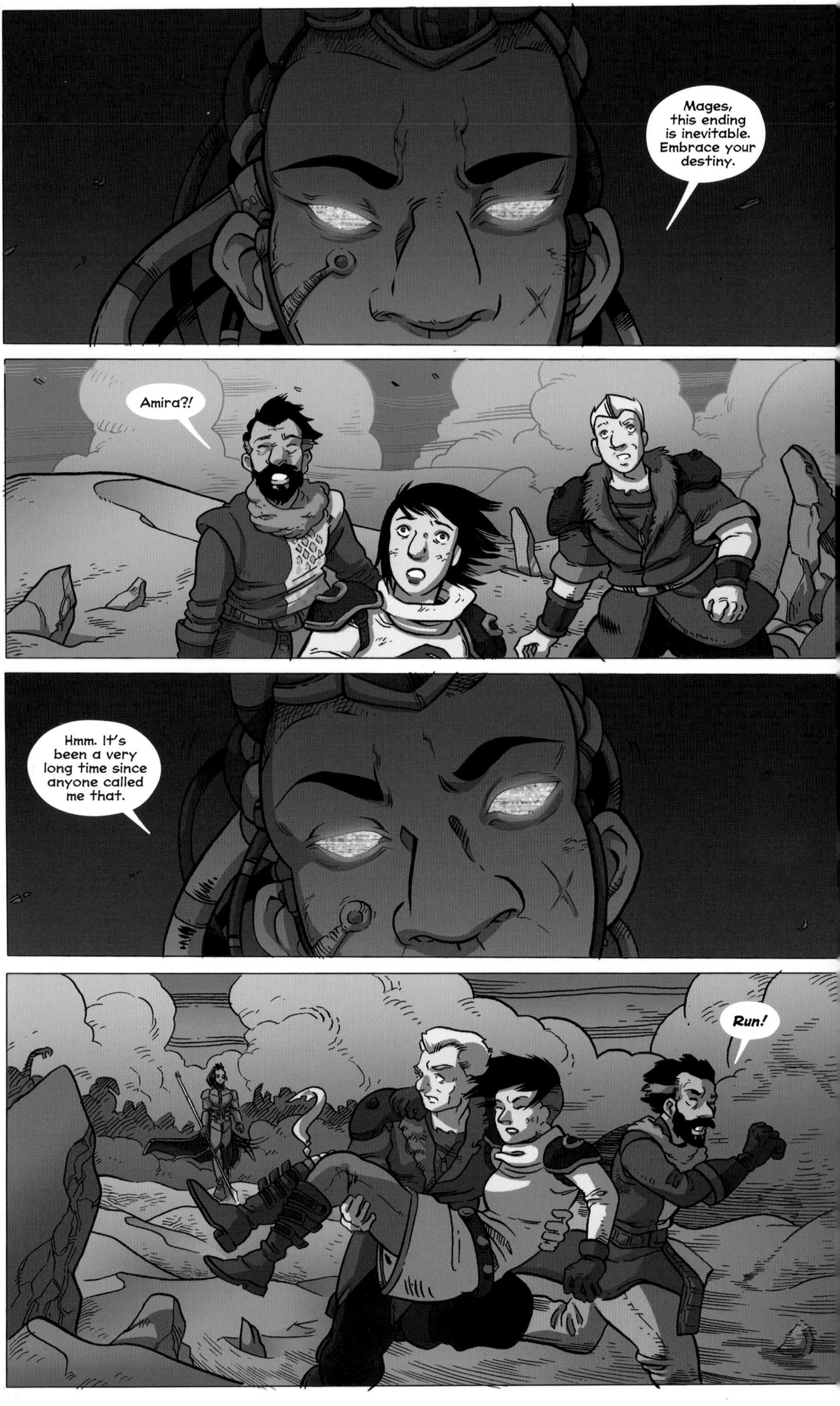
Mages, this ending is inevitable. Embrace your destiny.
Amira?!
Hmm. It's been a very long time since anyone called me that.
Run!

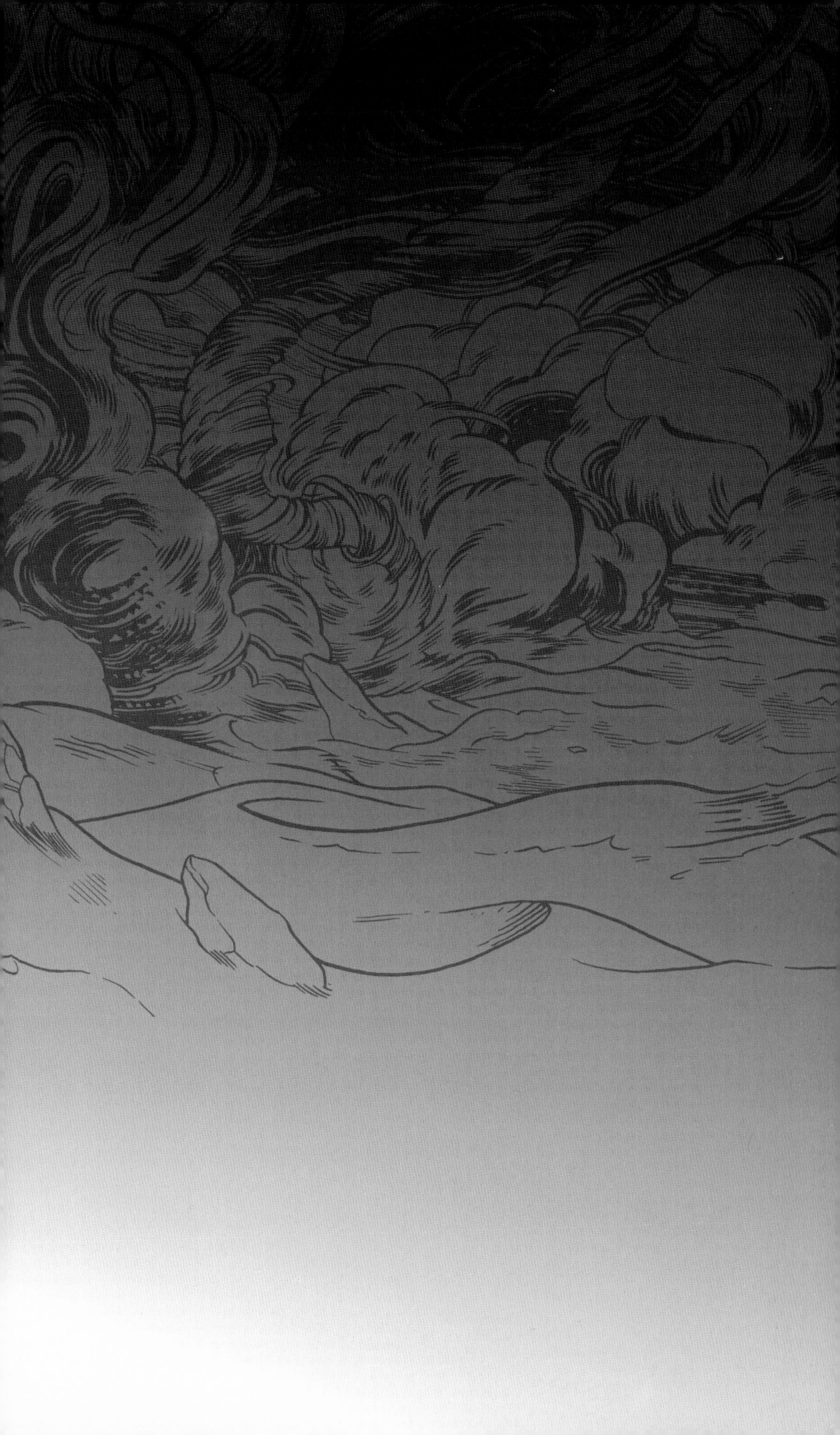

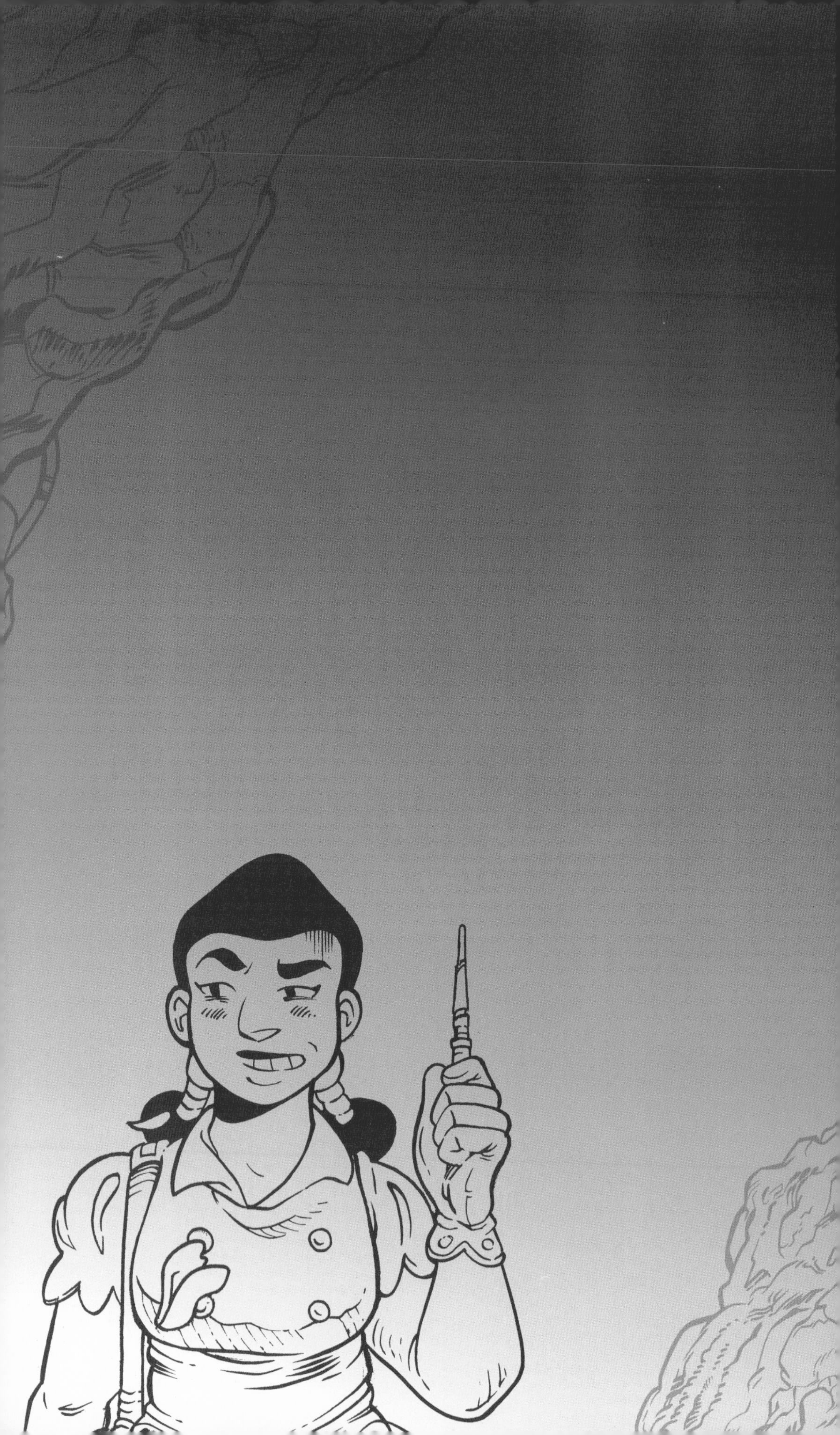

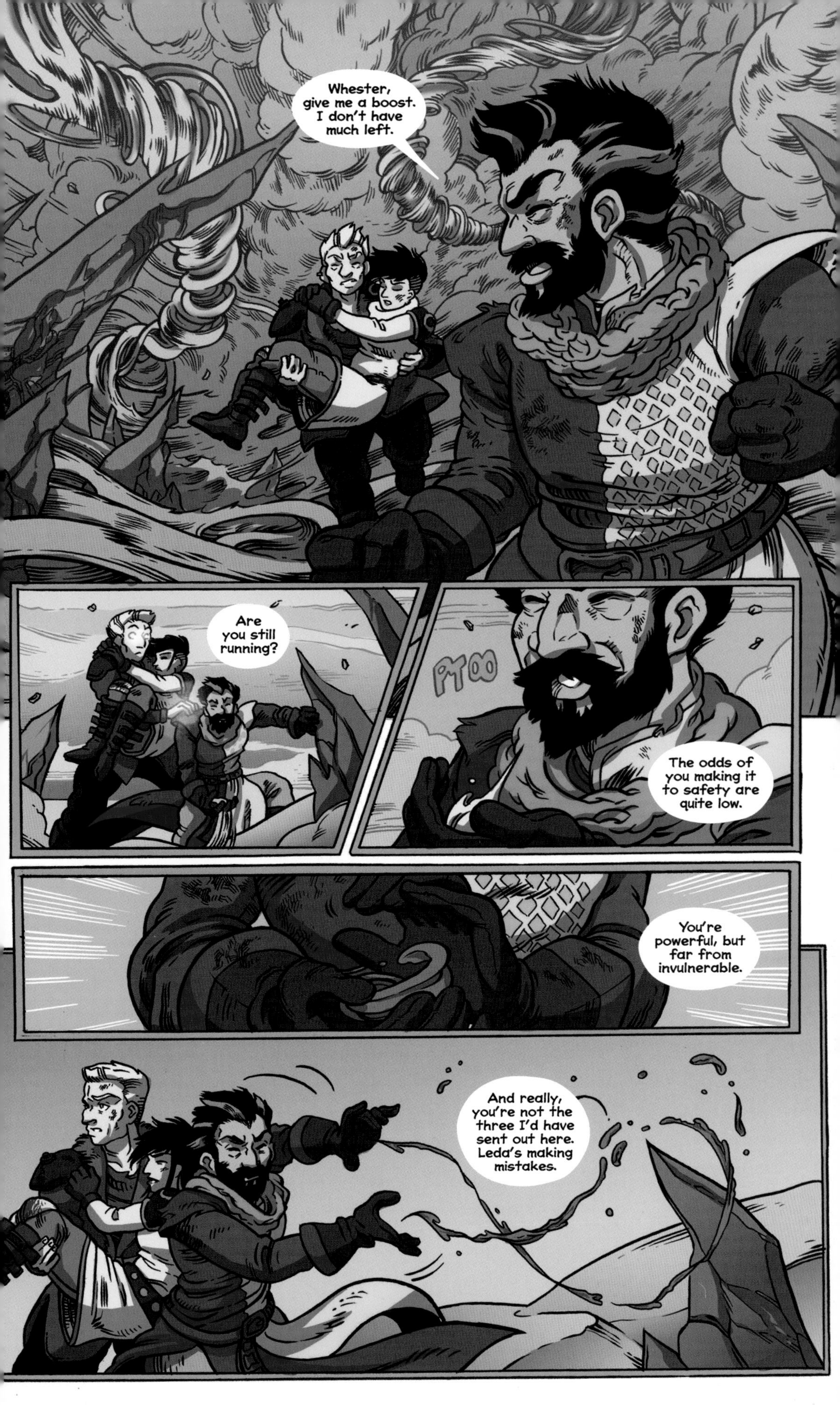
Whester, give me a boost. I don't have much left.
Are you still running?
PTOO
The odds of you making it to safety are quite low.
You're powerful, but far from invulnerable.
And really, you're not the three I'd have sent out here. Leda's making mistakes.

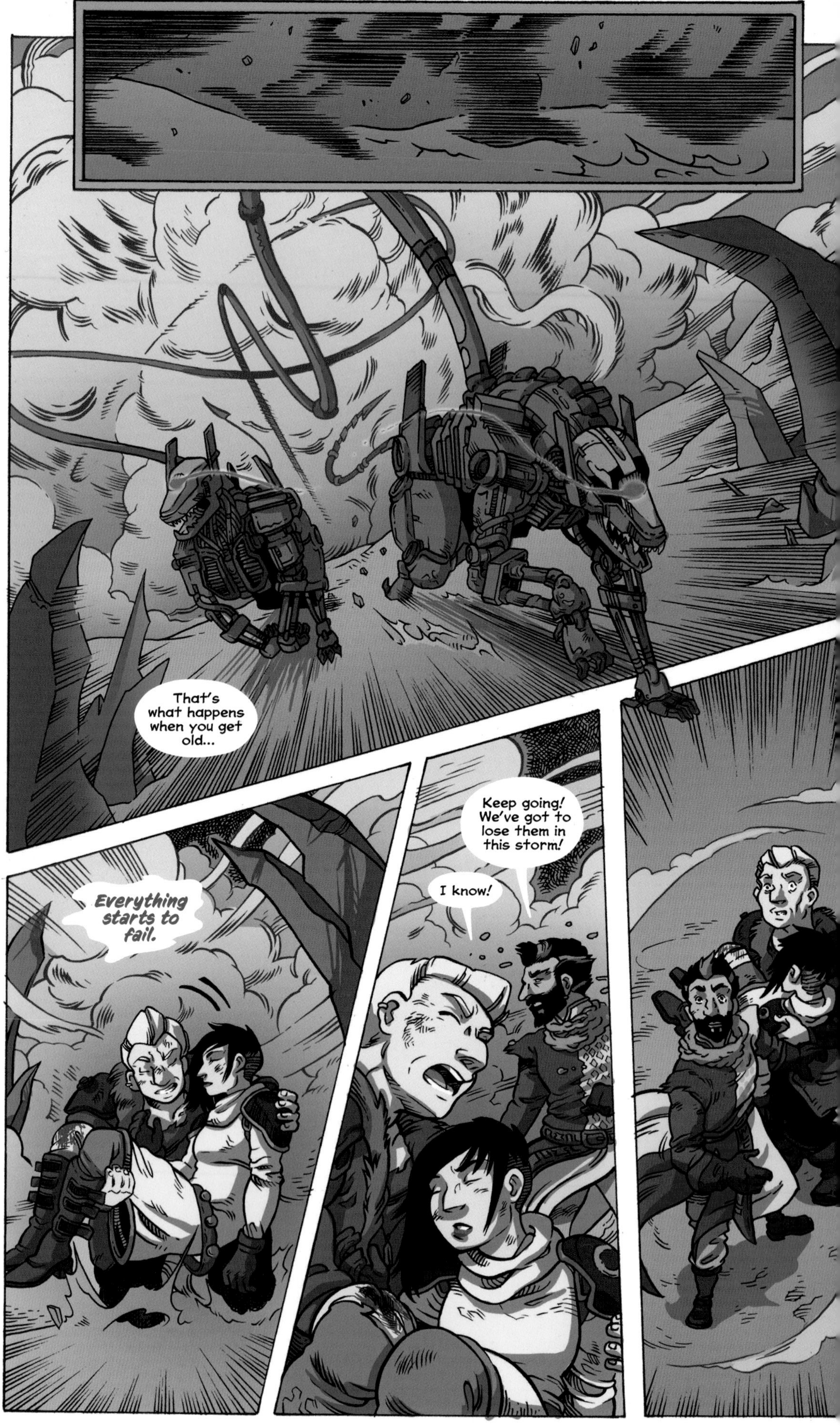
That's what happens when you get old...
Everything starts to fail.
Keep going! We've got to lose them in this storm!
I know!

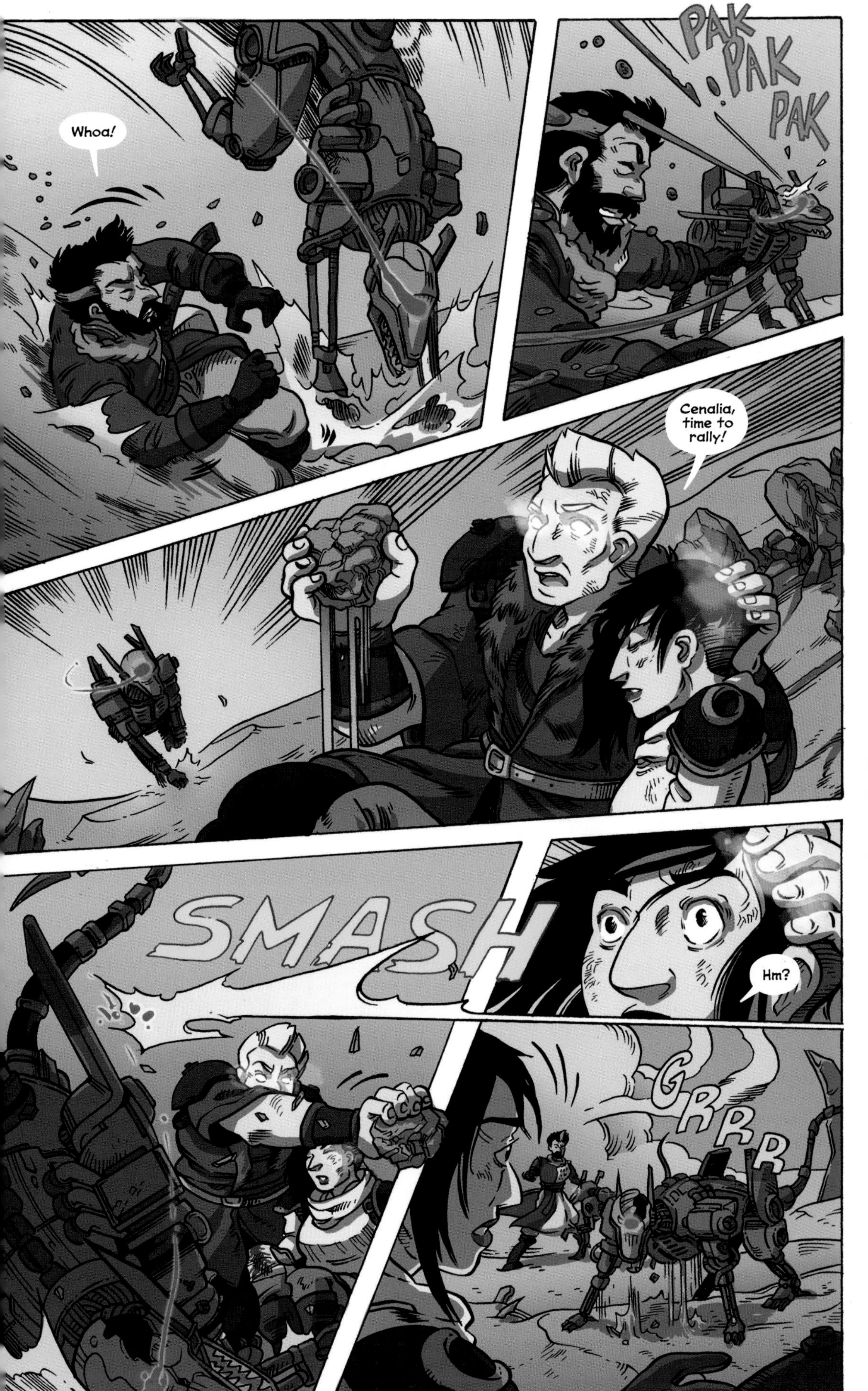
Whoa!
PAK
PAK
PAK
Cenalia, time to rally!
SMASH
Hm?
GRRR

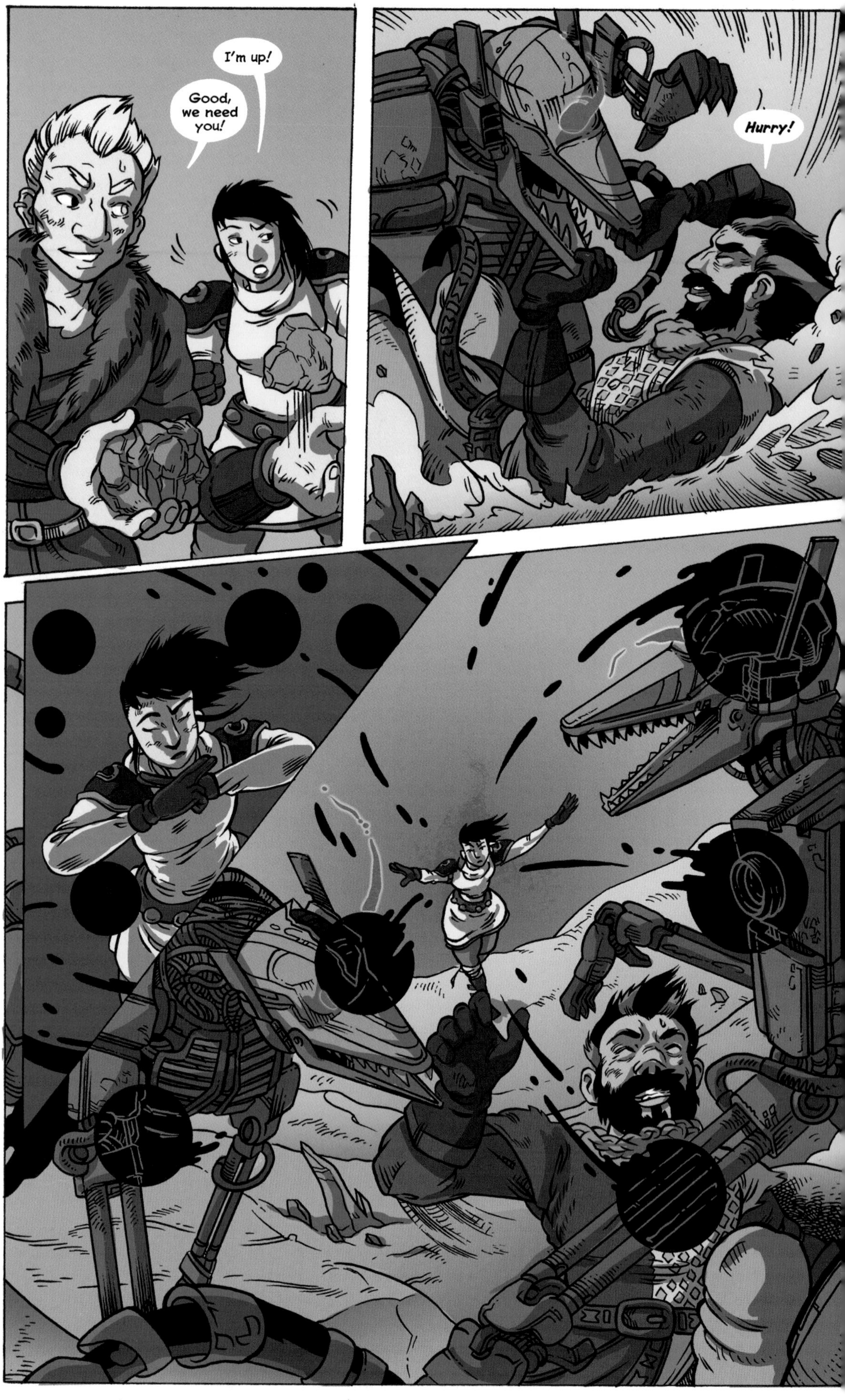
I'm up!
Good, we need you!
Hurry!

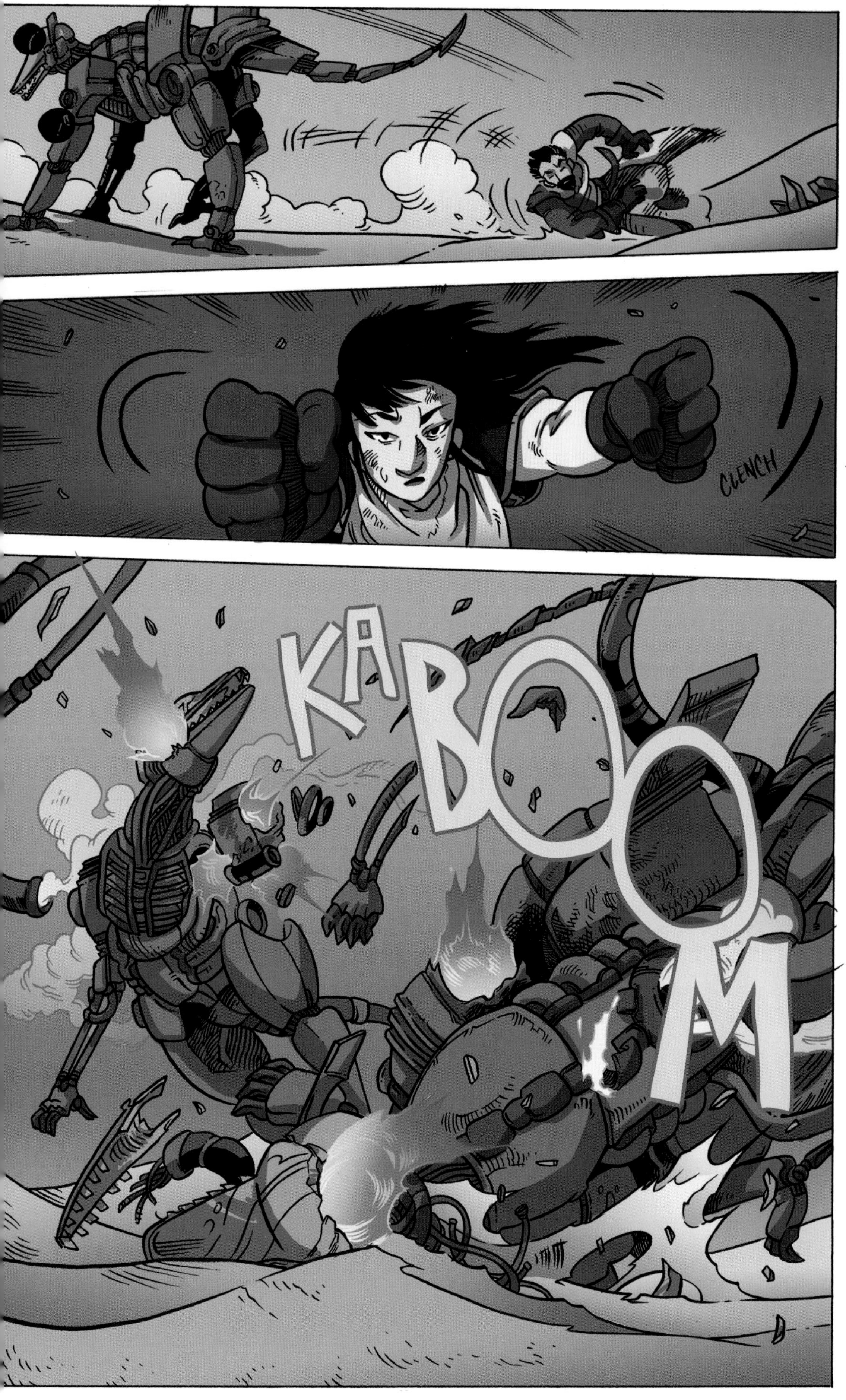
CLENCH
KABOOM

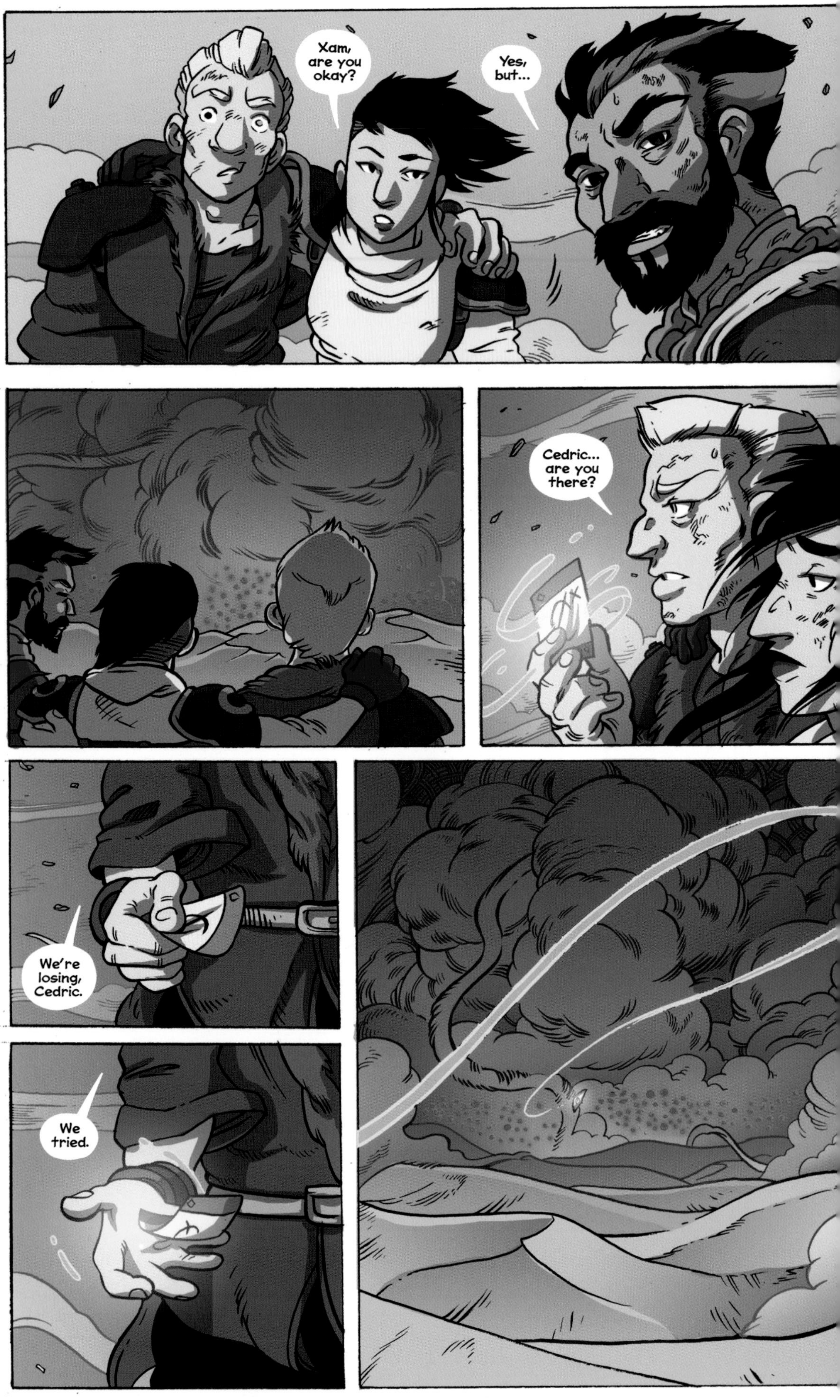
Xam, are you okay?
Yes, but...
Cedric... are you there?
We're losing, Cedric.
We tried.

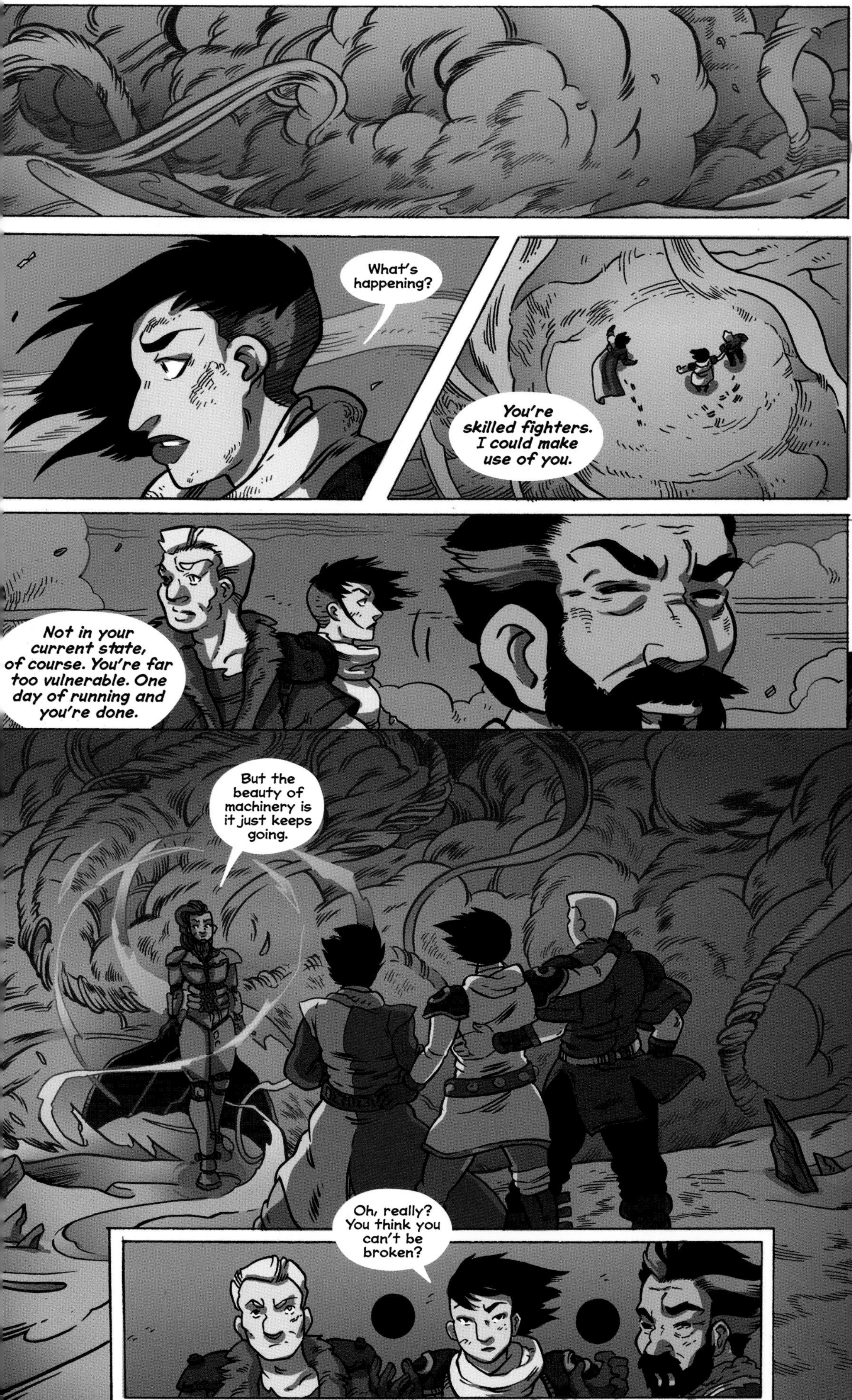
What's happening?
You're skilled fighters. I could make use of you.
Not in your current state, of course. You're far too vulnerable. One day of running and you're done.
But the beauty of machinery is it just keeps going.
Oh, really? You think you can't be broken?

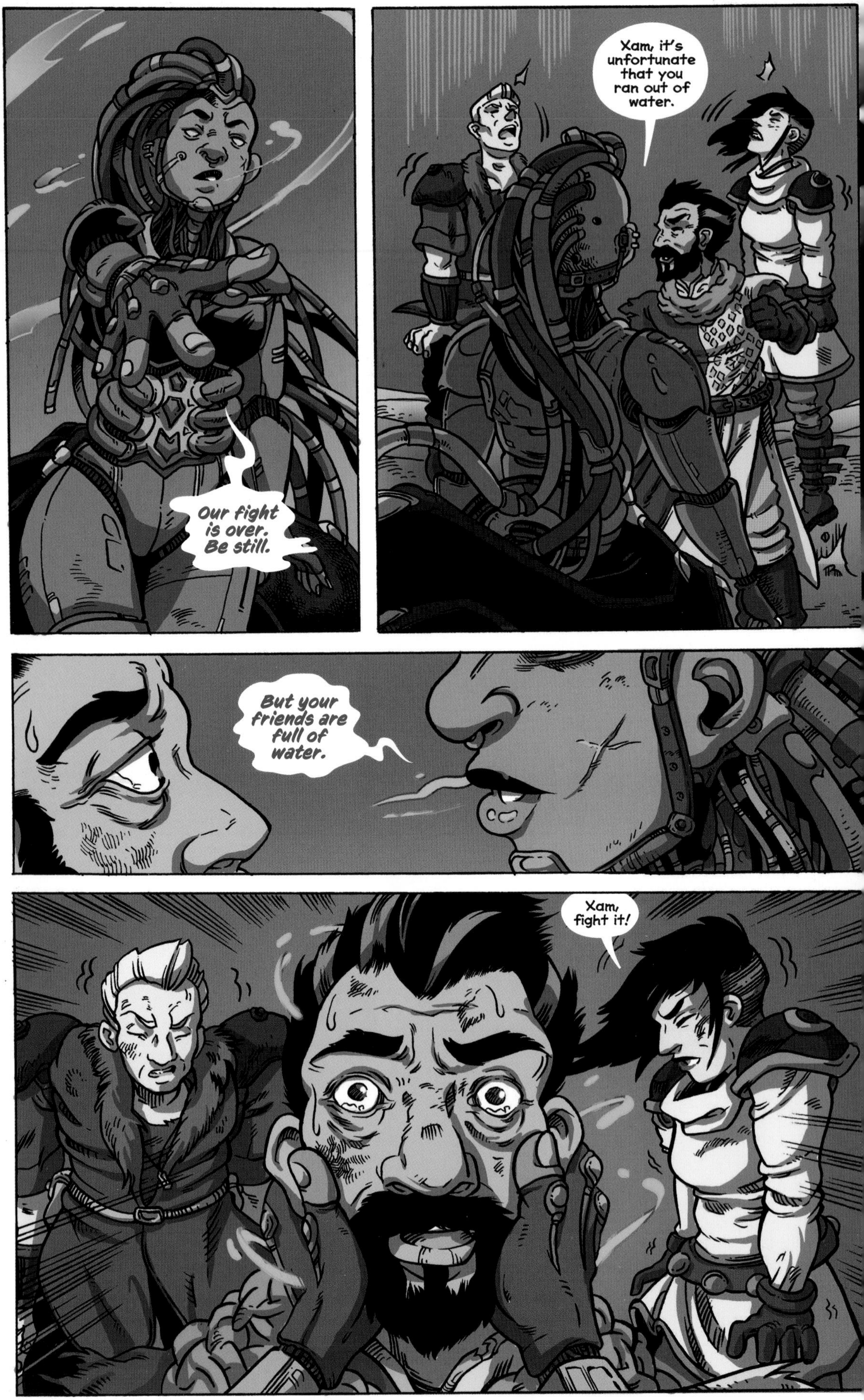
Our fight is over. Be still.
Xam, it's unfortunate that you ran out of water.
But your friends are full of water.
Xam, fight it!

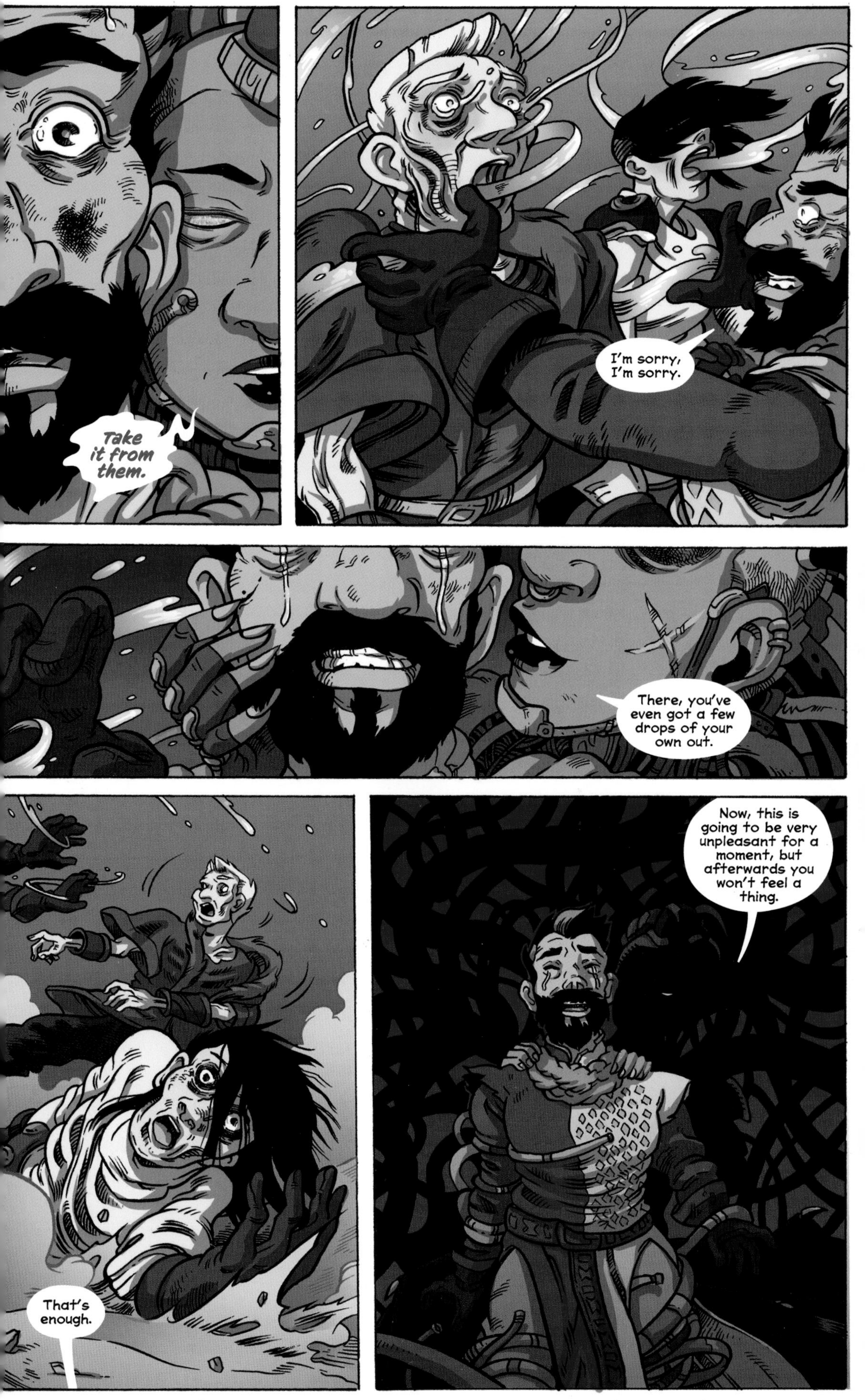
Take it from them.
I'm sorry, I'm sorry.
There, you've even got a few drops of your own out.
That's enough.
Now, this is going to be very unpleasant for a moment, but afterwards you won't feel a thing.

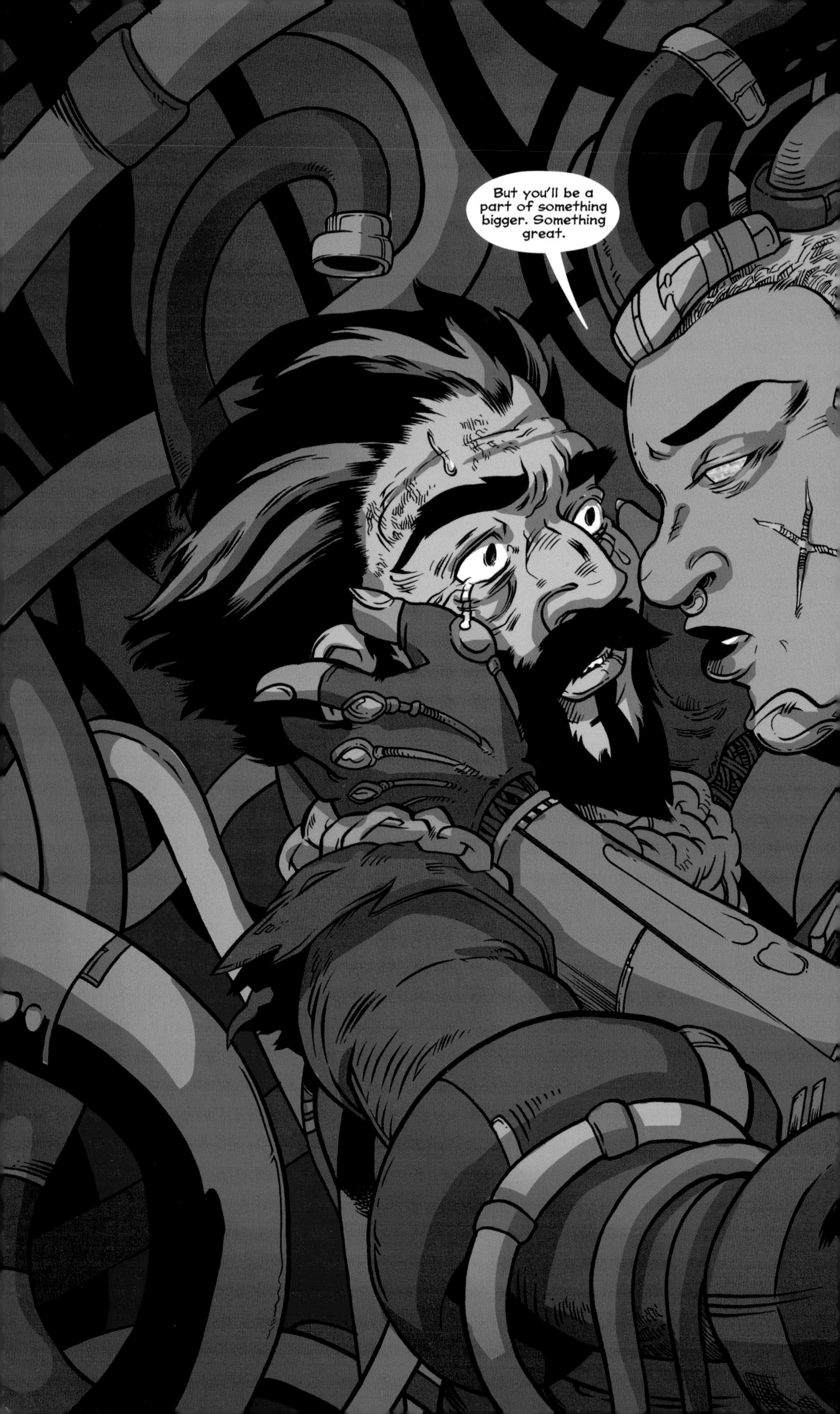
But you'll be a part of something bigger. Something great.

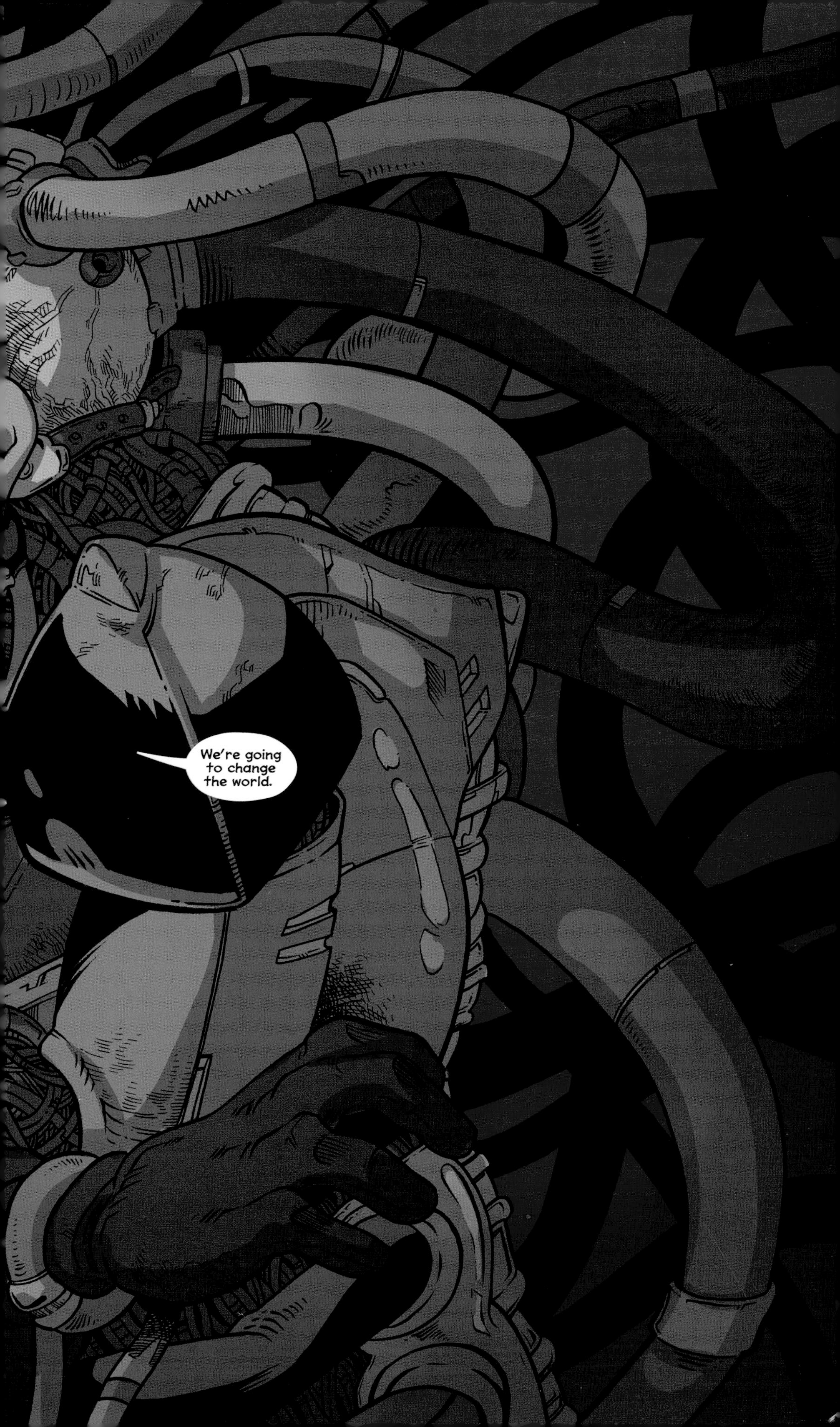
We're going to change the world.

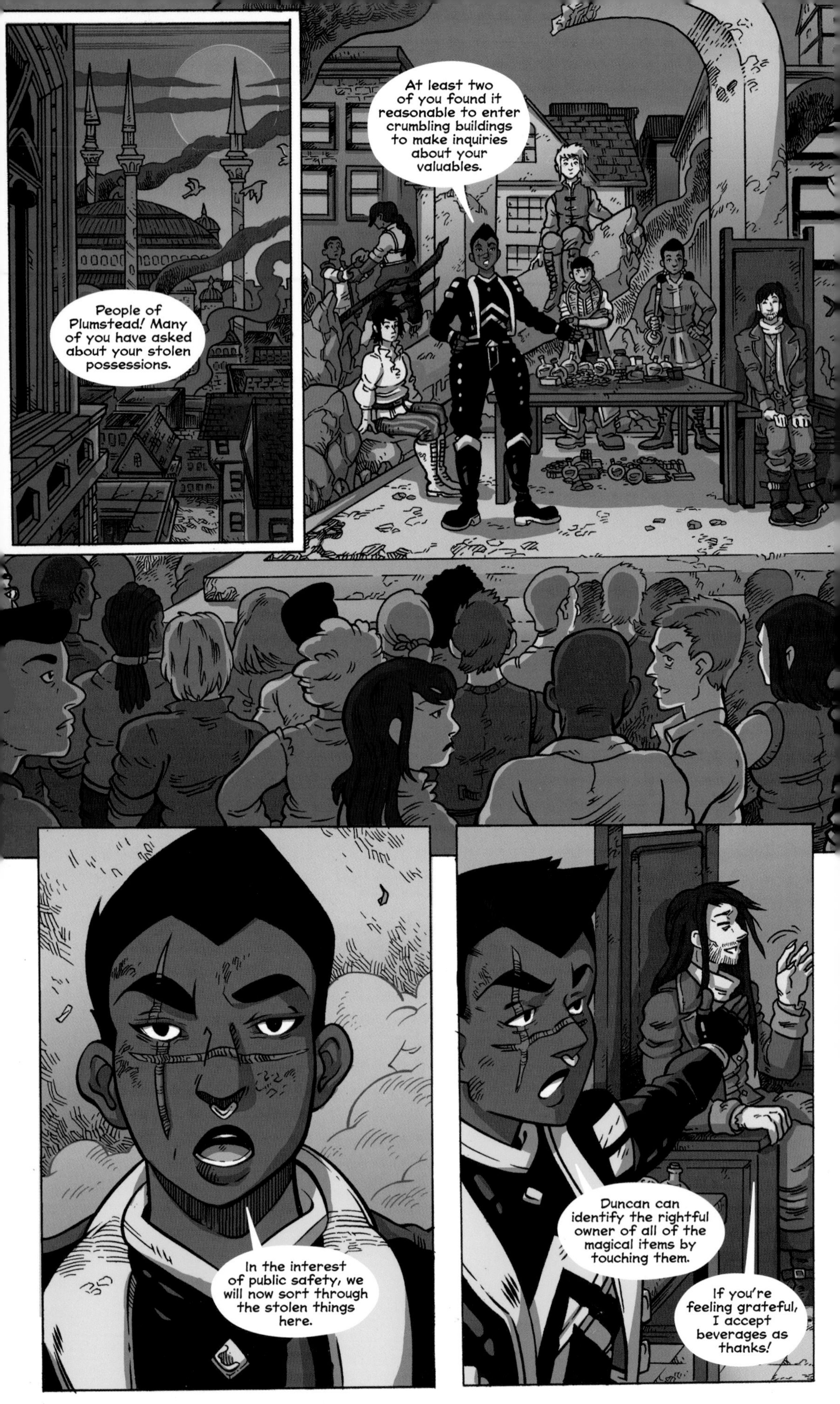
People of Plumstead! Many of you have asked about your stolen possessions.
At least two of you found it reasonable to enter crumbling buildings to make inquiries about your valuables.
In the interest of public safety, we will now sort through the stolen things here.
Duncan can identify the rightful owner of all of the magical items by touching them.
If you're feeling grateful, I accept beverages as thanks!

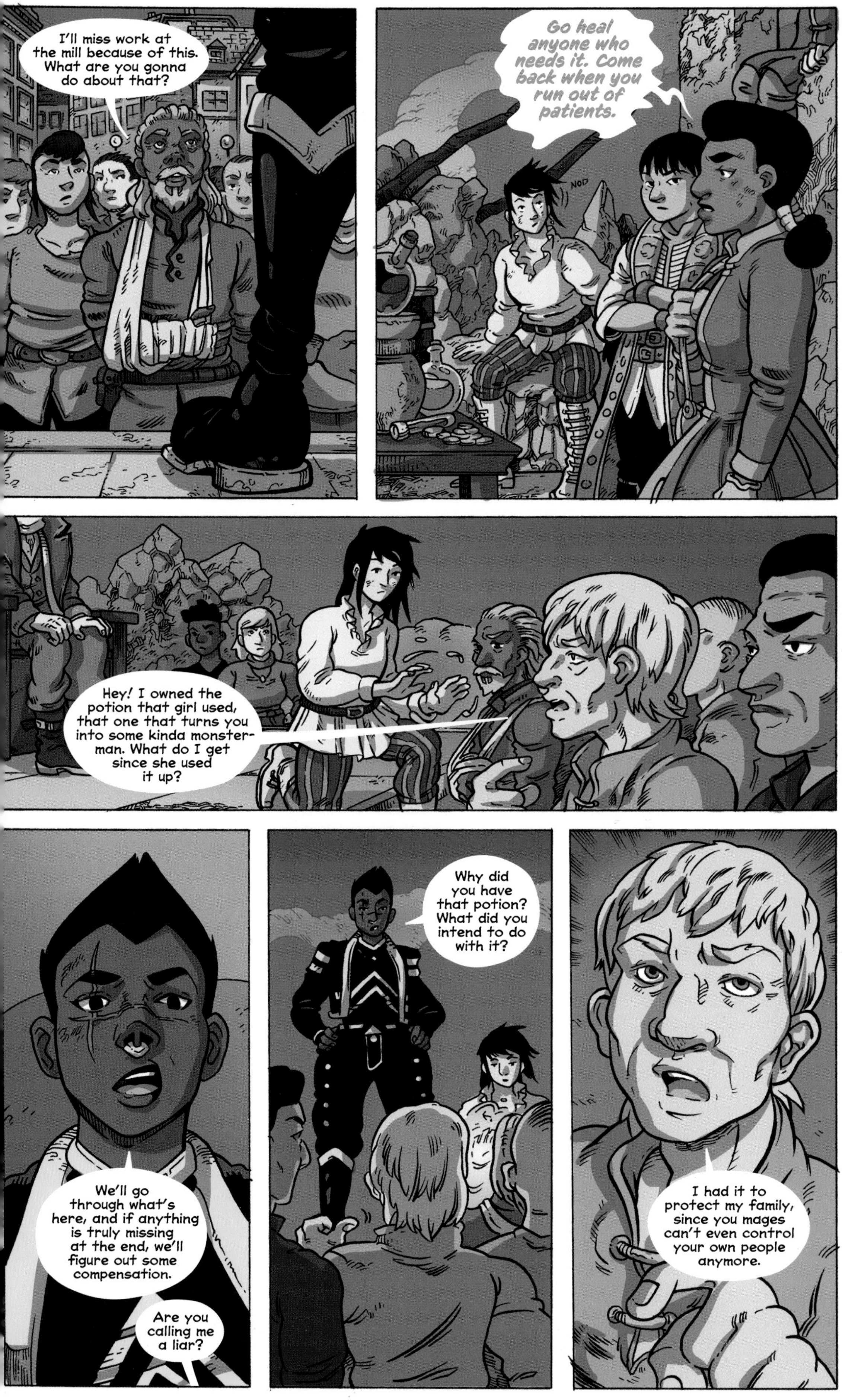
I'll miss work at the mill because of this. What are you gonna do about that?
Go heal anyone who needs it. Come back when you run out of patients.
NOD
Hey! I owned the potion that girl used, that one that turns you into some kinda monster-man. What do I get since she used it up?
We'll go through what's here, and if anything is truly missing at the end, we'll figure out some compensation.
Are you calling me a liar?
Why did you have that potion? What did you intend to do with it?
I had it to protect my family, since you mages can't even control your own people anymore.

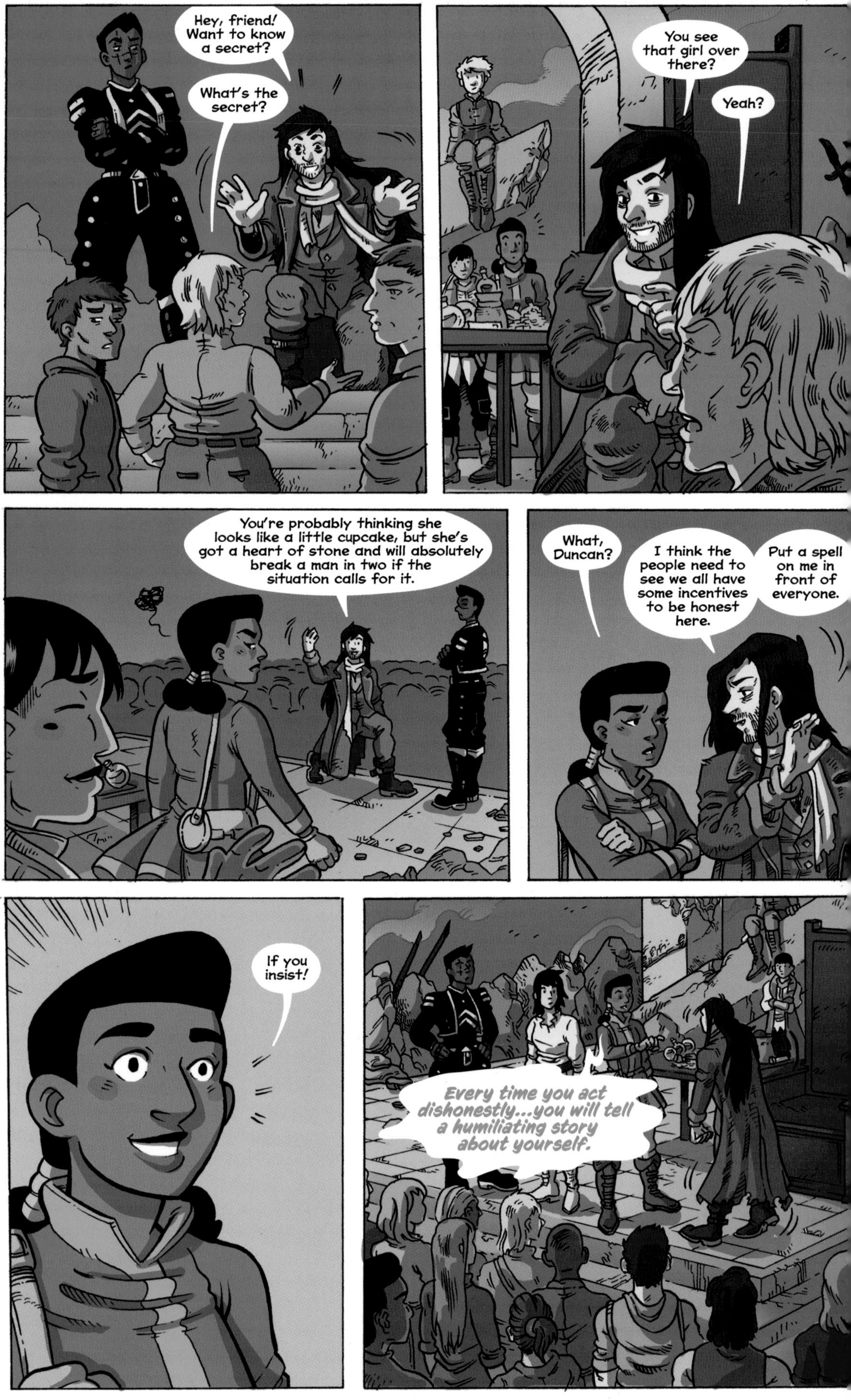
Hey, friend! Want to know a secret?
What's the secret?
You see that girl over there?
Yeah?
You're probably thinking she looks like a little cupcake, but she's got a heart of stone and will absolutely break a man in two if the situation calls for it.
What, Duncan?
I think the people need to see we all have some incentives to be honest here.
Put a spell on me in front of everyone.
If you insist!
Every time you act dishonestly...you will tell a humiliating story about yourself.

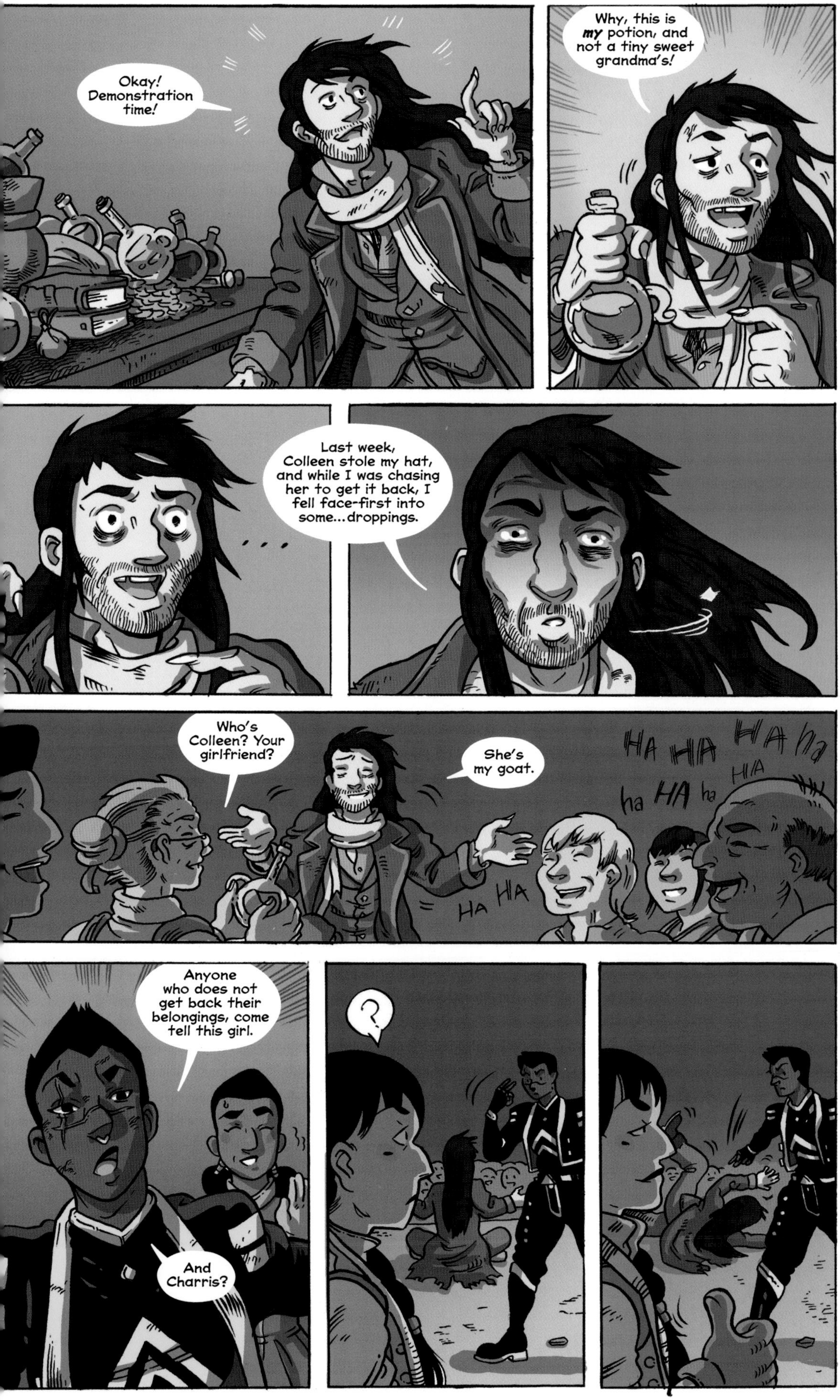
Okay! Demonstration time!
Why, this is my potion, and not a tiny sweet grandma's!
...
Last week, Colleen stole my hat, and while I was chasing her to get it back, I fell face-first into some...droppings.
Who's Colleen? Your girlfriend?
She's my goat.
HA HA HA ha ha HA ha HA
HA HA
Anyone who does not get back their belongings, come tell this girl.
And Charris?
?

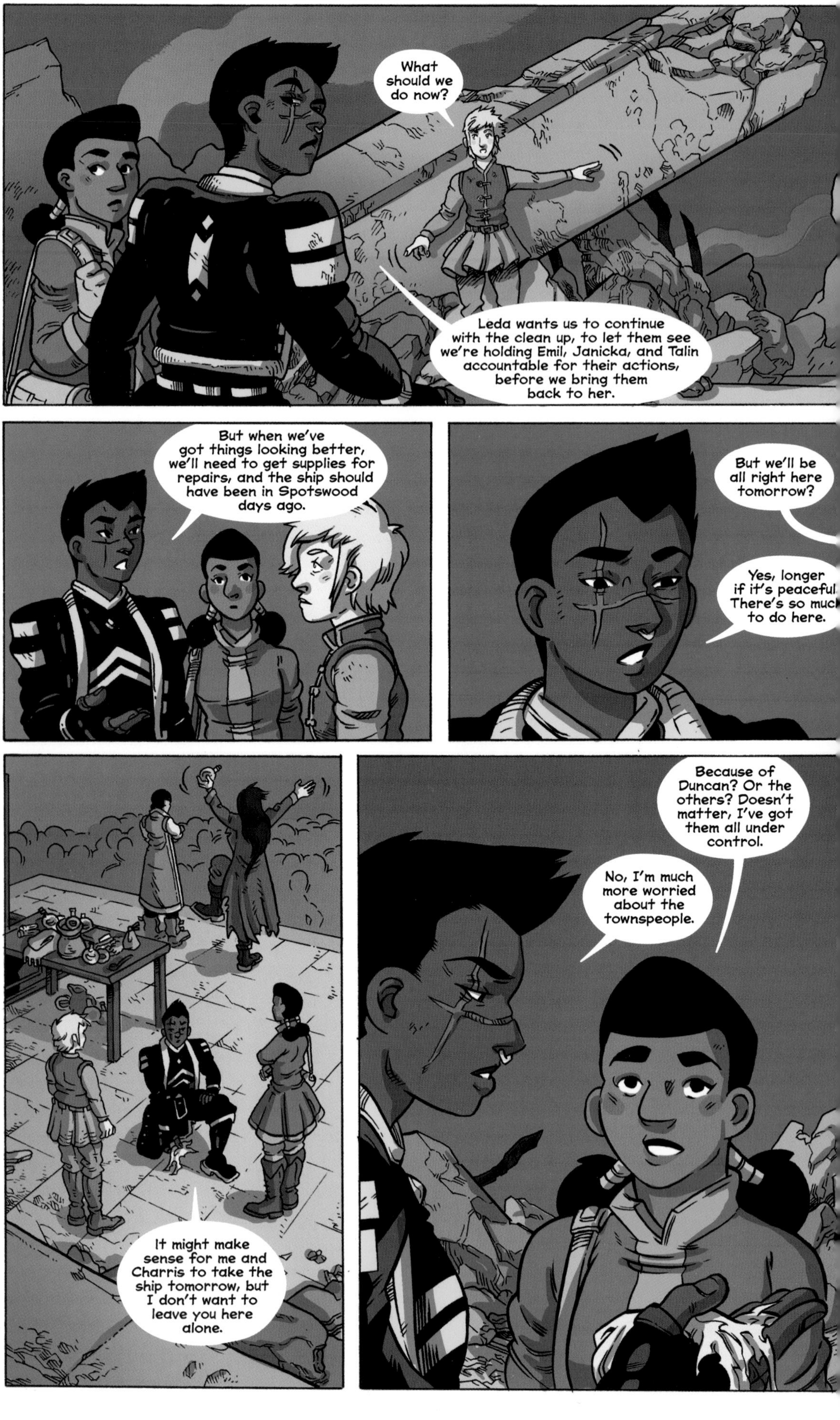
What should we do now?
Leda wants us to continue with the clean up, to let them see we're holding Emil, Janicka, and Talin accountable for their actions, before we bring them back to her.
But when we've got things looking better, we'll need to get supplies for repairs, and the ship should have been in Spotswood days ago.
But we'll be all right here tomorrow?
Yes, longer if it's peaceful. There's so muc to do here.
It might make sense for me and Charris to take the ship tomorrow, but I don't want to leave you here alone.
Because of Duncan? Or the others? Doesn't matter, I've got them all under control.
No, I'm much more worried about the townspeople.

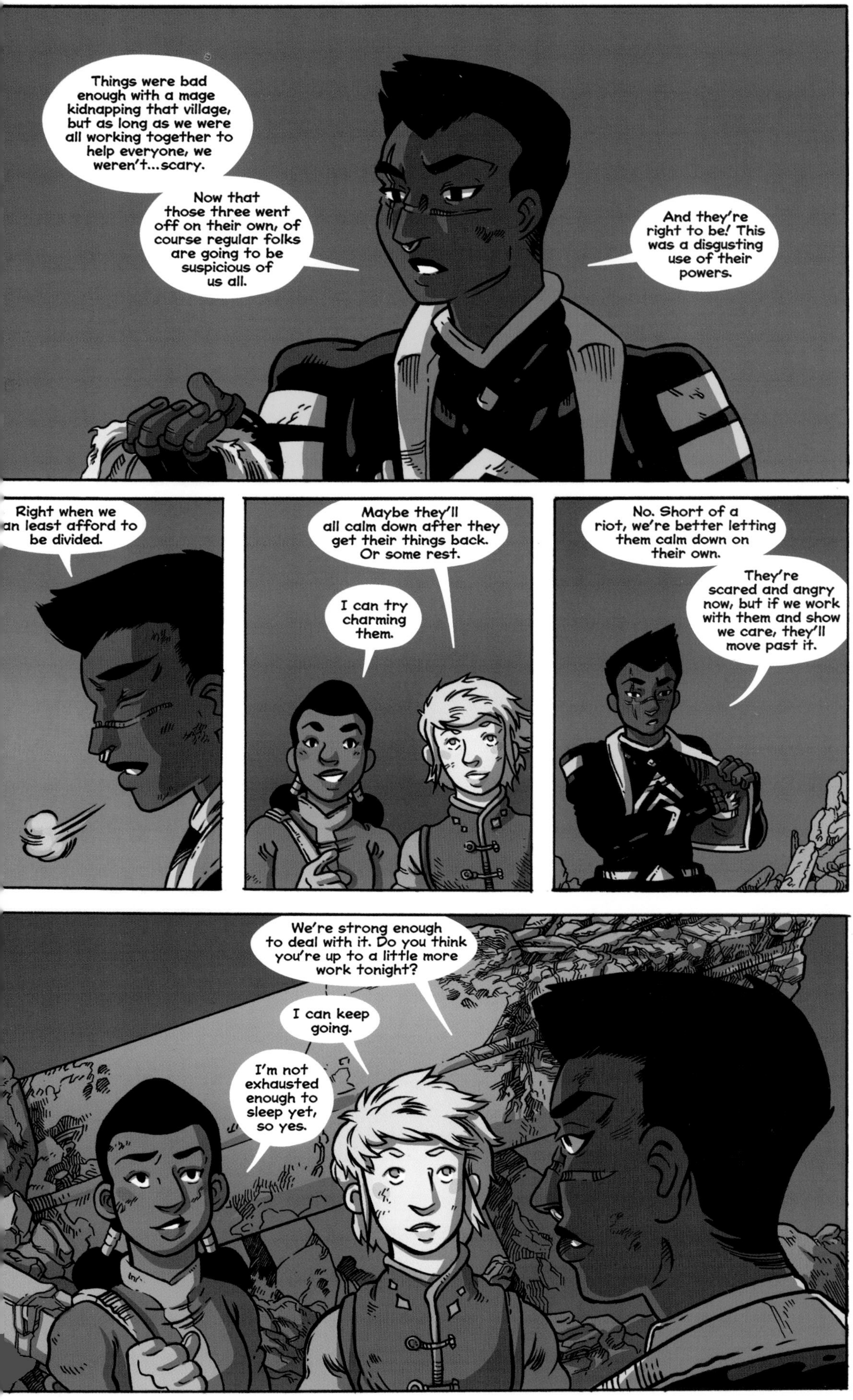
Things were bad enough with a mage kidnapping that village, but as long as we were all working together to help everyone, we weren't...scary.
Now that those three went off on their own, of course regular folks are going to be suspicious of us all.
And they're right to be! This was a disgusting use of their powers.
Right when we can least afford to be divided.
Maybe they'll all calm down after they get their things back. Or some rest.
I can try charming them.
No. Short of a riot, we're better letting them calm down on their own.
They're scared and angry now, but if we work with them and show we care, they'll move past it.
We're strong enough to deal with it. Do you think you're up to a little more work tonight?
I can keep going.
I'm not exhausted enough to sleep yet, so yes.

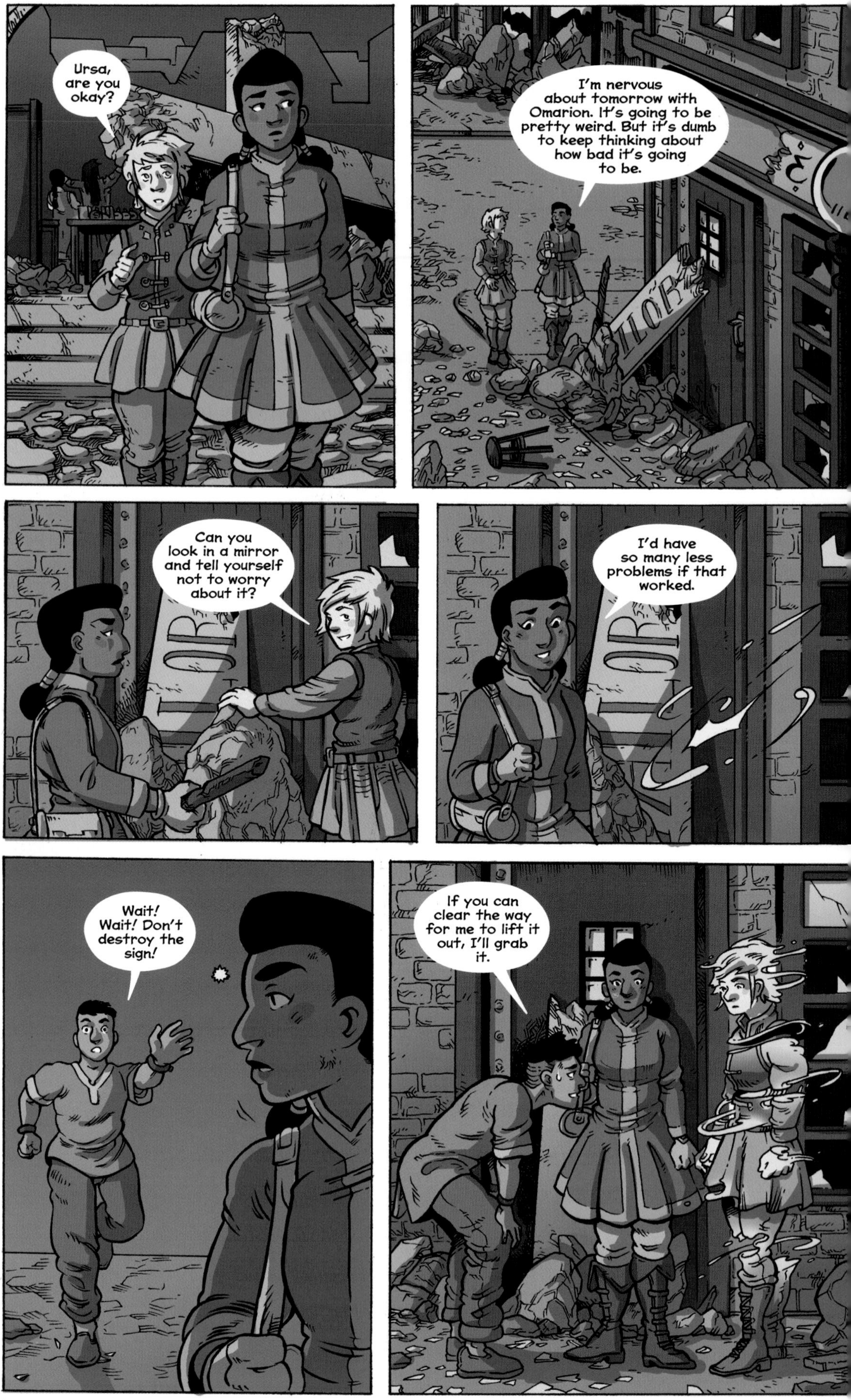
Ursa, are you okay?
I'm nervous about tomorrow with Omarion. It's going to be pretty weird. But it's dumb to keep thinking about how bad it's going to be.
Can you look in a mirror and tell yourself not to worry about it?
I'd have so many less problems if that worked.
Wait! Wait! Don't destroy the sign!
If you can clear the way for me to lift it out, I'll grab it.

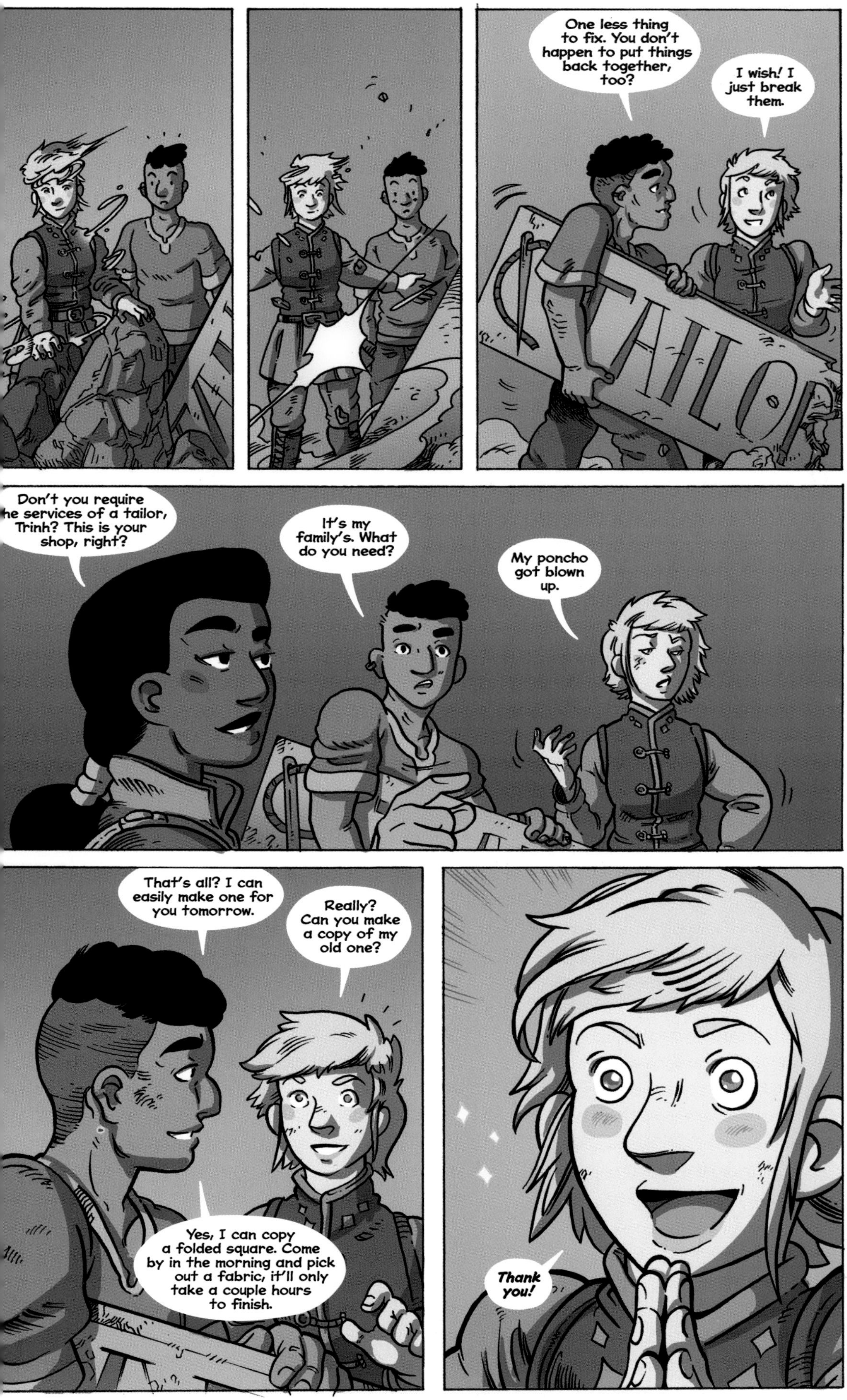

One less thing to fix. You don't happen to put things back together, too?
I wish! I just break them.
TAILOR
Don't you require he services of a tailor, Trinh? This is your shop, right?
It's my family's. What do you need?
My poncho got blown up.
That's all? I can easily make one for you tomorrow.
Really? Can you make a copy of my old one?
Yes, I can copy a folded square. Come by in the morning and pick out a fabric, it'll only take a couple hours to finish.
Thank you!

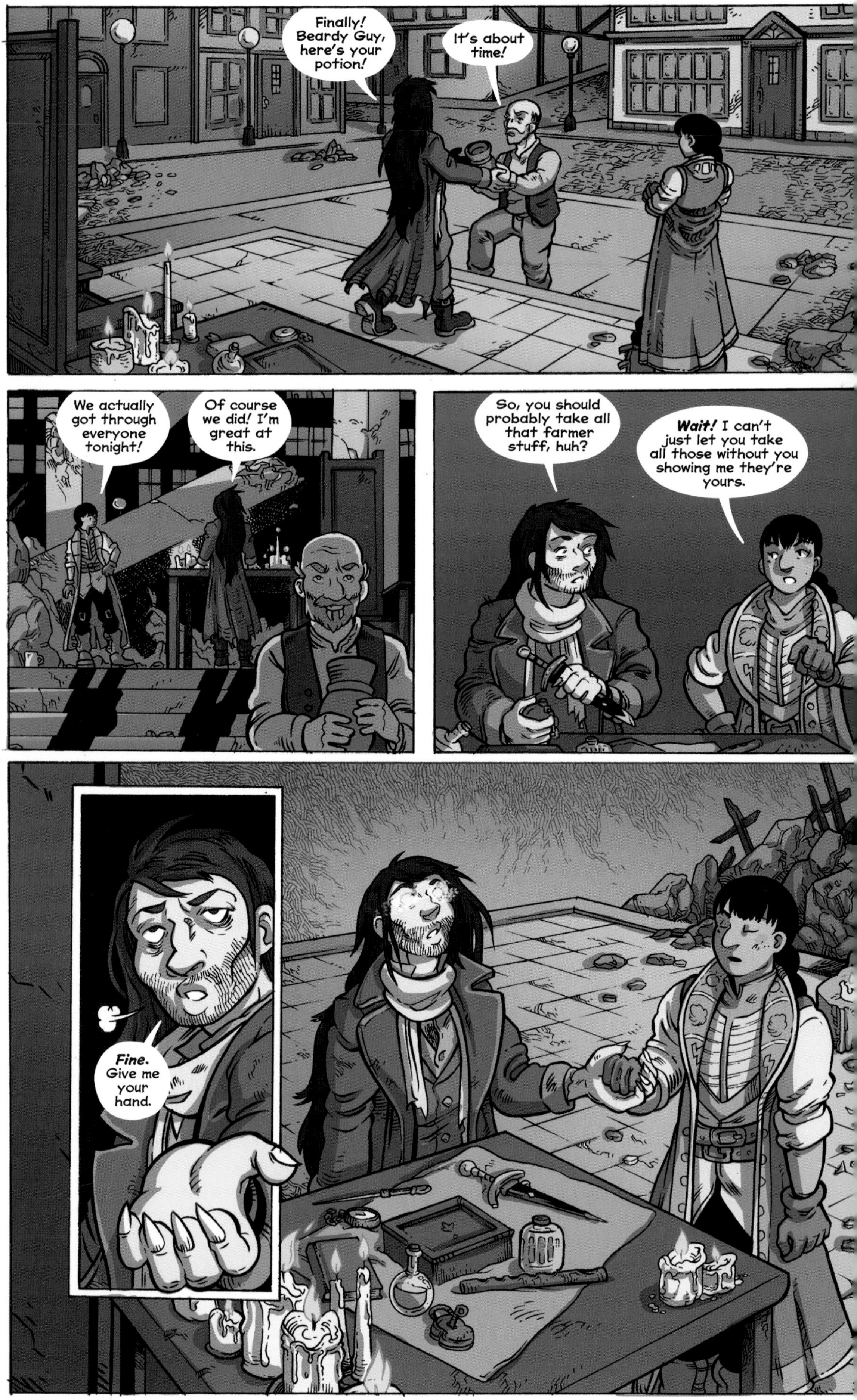
Finally! Beardy Guy, here's your potion!
It's about time!
We actually got through everyone tonight!
Of course we did! I'm great at this.
So, you should probably take all that farmer stuff, huh?
Wait! I can't just let you take all those without you showing me they're yours.
Fine. Give me your hand.

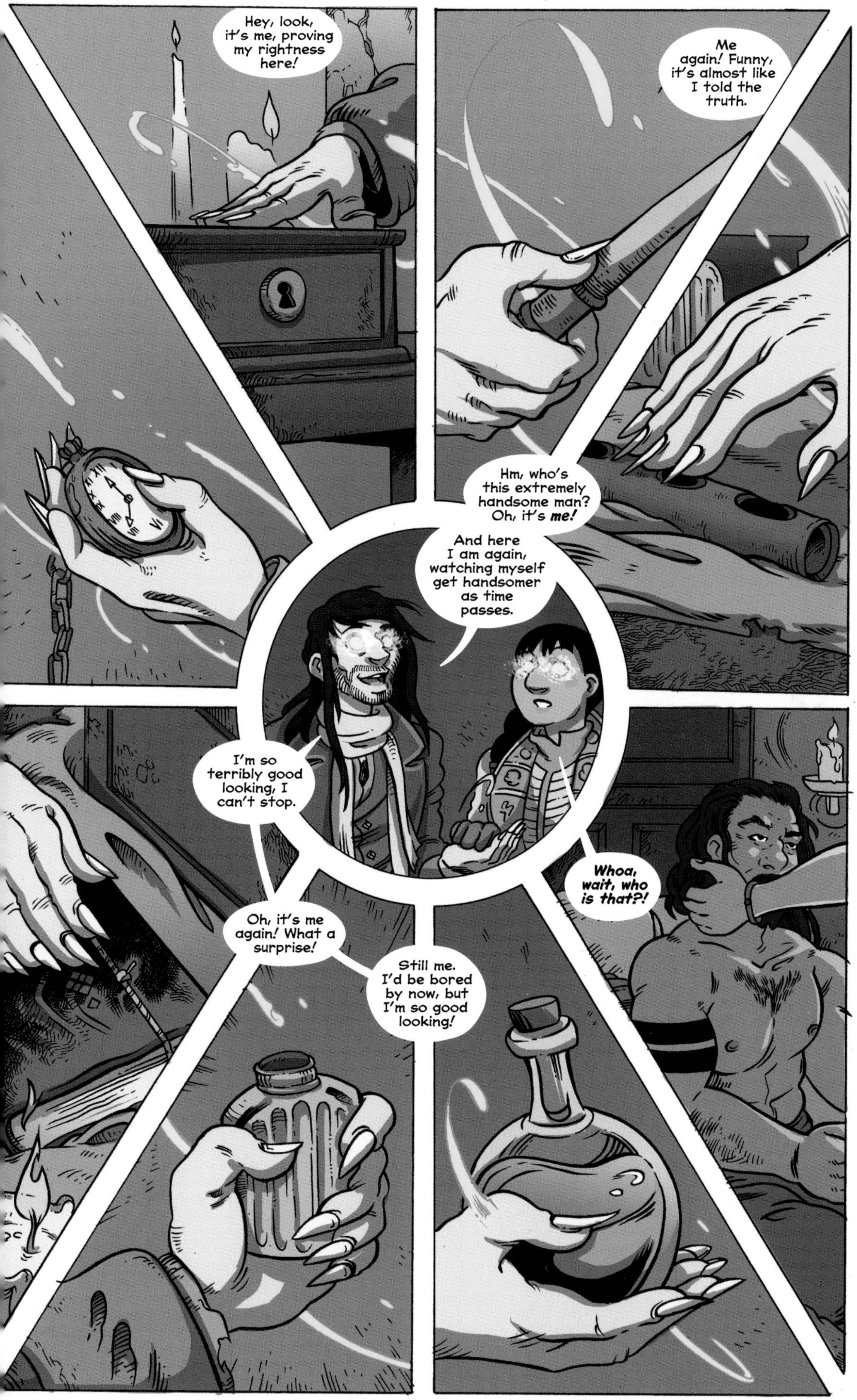

Hey, look, it's me, proving my rightness here!
Me again! Funny, it's almost like I told the truth.
Hm, who's this extremely handsome man? Oh, it's *me!*
And here I am again, watching myself get handsomer as time passes.
I'm so terribly good looking, I can't stop.
Whoa, wait, who is that?!
Oh, it's me again! What a surprise!
Still me. I'd be bored by now, but I'm so good looking!

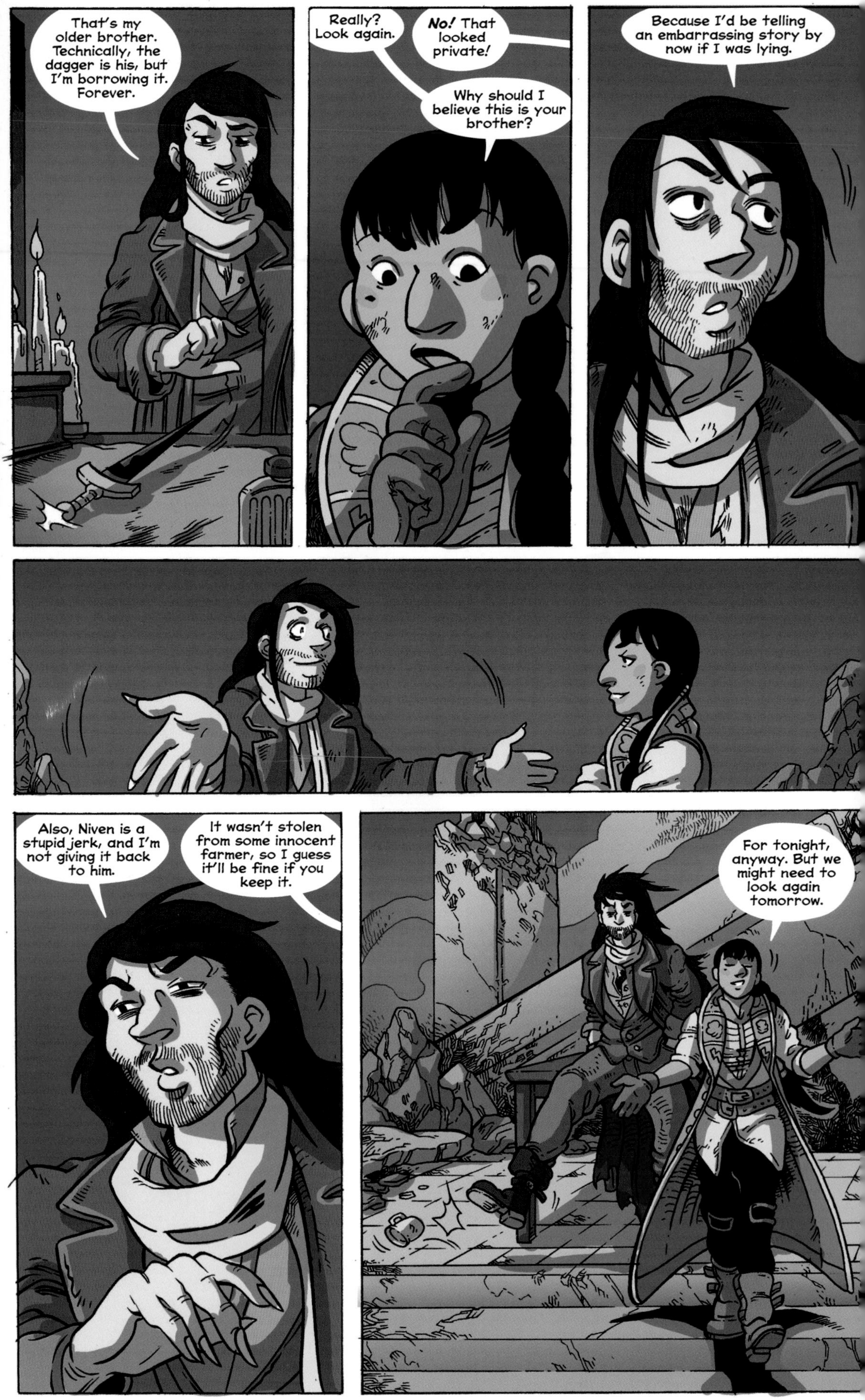
That's my older brother. Technically, the dagger is his, but I'm borrowing it. Forever.
Really? Look again.
No! That looked private!
Why should I believe this is your brother?
Because I'd be telling an embarrassing story by now if I was lying.
Also, Niven is a stupid jerk, and I'm not giving it back to him.
It wasn't stolen from some innocent farmer, so I guess it'll be fine if you keep it.
For tonight, anyway. But we might need to look again tomorrow.

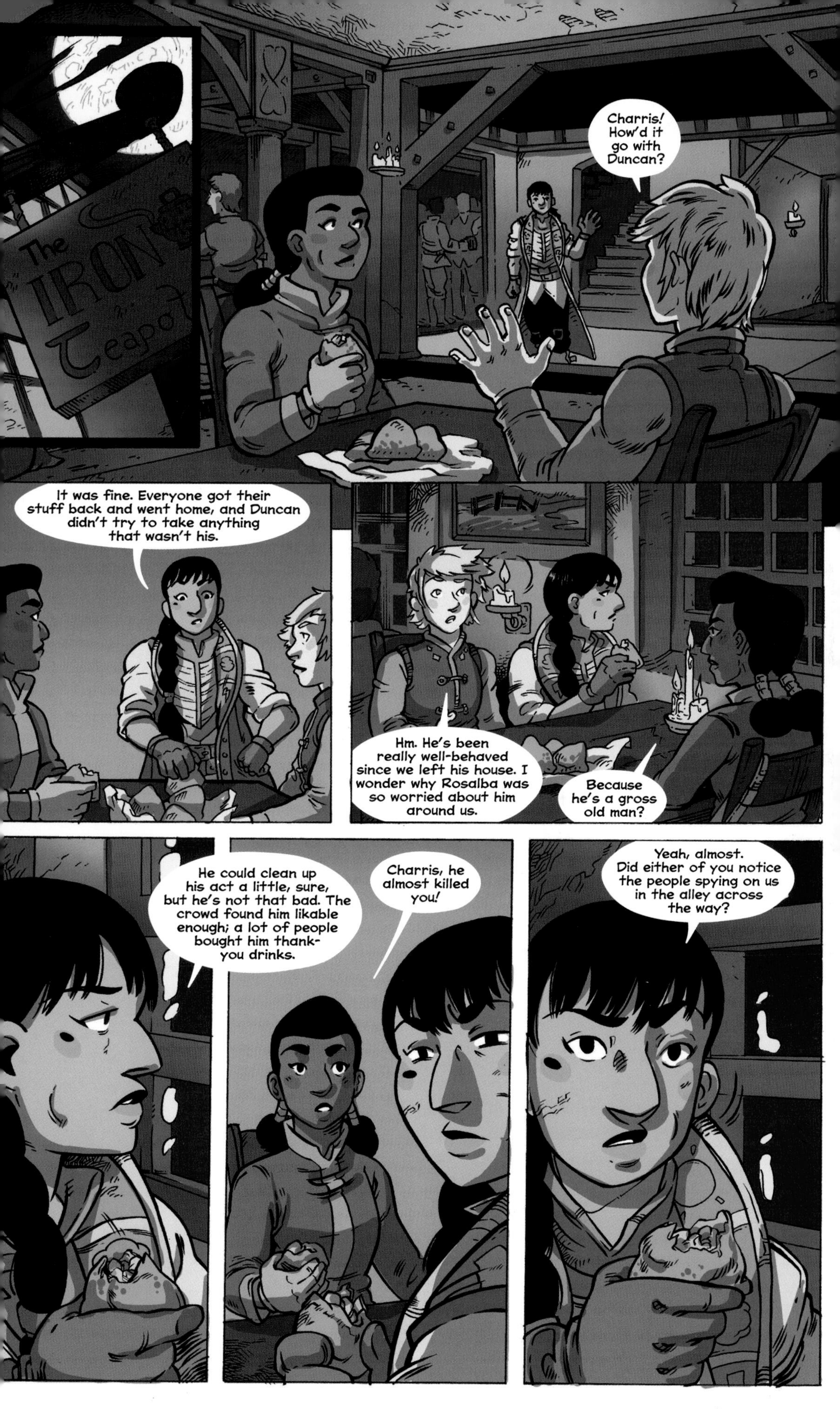
The IRON Teapot
Charris! How'd it go with Duncan?
It was fine. Everyone got their stuff back and went home, and Duncan didn't try to take anything that wasn't his.
Hm. He's been really well-behaved since we left his house. I wonder why Rosalba was so worried about him around us.
Because he's a gross old man?
He could clean up his act a little, sure, but he's not that bad. The crowd found him likable enough; a lot of people bought him thank-you drinks.
Charris, he almost killed you!
Yeah, almost. Did either of you notice the people spying on us in the alley across the way?

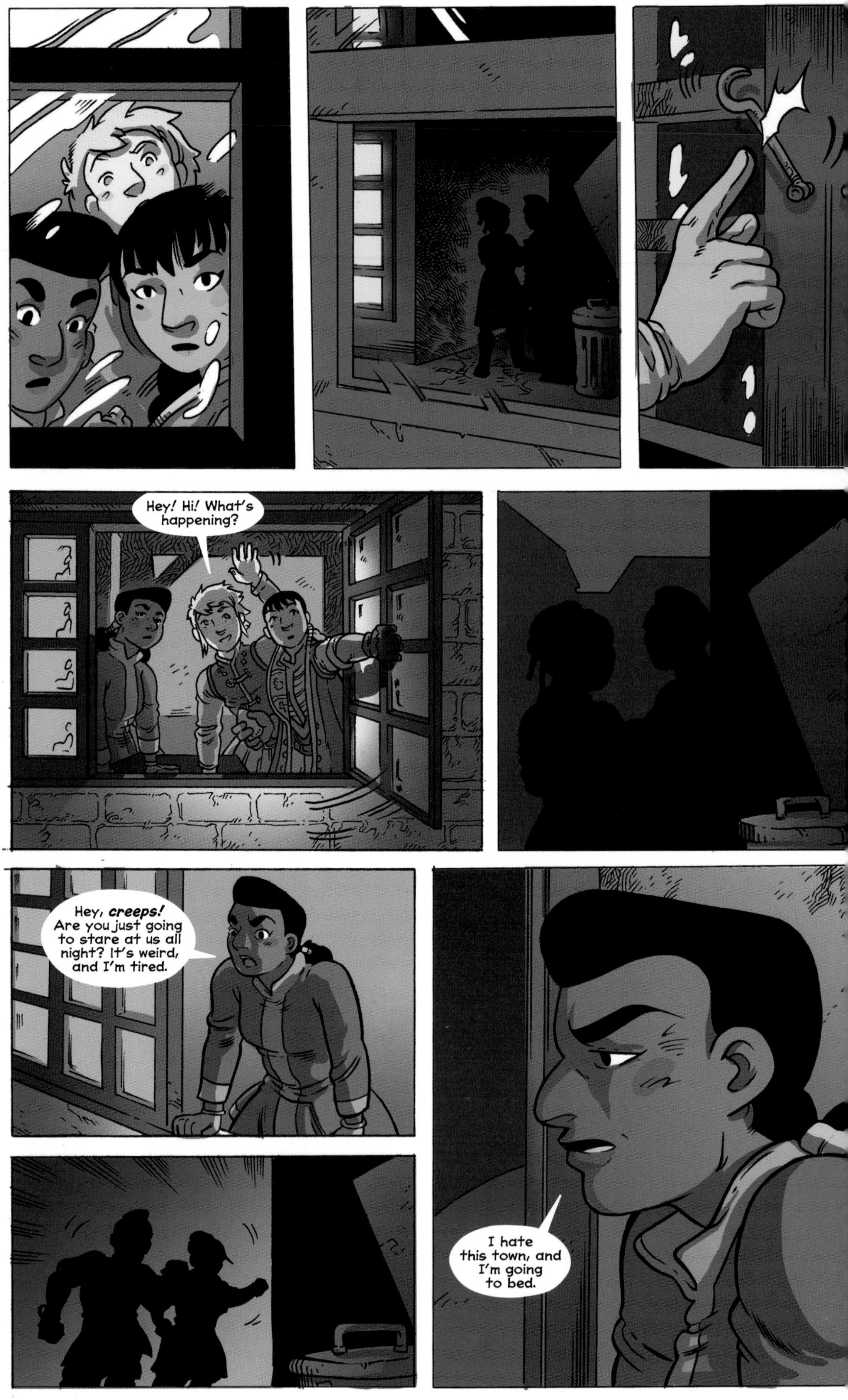
Hey! Hi! What's happening?
Hey, ***creeps!*** Are you just going to stare at us all night? It's weird, and I'm tired.
I hate this town, and I'm going to bed.

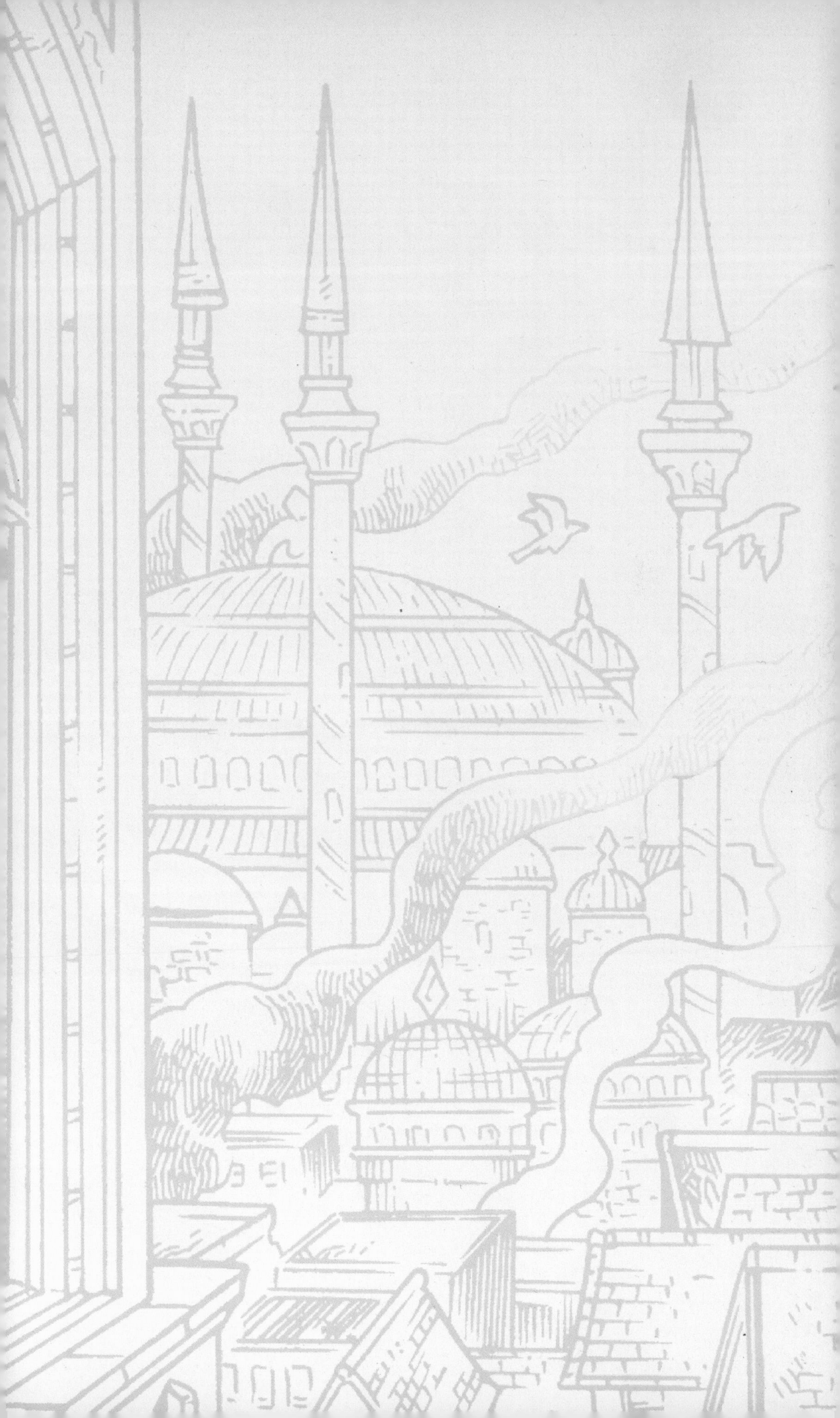

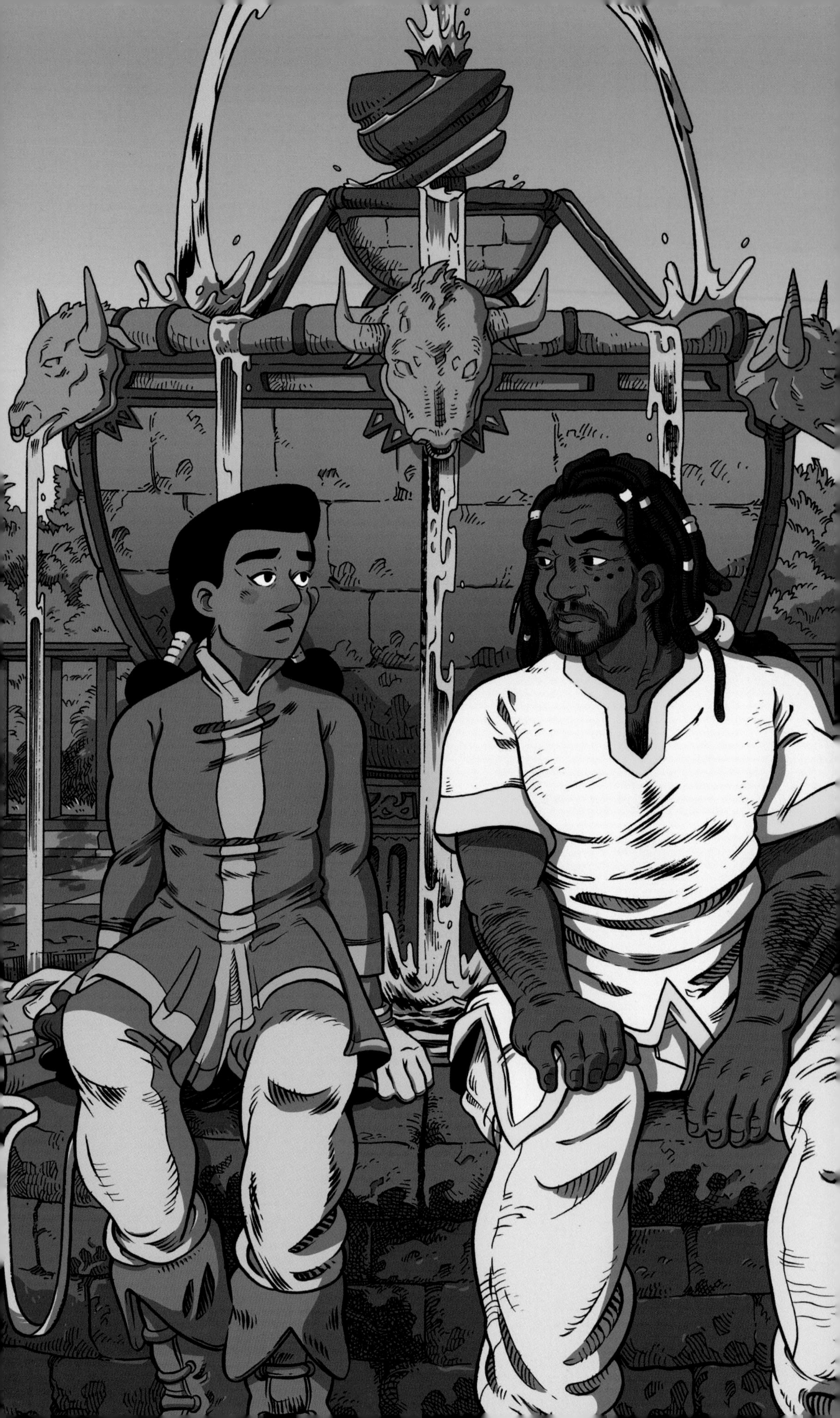

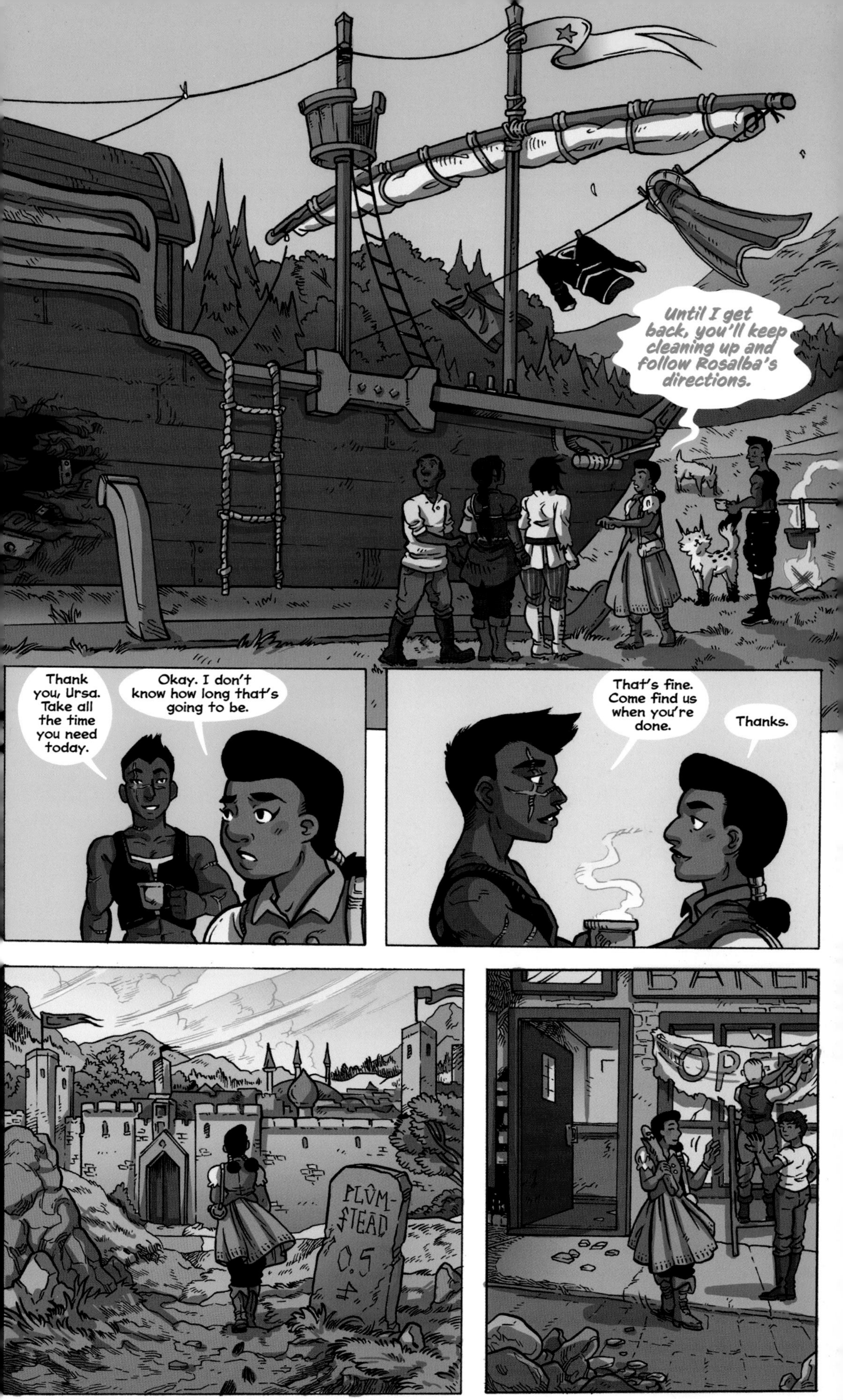
Until I get back, you'll keep cleaning up and follow Rosalba's directions.
Thank you, Ursa. Take all the time you need today.
Okay. I don't know how long that's going to be.
That's fine. Come find us when you're done.
Thanks.
PLÛM-
STEAD
0.5

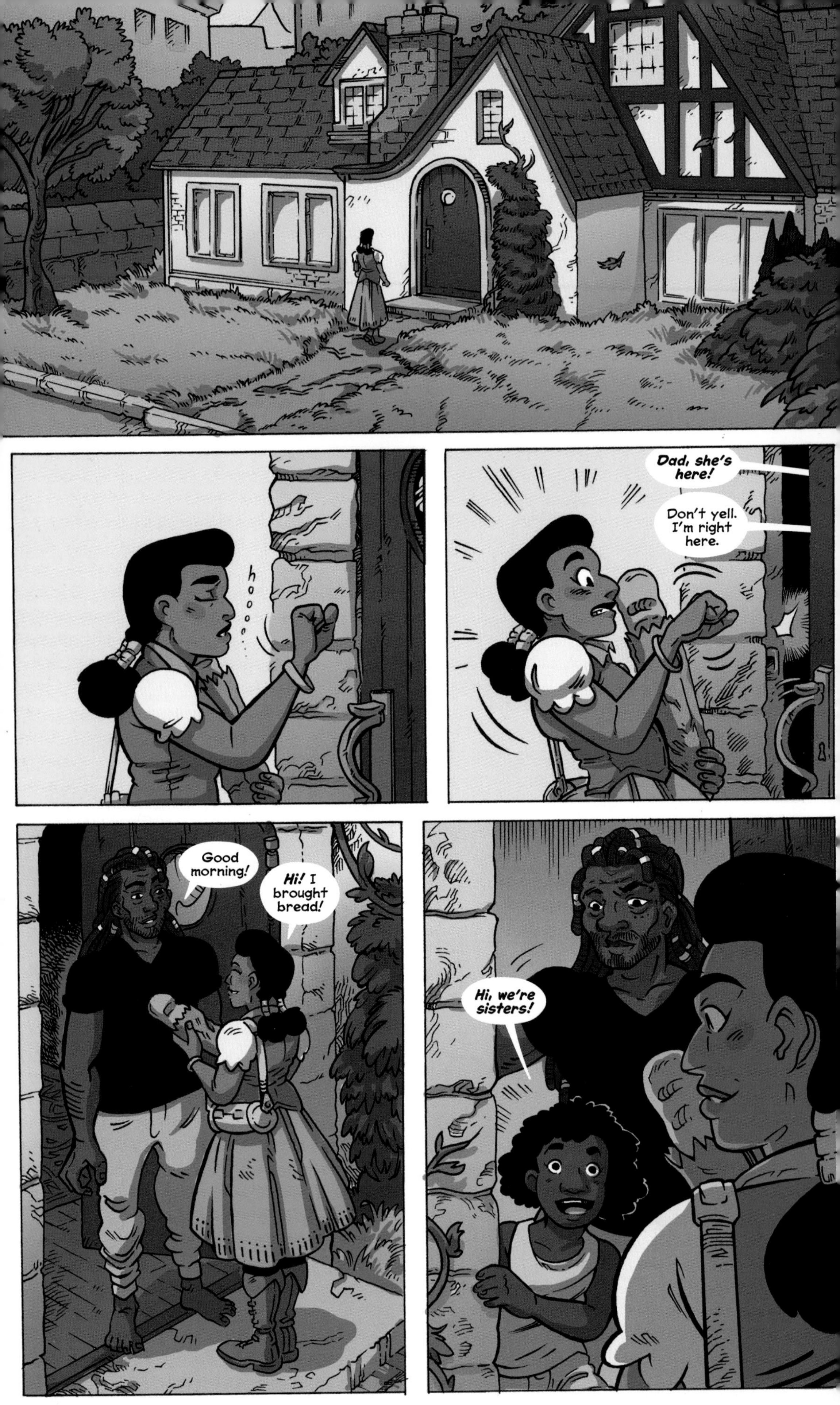
hoooo...
Dad, she's here!
Don't yell. I'm right here.
Good morning!
Hi! I brought bread!
Hi, we're sisters!

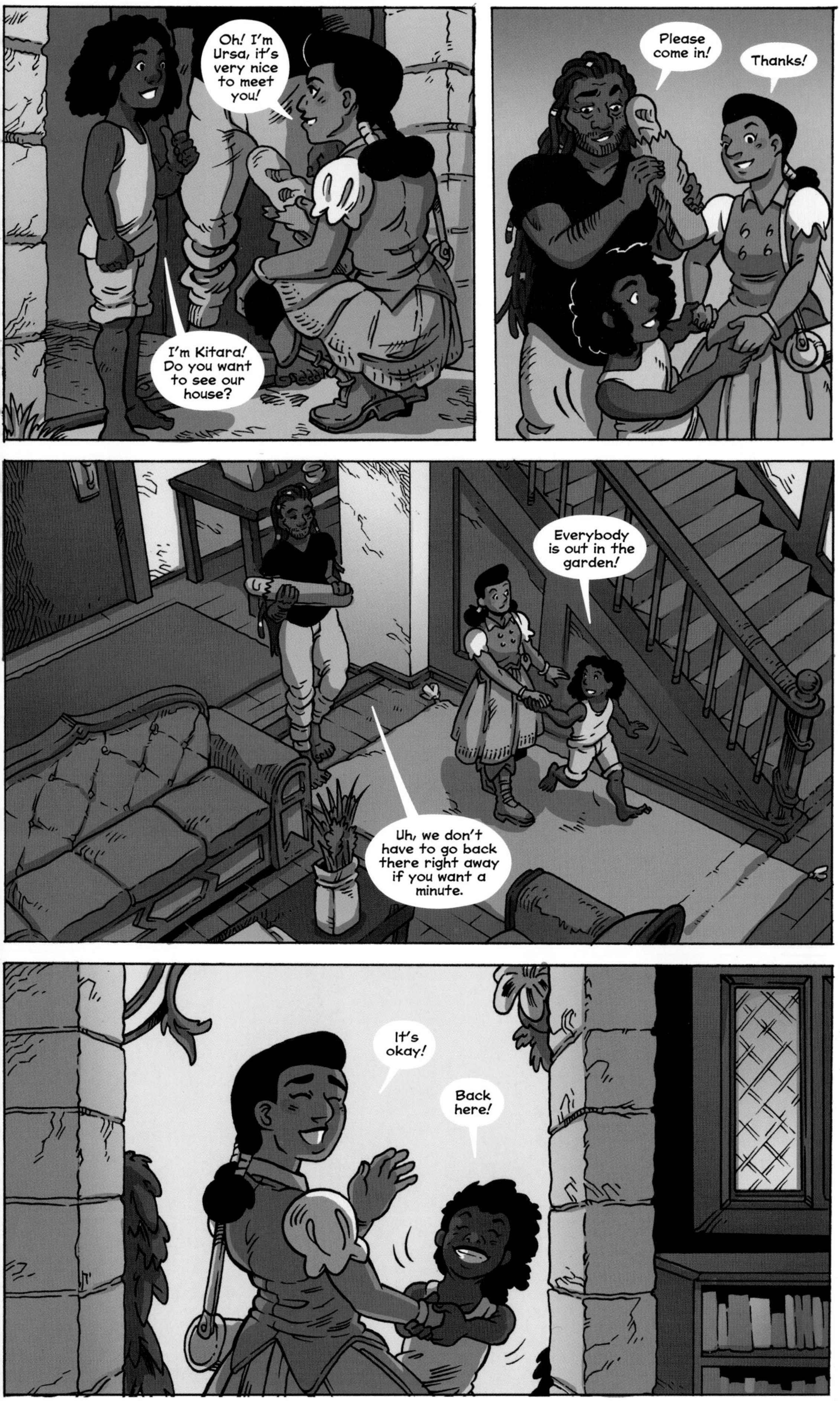
Oh! I'm Ursa, it's very nice to meet you!
I'm Kitara! Do you want to see our house?
Please come in!
Thanks!
Everybody is out in the garden!
Uh, we don't have to go back there right away if you want a minute.
It's okay!
Back here!

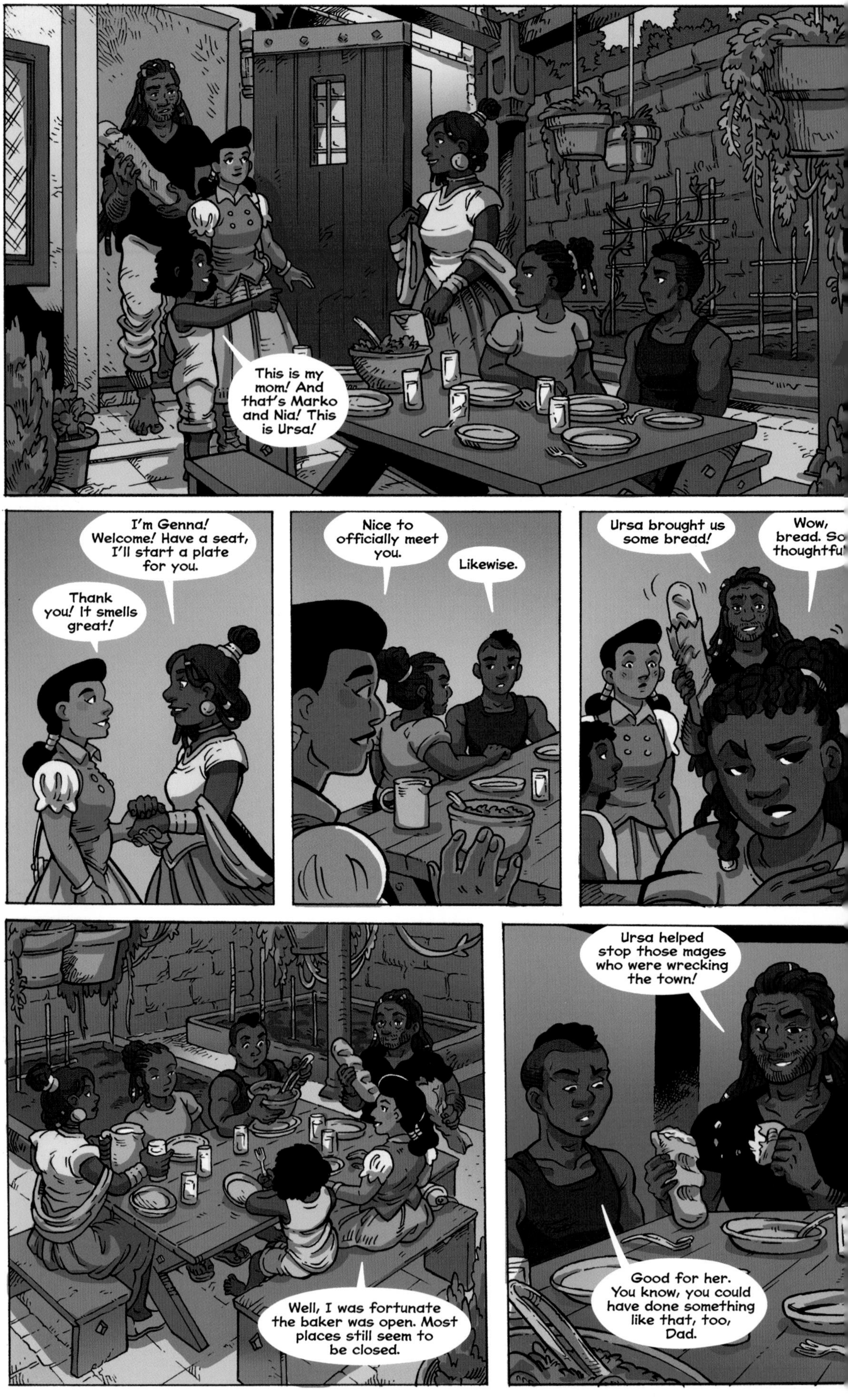
This is my mom! And that's Marko and Nia! This is Ursa!
I'm Genna! Welcome! Have a seat, I'll start a plate for you.
Thank you! It smells great!
Nice to officially meet you.
Likewise.
Ursa brought us some bread!
Wow, bread. So thoughtfu
Well, I was fortunate the baker was open. Most places still seem to be closed.
Ursa helped stop those mages who were wrecking the town!
Good for her. You know, you could have done something like that, too, Dad.

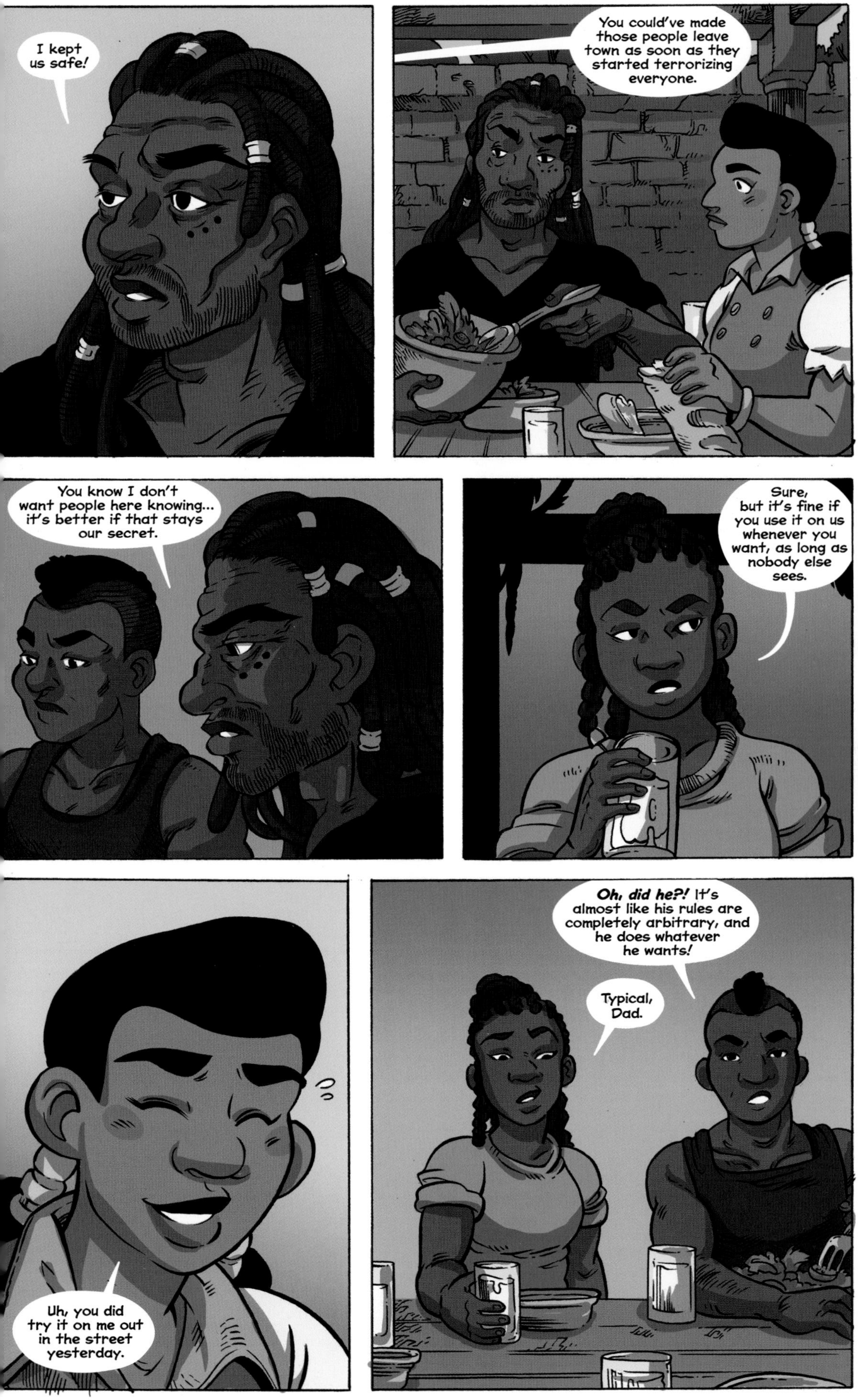
I kept us safe!
You could've made those people leave town as soon as they started terrorizing everyone.
You know I don't want people here knowing... it's better if that stays our secret.
Sure, but it's fine if you use it on us whenever you want, as long as nobody else sees.
Uh, you did try it on me out in the street yesterday.
Oh, did he?! It's almost like his rules are completely arbitrary, and he does whatever he wants!
Typical, Dad.

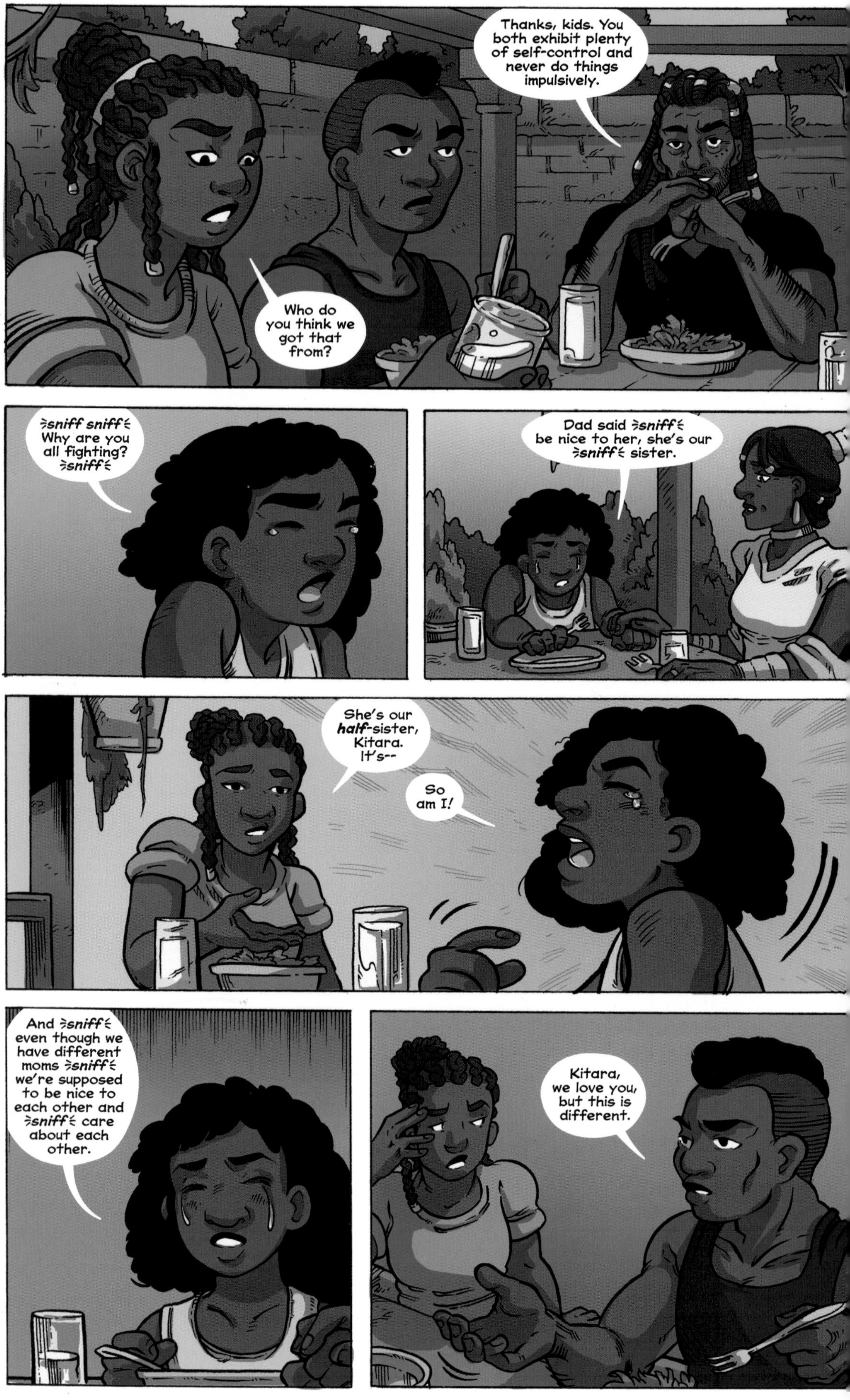

Thanks, kids. You both exhibit plenty of self-control and never do things impulsively.
Who do you think we got that from?
⋟sniff sniff⋞ Why are you all fighting? ⋟sniff⋞
Dad said ⋟sniff⋞ be nice to her, she's our ⋟sniff⋞ sister.
She's our ***half***-sister, Kitara. It's--
So am I!
And ⋟sniff⋞ even though we have different moms ⋟sniff⋞ we're supposed to be nice to each other and ⋟sniff⋞ care about each other.
Kitara, we love you, but this is different.

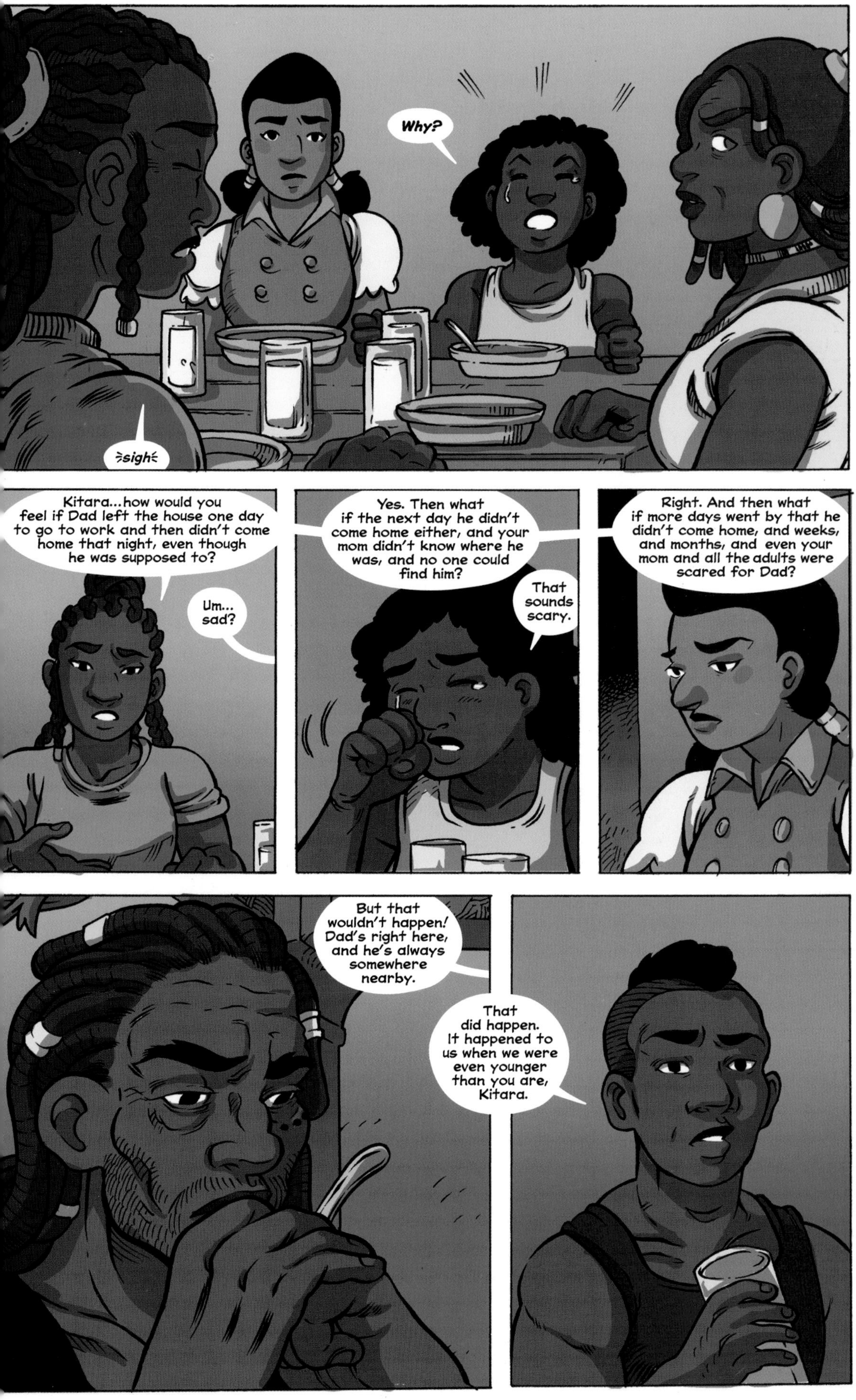
Why?
sigh
Kitara...how would you feel if Dad left the house one day to go to work and then didn't come home that night, even though he was supposed to?
Um... sad?
Yes. Then what if the next day he didn't come home either, and your mom didn't know where he was, and no one could find him?
That sounds scary.
Right. And then what if more days went by that he didn't come home, and weeks, and months, and even your mom and all the adults were scared for Dad?
But that wouldn't happen! Dad's right here, and he's always somewhere nearby.
That did happen. It happened to us when we were even younger than you are, Kitara.

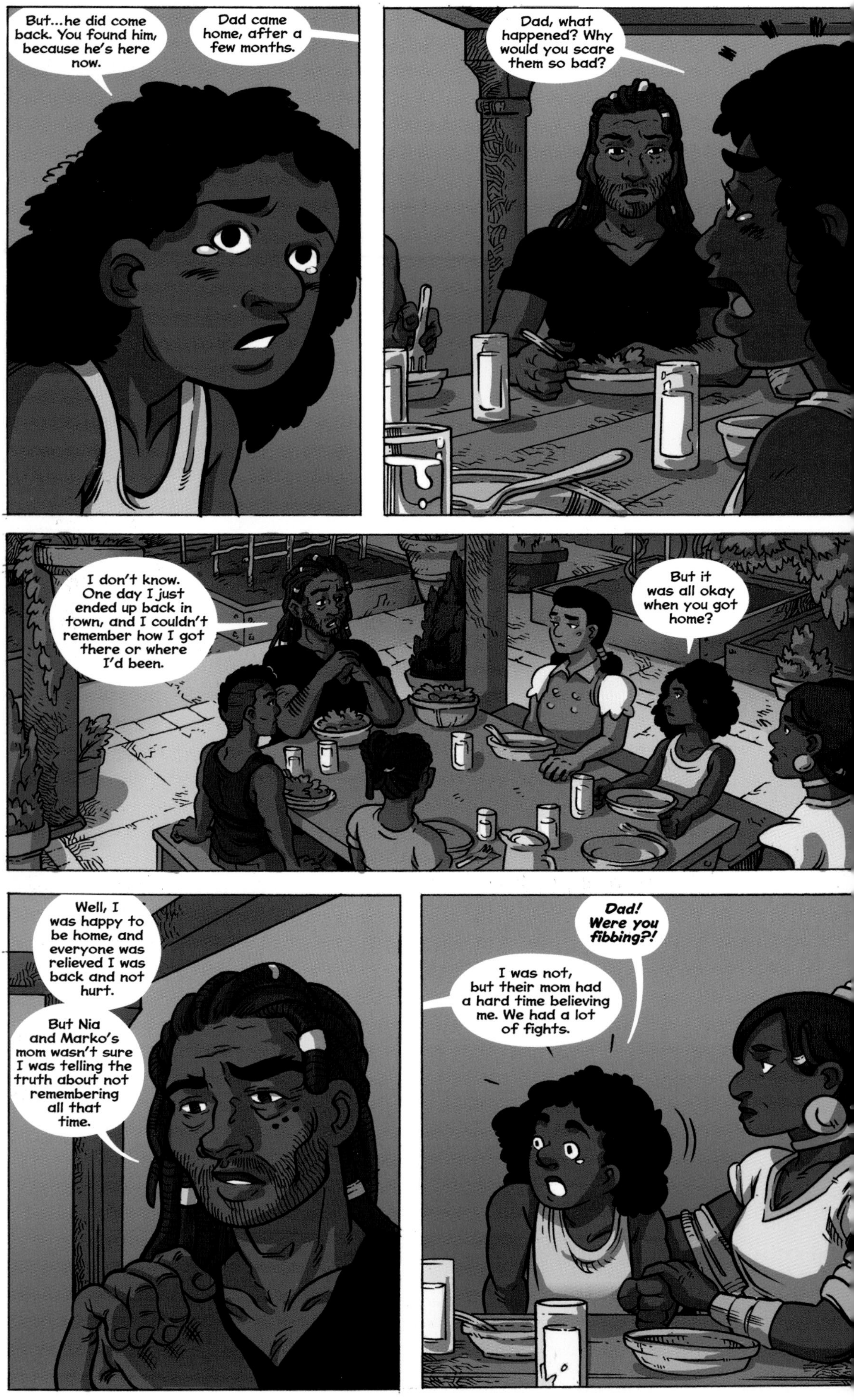

But...he did come back. You found him, because he's here now.
Dad came home, after a few months.
Dad, what happened? Why would you scare them so bad?
I don't know. One day I just ended up back in town, and I couldn't remember how I got there or where I'd been.
But it was all okay when you got home?
Well, I was happy to be home, and everyone was relieved I was back and not hurt.
But Nia and Marko's mom wasn't sure I was telling the truth about not remembering all that time.
Dad! Were you fibbing?!
I was not, but their mom had a hard time believing me. We had a lot of fights.

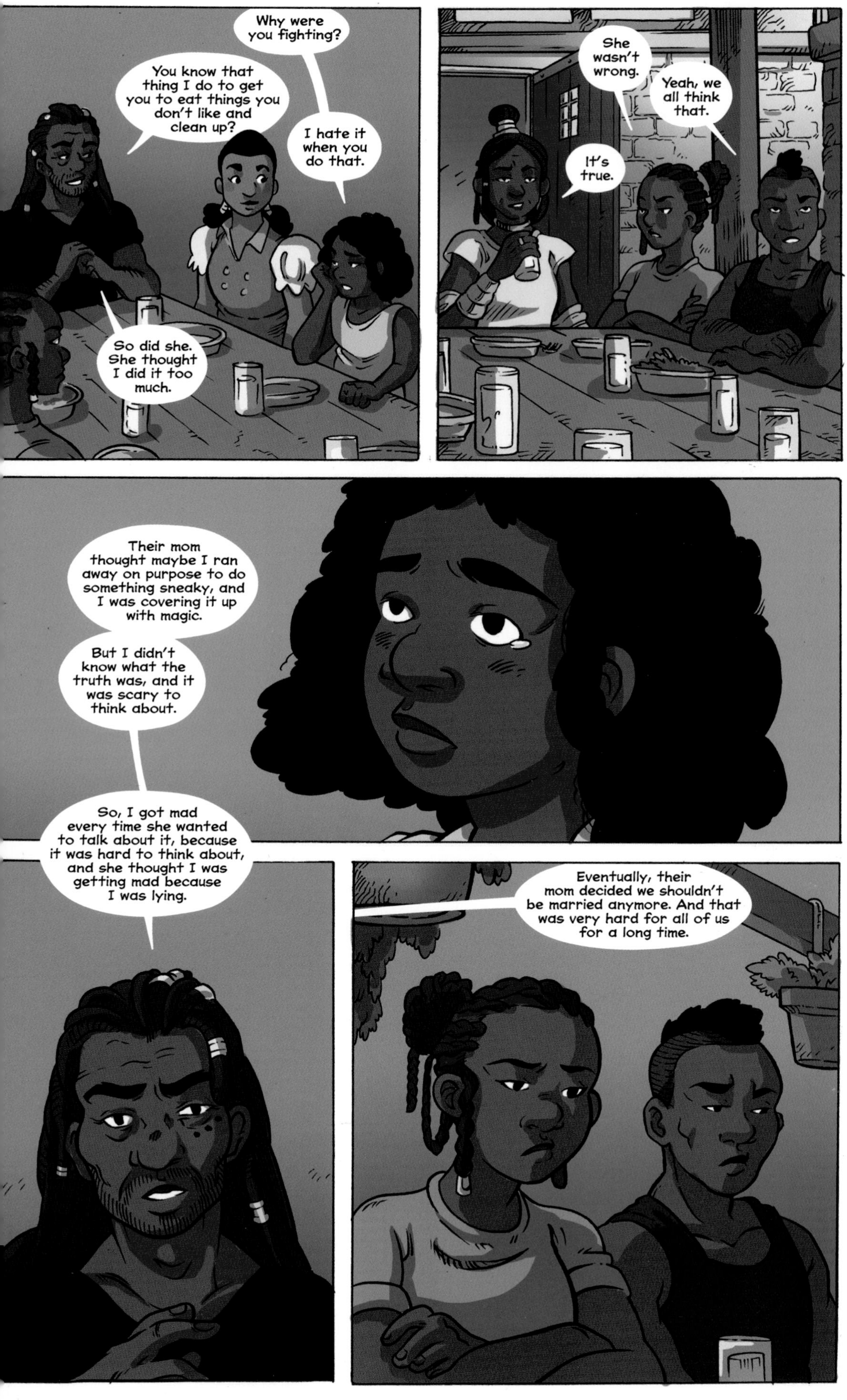
Why were you fighting?
You know that thing I do to get you to eat things you don't like and clean up?
I hate it when you do that.
So did she. She thought I did it too much.
She wasn't wrong.
Yeah, we all think that.
It's true.
Their mom thought maybe I ran away on purpose to do something sneaky, and I was covering it up with magic.
But I didn't know what the truth was, and it was scary to think about.
So, I got mad every time she wanted to talk about it, because it was hard to think about, and she thought I was getting mad because I was lying.
Eventually, their mom decided we shouldn't be married anymore. And that was very hard for all of us for a long time.

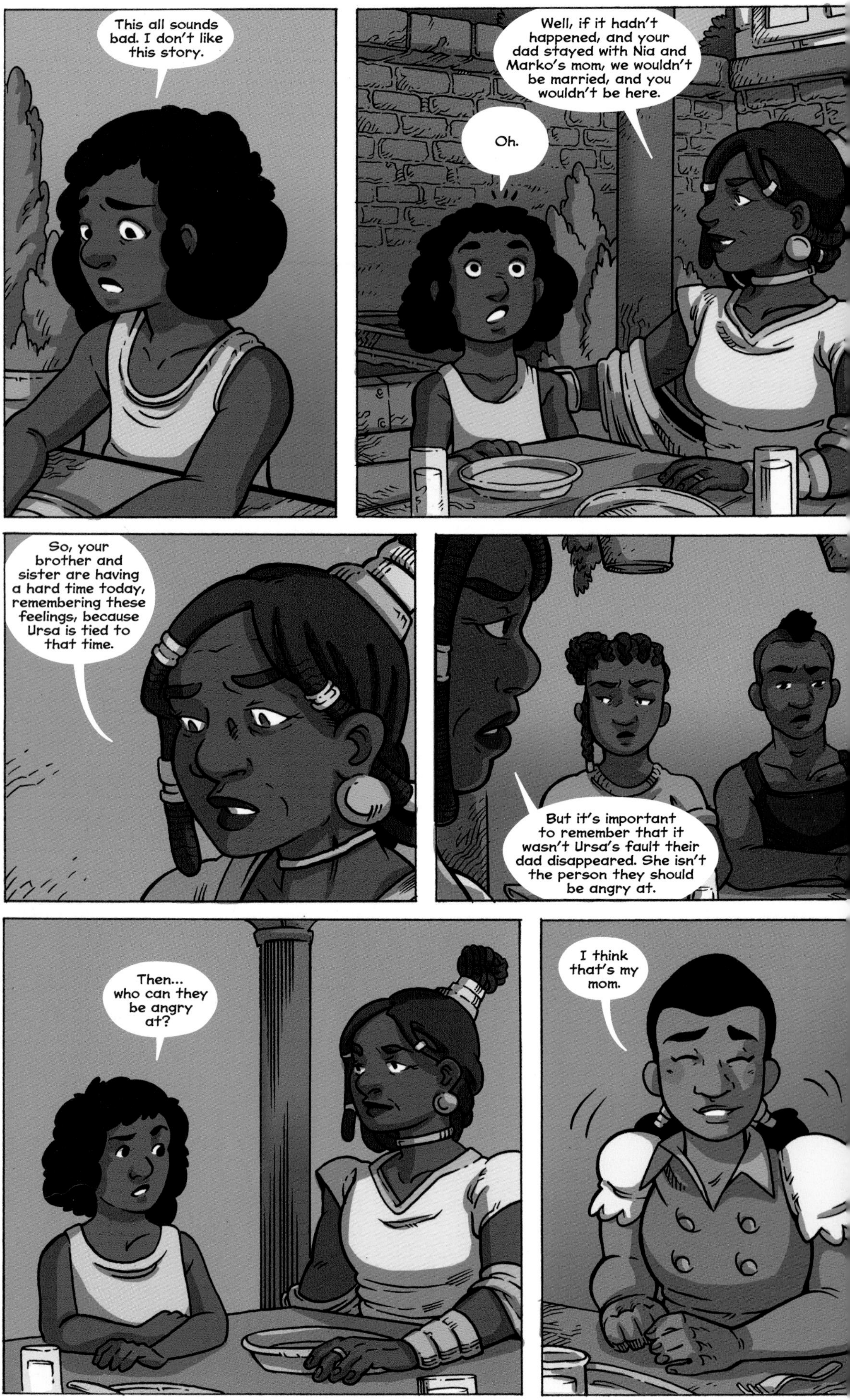
This all sounds bad. I don't like this story.
Well, if it hadn't happened, and your dad stayed with Nia and Marko's mom, we wouldn't be married, and you wouldn't be here.
Oh.
So, your brother and sister are having a hard time today, remembering these feelings, because Ursa is tied to that time.
But it's important to remember that it wasn't Ursa's fault their dad disappeared. She isn't the person they should be angry at.
Then... who can they be angry at?
I think that's my mom.

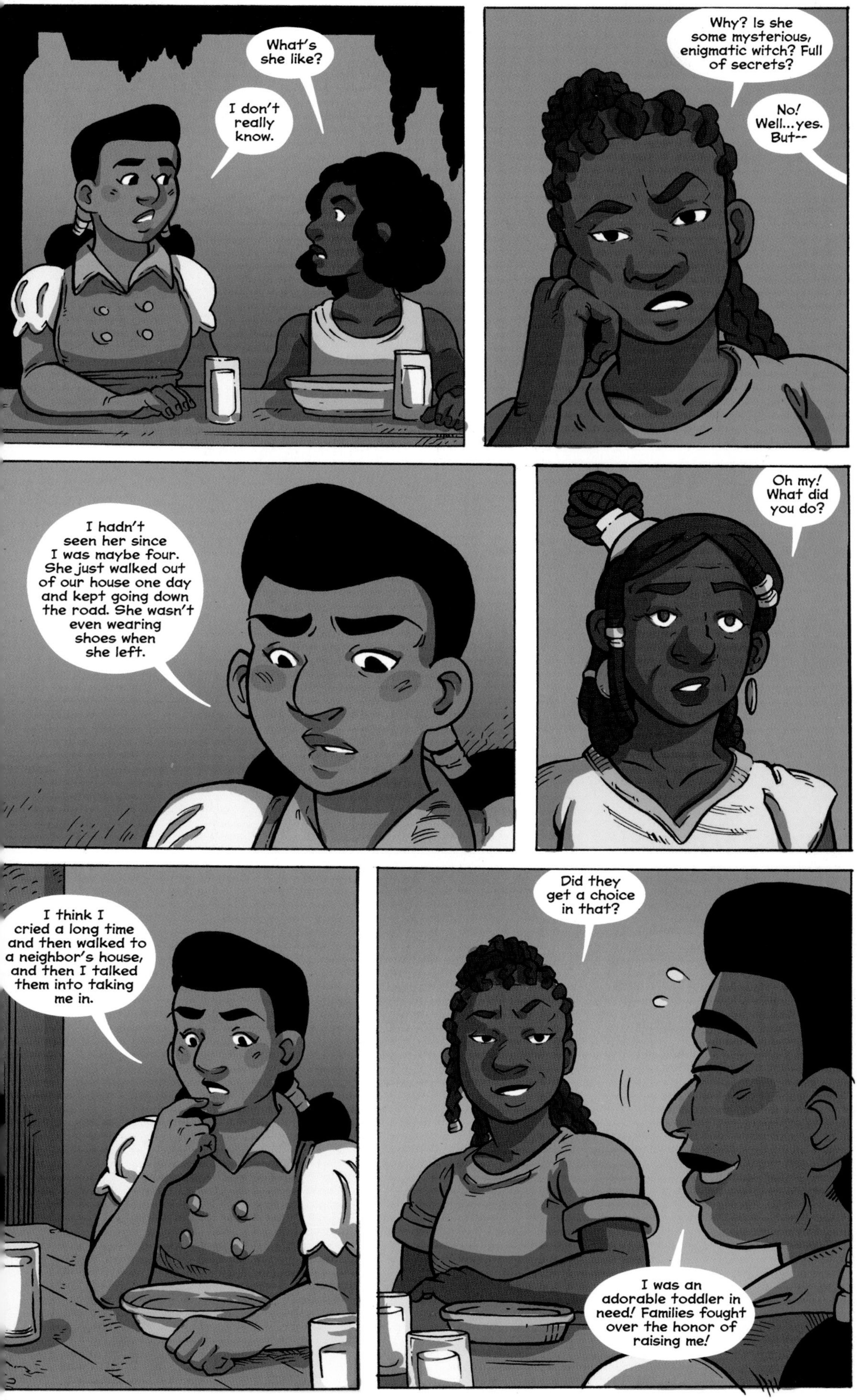
What's she like?
I don't really know.
Why? Is she some mysterious, enigmatic witch? Full of secrets?
No! Well...yes. But--
I hadn't seen her since I was maybe four. She just walked out of our house one day and kept going down the road. She wasn't even wearing shoes when she left.
Oh my! What did you do?
I think I cried a long time and then walked to a neighbor's house, and then I talked them into taking me in.
Did they get a choice in that?
I was an adorable toddler in need! Families fought over the honor of raising me!

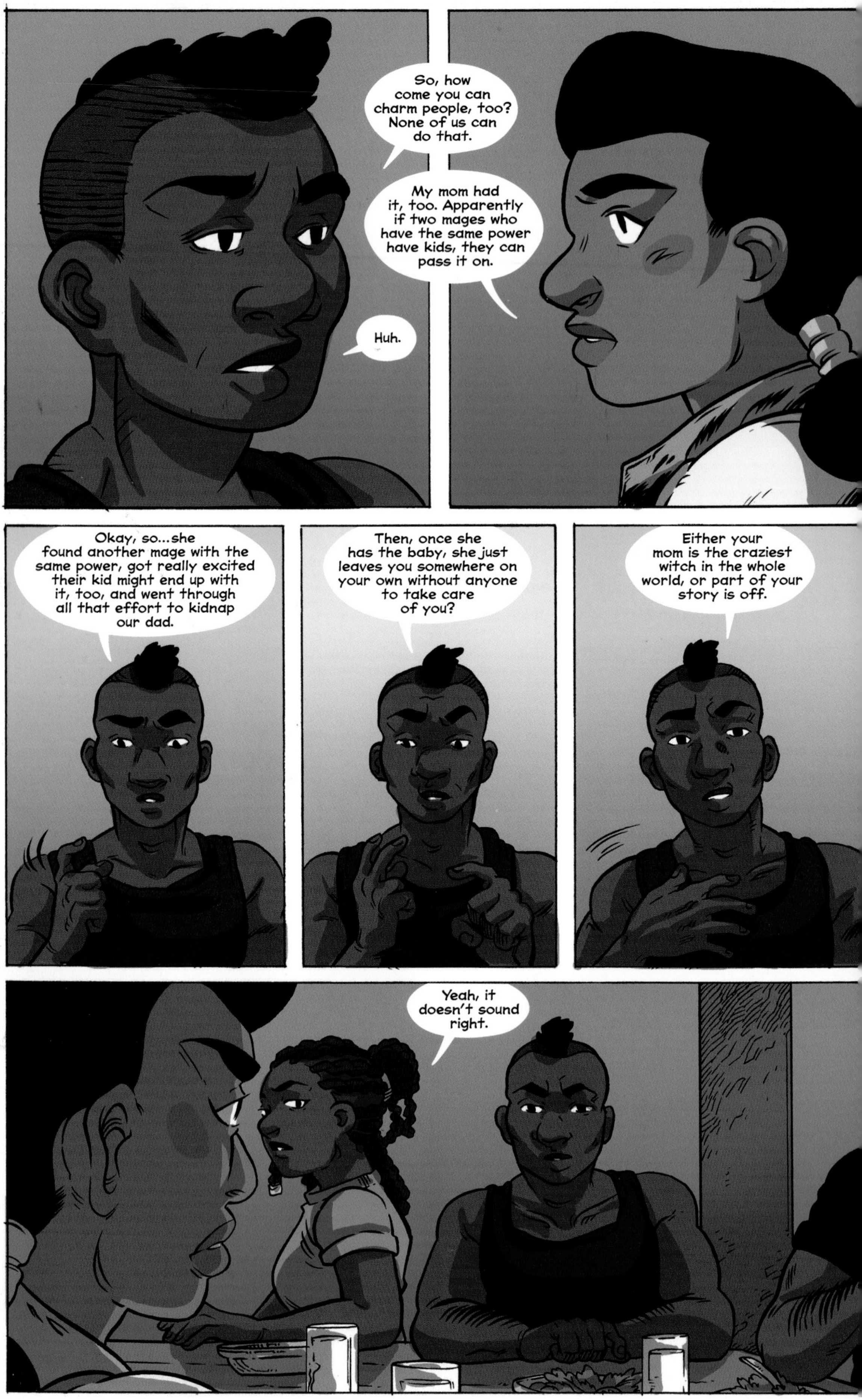
So, how come you can charm people, too? None of us can do that.
My mom had it, too. Apparently if two mages who have the same power have kids, they can pass it on.
Huh.
Okay, so...she found another mage with the same power, got really excited their kid might end up with it, too, and went through all that effort to kidnap our dad.
Then, once she has the baby, she just leaves you somewhere on your own without anyone to take care of you?
Either your mom is the craziest witch in the whole world, or part of your story is off.
Yeah, it doesn't sound right.

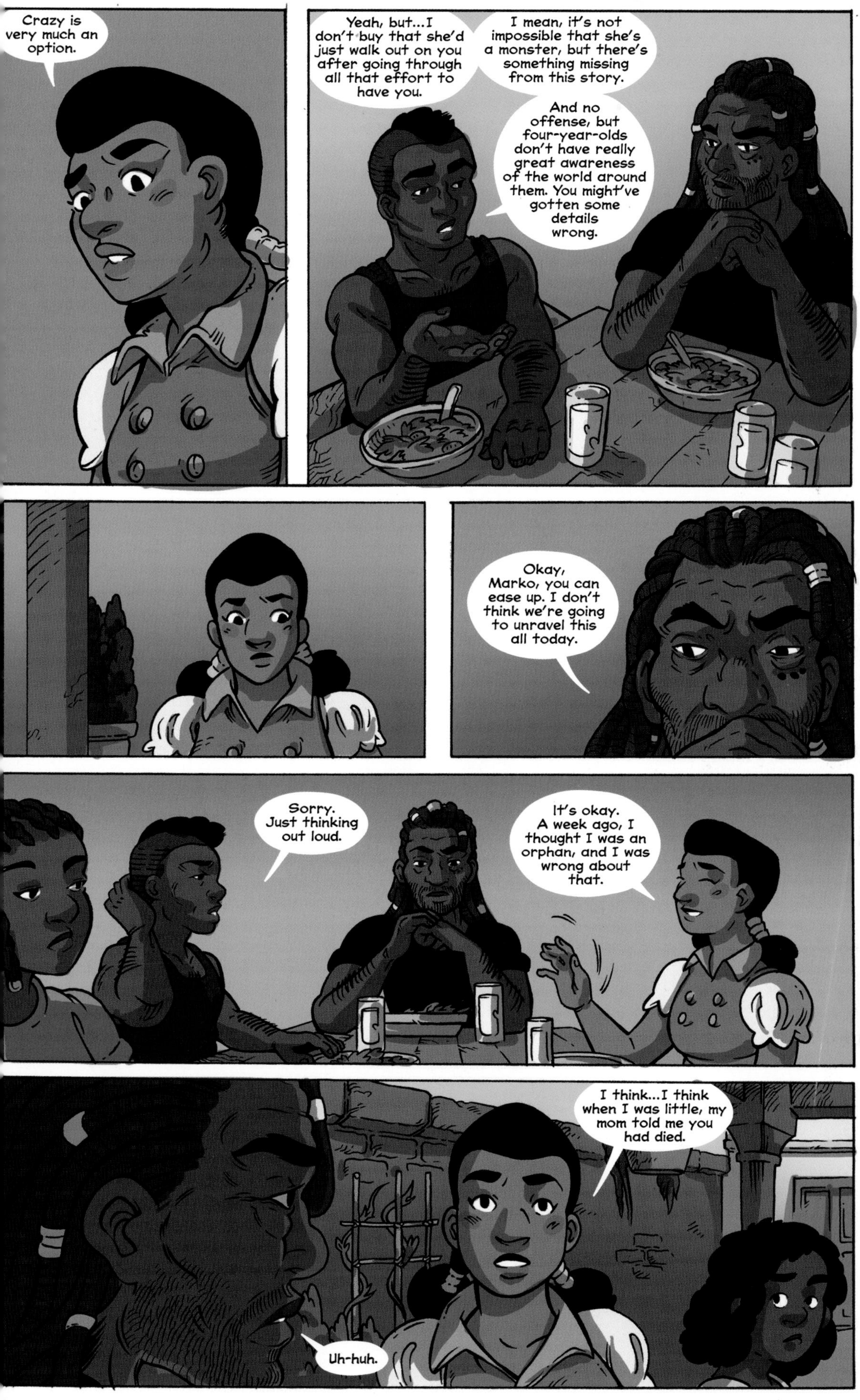
Crazy is very much an option.
Yeah, but...I don't buy that she'd just walk out on you after going through all that effort to have you.
I mean, it's not impossible that she's a monster, but there's something missing from this story.
And no offense, but four-year-olds don't have really great awareness of the world around them. You might've gotten some details wrong.
Okay, Marko, you can ease up. I don't think we're going to unravel this all today.
Sorry. Just thinking out loud.
It's okay. A week ago, I thought I was an orphan, and I was wrong about that.
I think...I think when I was little, my mom told me you had died.
Uh-huh.

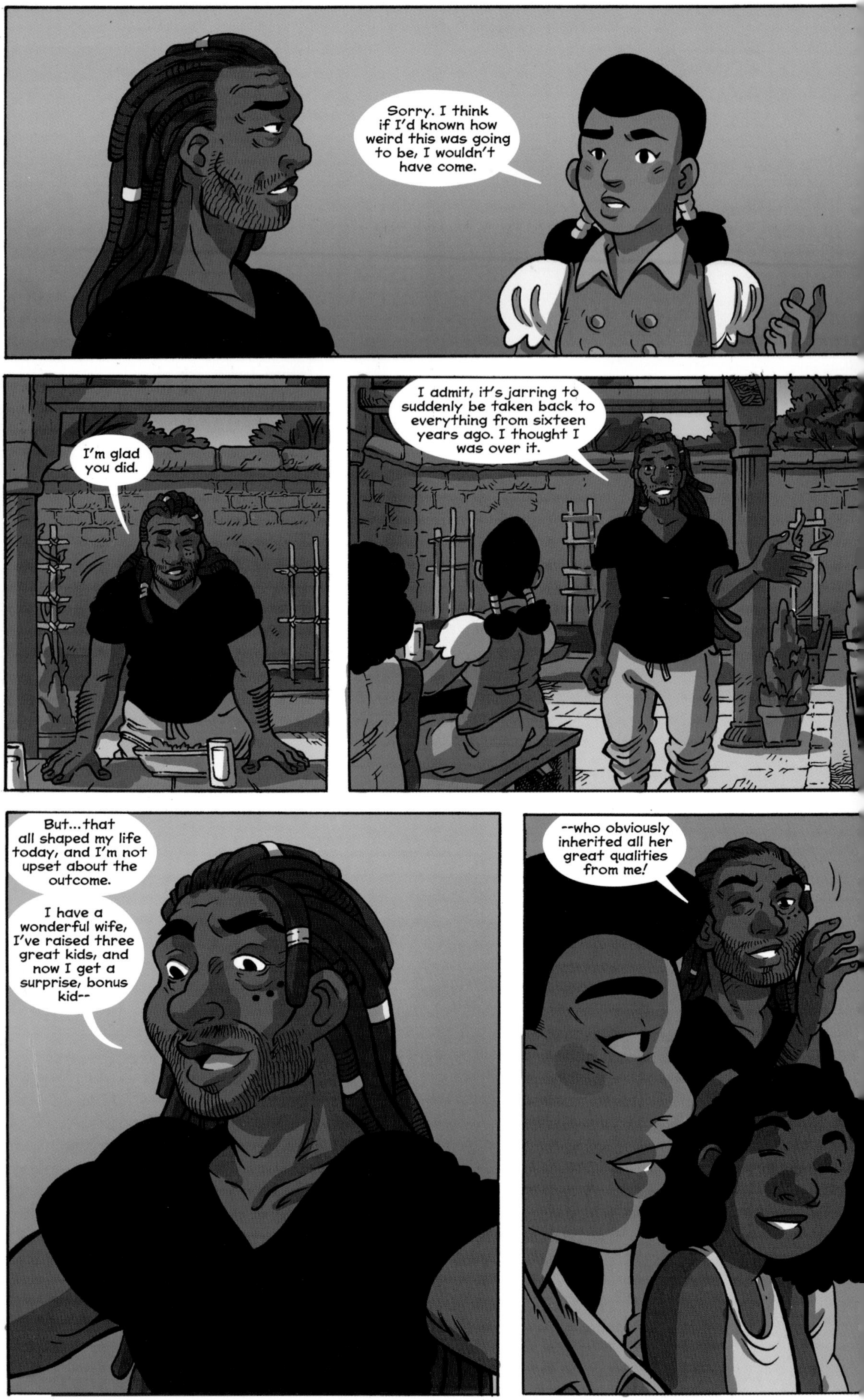
Sorry. I think if I'd known how weird this was going to be, I wouldn't have come.
I'm glad you did.
I admit, it's jarring to suddenly be taken back to everything from sixteen years ago. I thought I was over it.
But...that all shaped my life today, and I'm not upset about the outcome.
I have a wonderful wife, I've raised three great kids, and now I get a surprise, bonus kid--
--who obviously inherited all her great qualities from me!

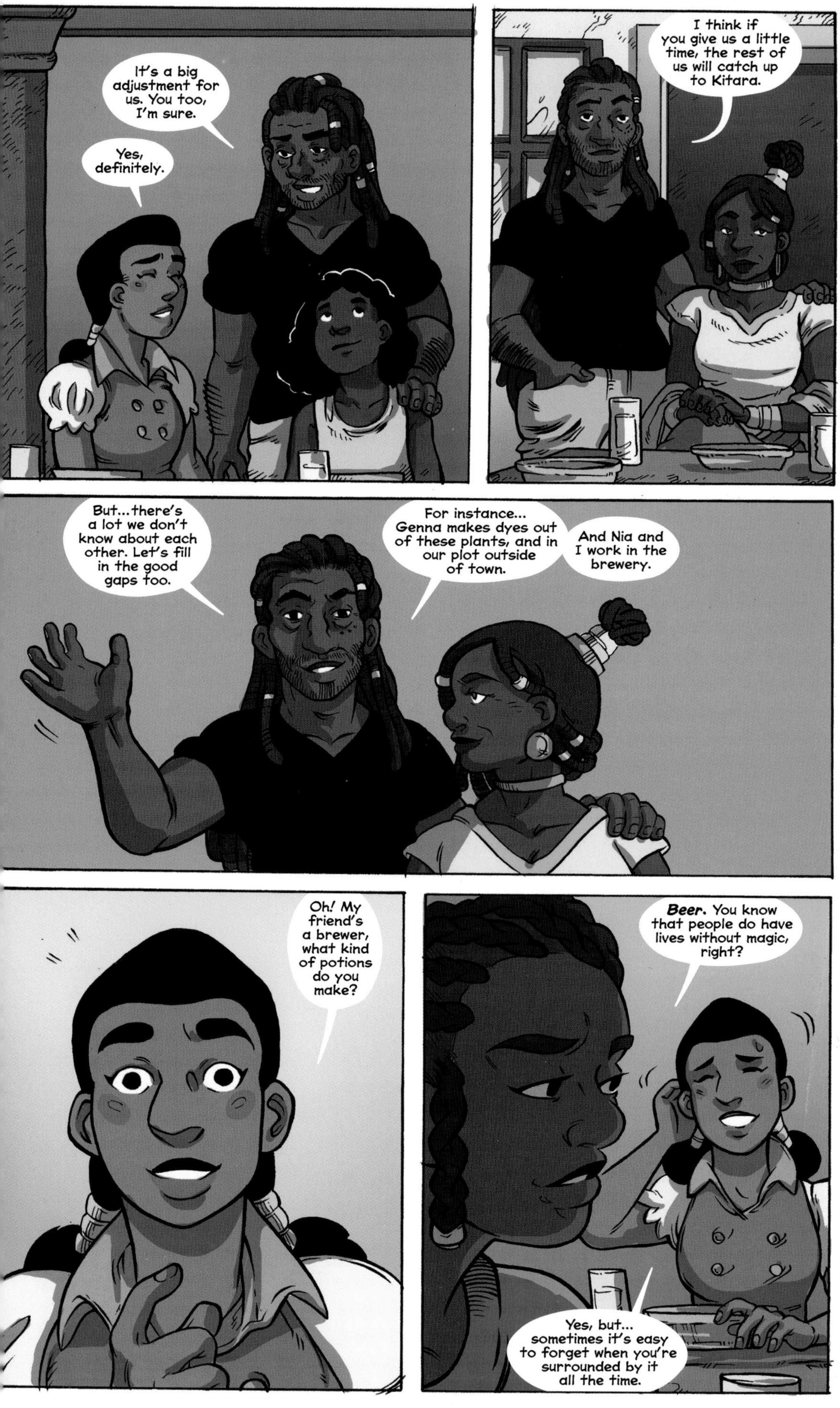
It's a big adjustment for us. You too, I'm sure.
Yes, definitely.
I think if you give us a little time, the rest of us will catch up to Kitara.
But...there's a lot we don't know about each other. Let's fill in the good gaps too.
For instance... Genna makes dyes out of these plants, and in our plot outside of town.
And Nia and I work in the brewery.
Oh! My friend's a brewer, what kind of potions do you make?
Beer. You know that people do have lives without magic, right?
Yes, but... sometimes it's easy to forget when you're surrounded by it all the time.

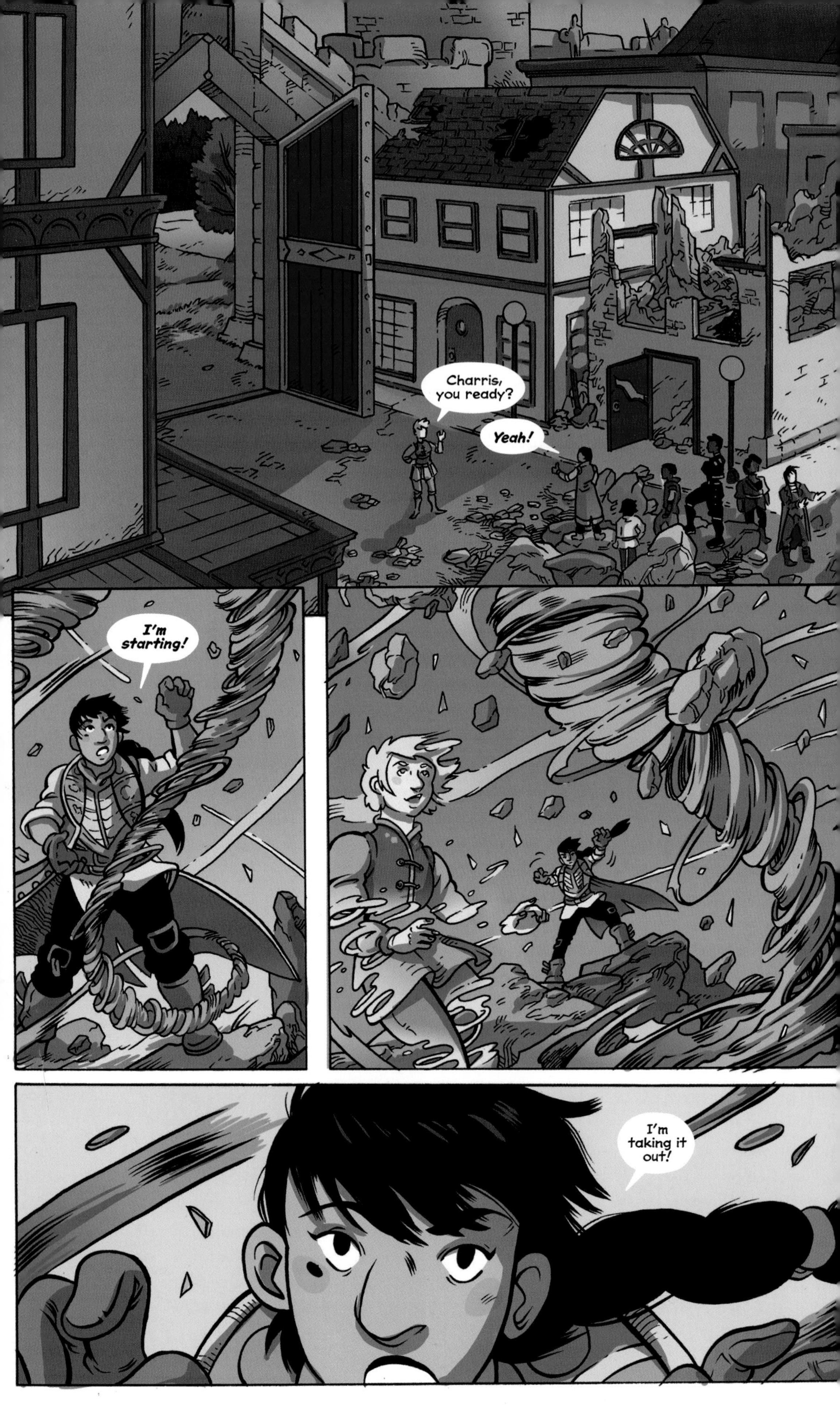
Charris, you ready?
Yeah!
I'm starting!
I'm taking it out!

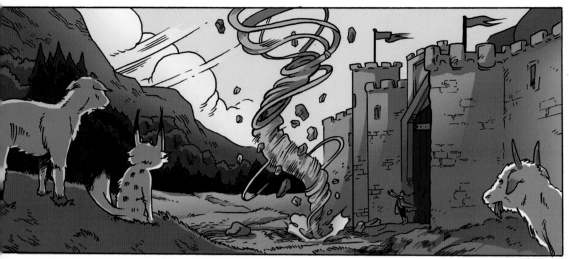

SNAP

Well done! Things are looking much better in there.

I'll make it rain over town tonight, that should help a little.

Good idea. I'm going to have Janicka, Emil, and Talin keep sweeping up. There's not much left to do, but the town likes seeing them get punished.

Rosalba, that's not a good reason...

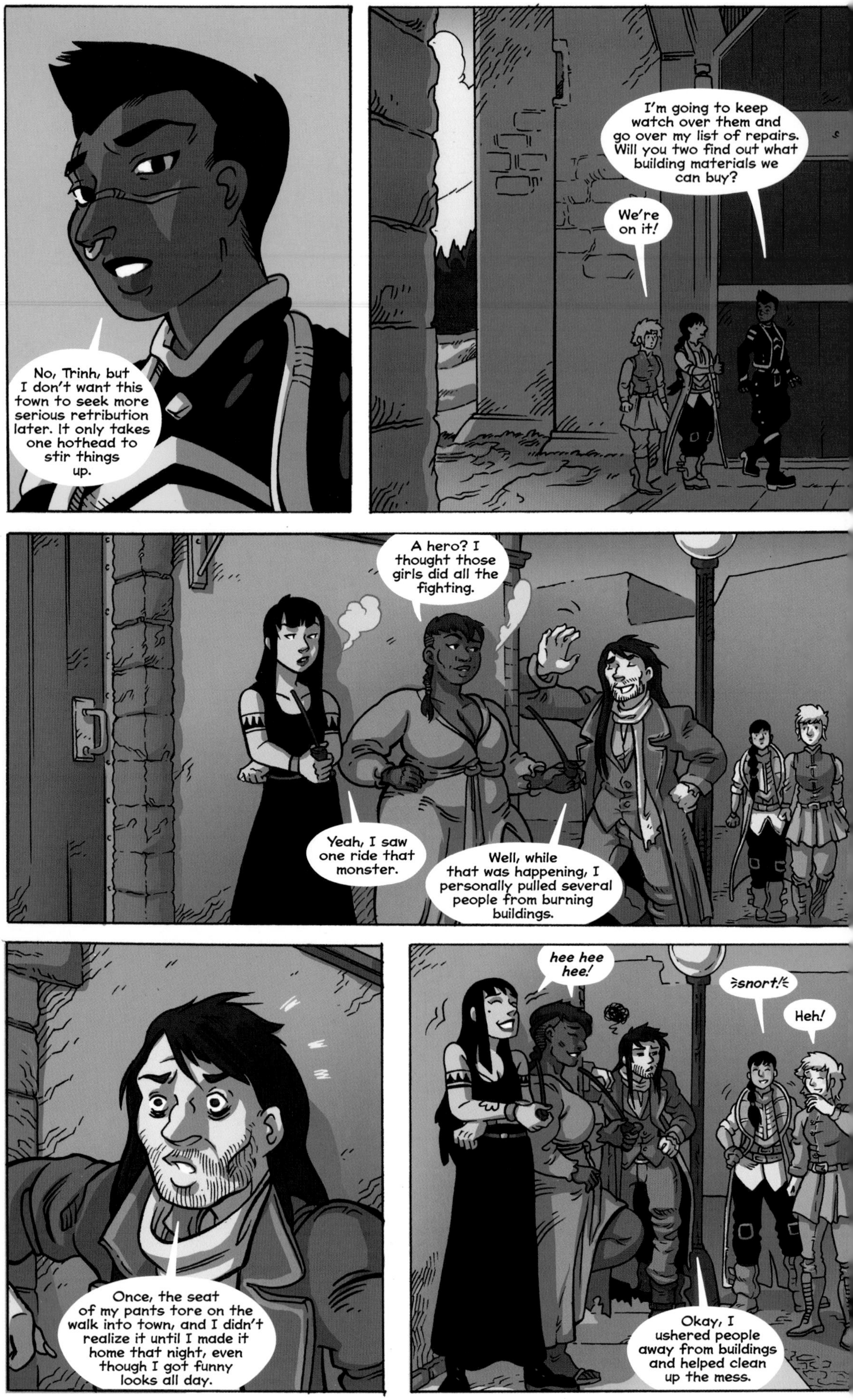
No, Trinh, but I don't want this town to seek more serious retribution later. It only takes one hothead to stir things up.
I'm going to keep watch over them and go over my list of repairs. Will you two find out what building materials we can buy?
We're on it!
A hero? I thought those girls did all the fighting.
Yeah, I saw one ride that monster.
Well, while that was happening, I personally pulled several people from burning buildings.
Once, the seat of my pants tore on the walk into town, and I didn't realize it until I made it home that night, even though I got funny looks all day.
hee hee hee!
snort!
Heh!
Okay, I ushered people away from buildings and helped clean up the mess.

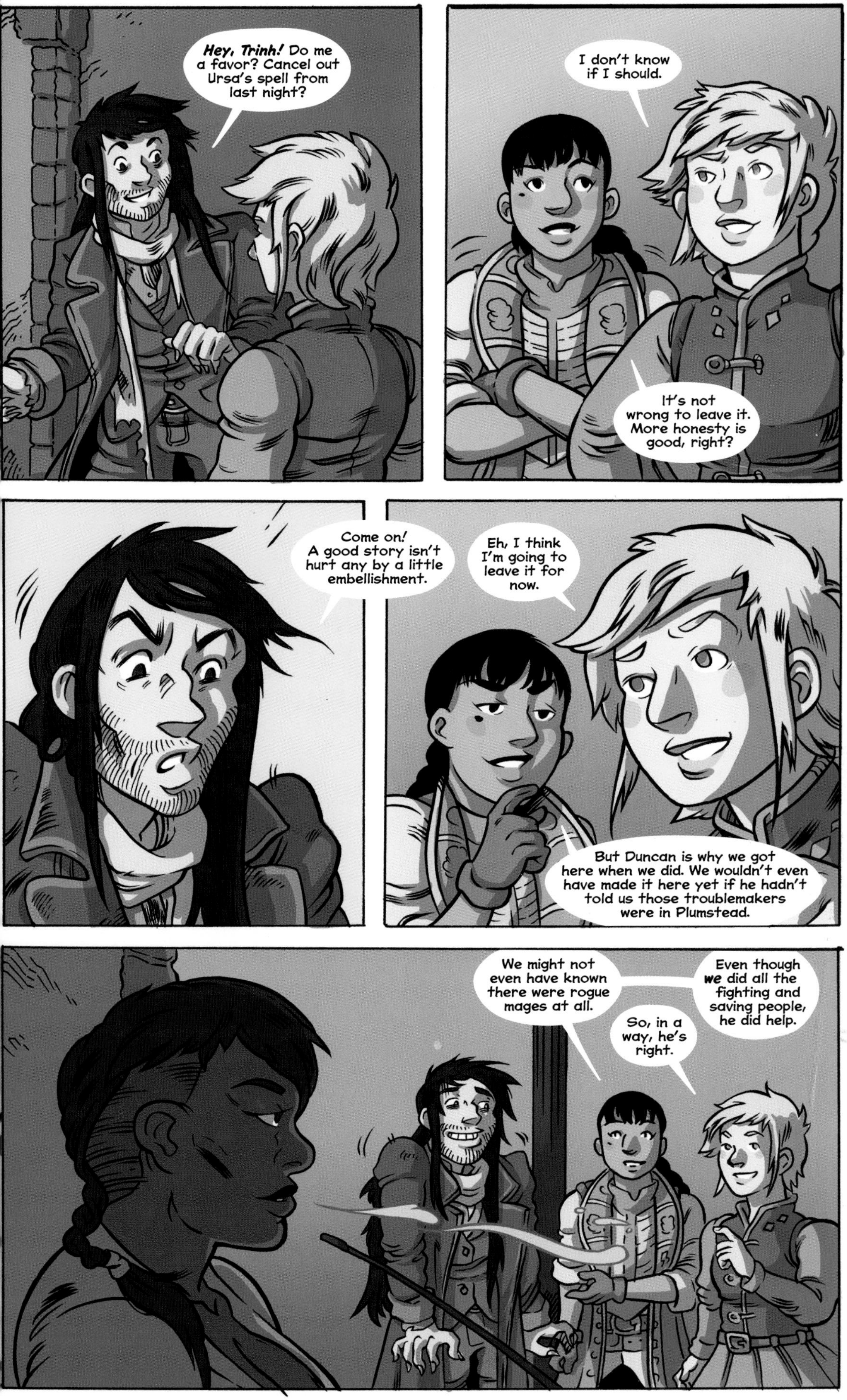

Hey, Trinh! Do me a favor? Cancel out Ursa's spell from last night?
I don't know if I should.
It's not wrong to leave it. More honesty is good, right?
Come on! A good story isn't hurt any by a little embellishment.
Eh, I think I'm going to leave it for now.
But Duncan is why we got here when we did. We wouldn't even have made it here yet if he hadn't told us those troublemakers were in Plumstead.
We might not even have known there were rogue mages at all.
Even though ***we*** did all the fighting and saving people, he did help.
So, in a way, he's right.

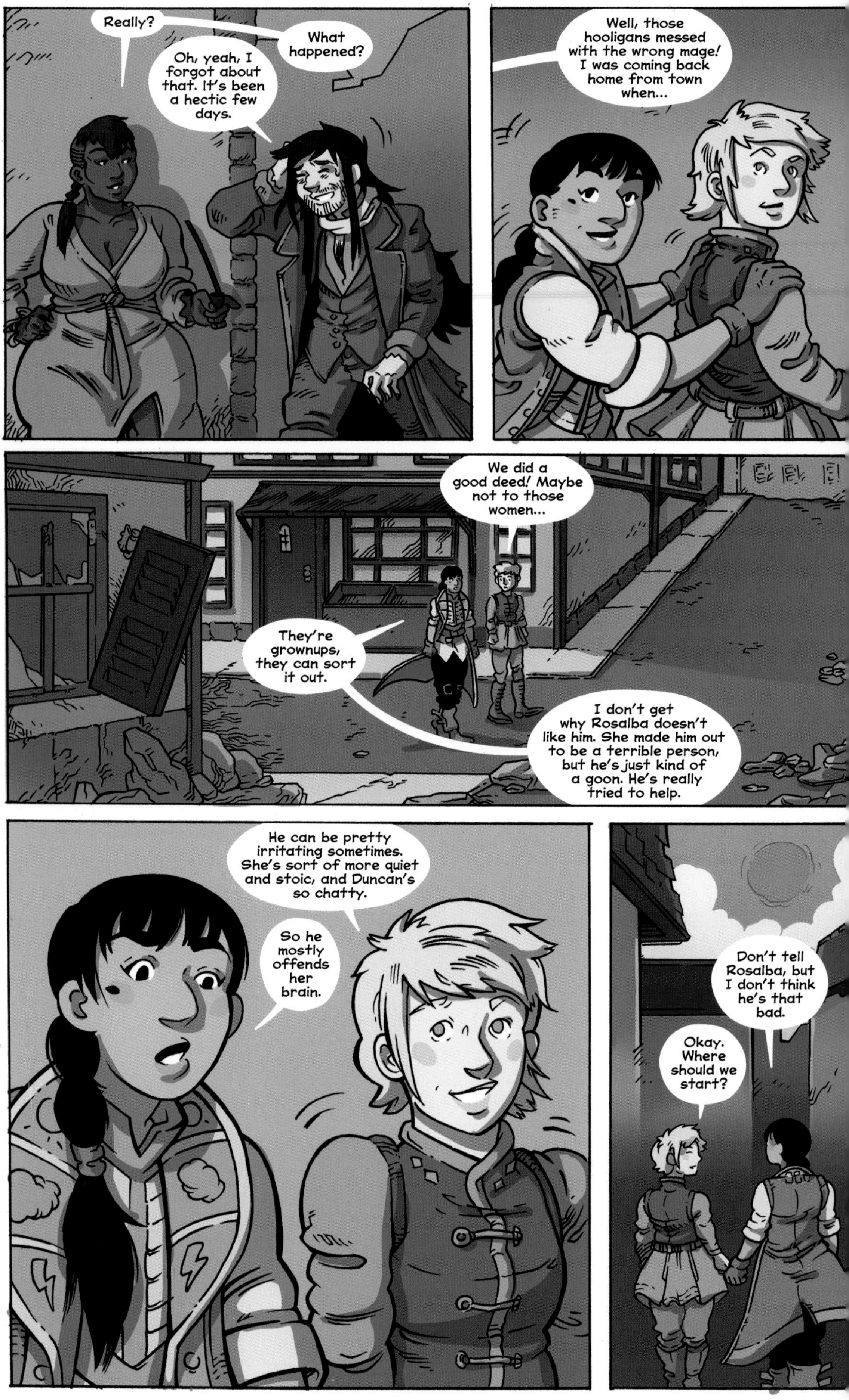
Really?
What happened?
Oh, yeah, I forgot about that. It's been a hectic few days.
Well, those hooligans messed with the wrong mage! I was coming back home from town when...
We did a good deed! Maybe not to those women...
They're grownups, they can sort it out.
I don't get why Rosalba doesn't like him. She made him out to be a terrible person, but he's just kind of a goon. He's really tried to help.
He can be pretty irritating sometimes. She's sort of more quiet and stoic, and Duncan's so chatty.
So he mostly offends her brain.
Don't tell Rosalba, but I don't think he's that bad.
Okay. Where should we start?

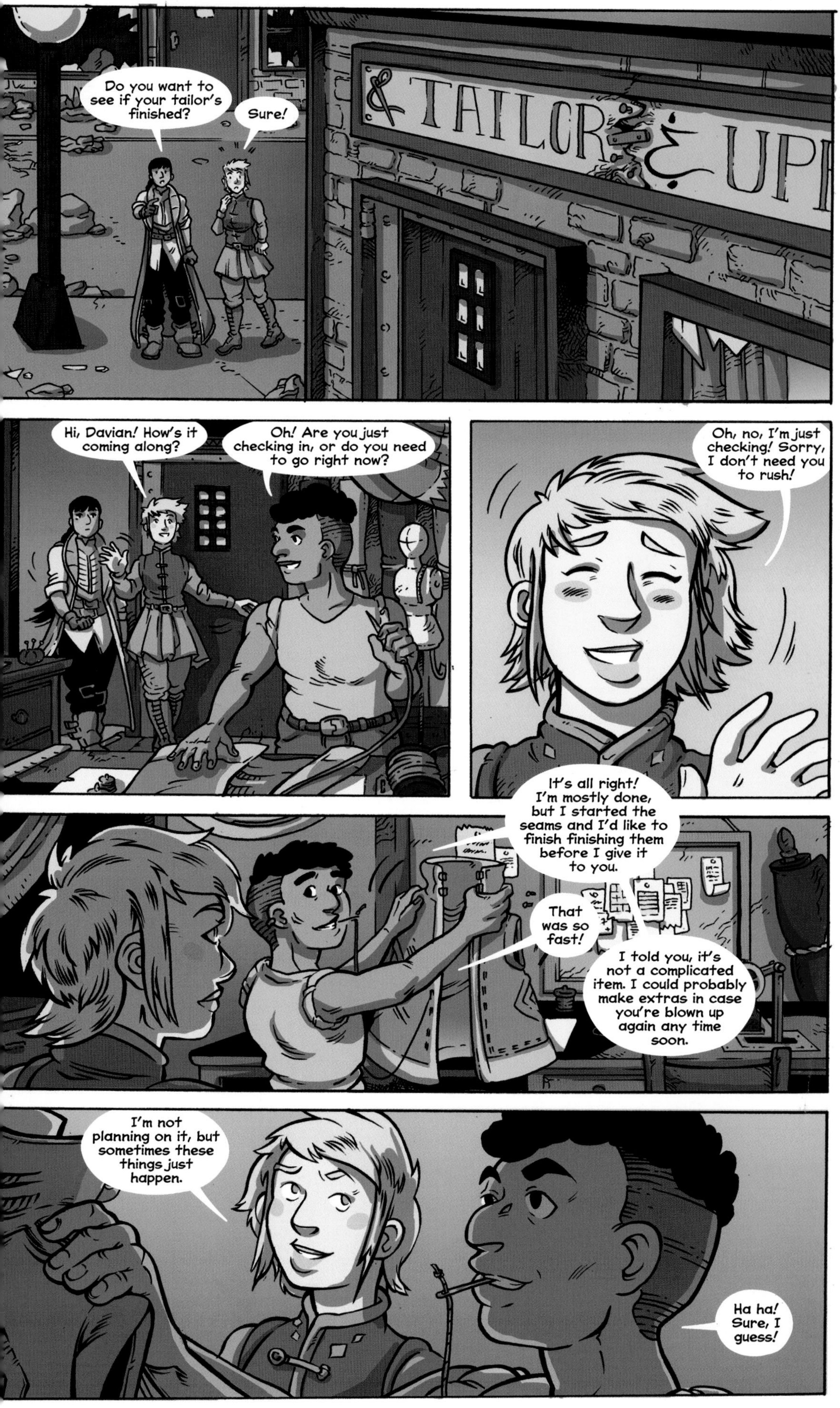
& TAILOR & UP
Do you want to see if your tailor's finished?
Sure!
Hi, Davian! How's it coming along?
Oh! Are you just checking in, or do you need to go right now?
Oh, no, I'm just checking! Sorry, I don't need you to rush!
It's all right! I'm mostly done, but I started the seams and I'd like to finish finishing them before I give it to you.
That was so fast!
I told you, it's not a complicated item. I could probably make extras in case you're blown up again any time soon.
I'm not planning on it, but sometimes these things just happen.
Ha ha! Sure, I guess!

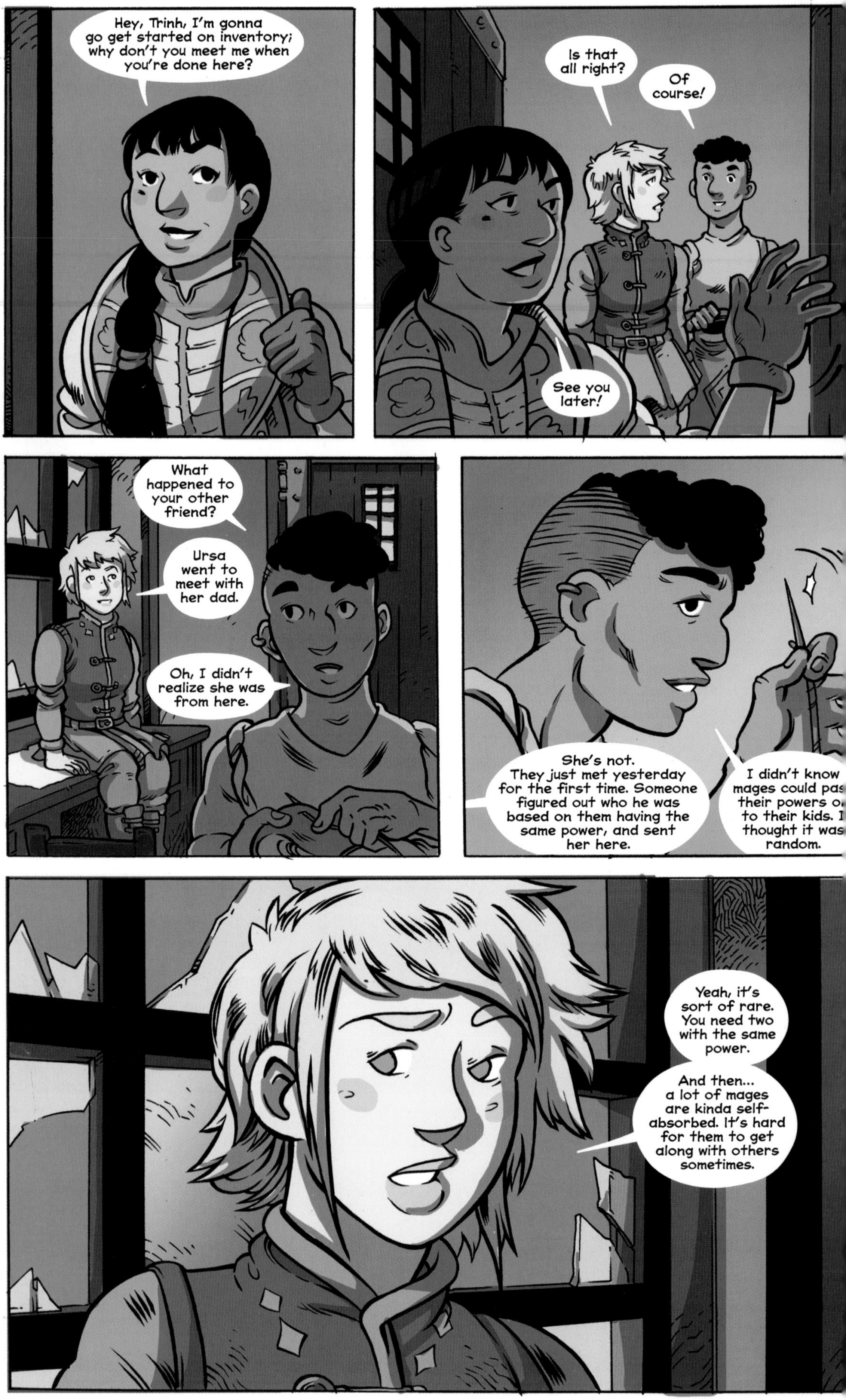
Hey, Trinh, I'm gonna go get started on inventory; why don't you meet me when you're done here?
Is that all right?
Of course!
See you later!
What happened to your other friend?
Ursa went to meet with her dad.
Oh, I didn't realize she was from here.
She's not. They just met yesterday for the first time. Someone figured out who he was based on them having the same power, and sent her here.
I didn't know mages could pas their powers o to their kids. I thought it was random.
Yeah, it's sort of rare. You need two with the same power.
And then... a lot of mages are kinda self-absorbed. It's hard for them to get along with others sometimes.

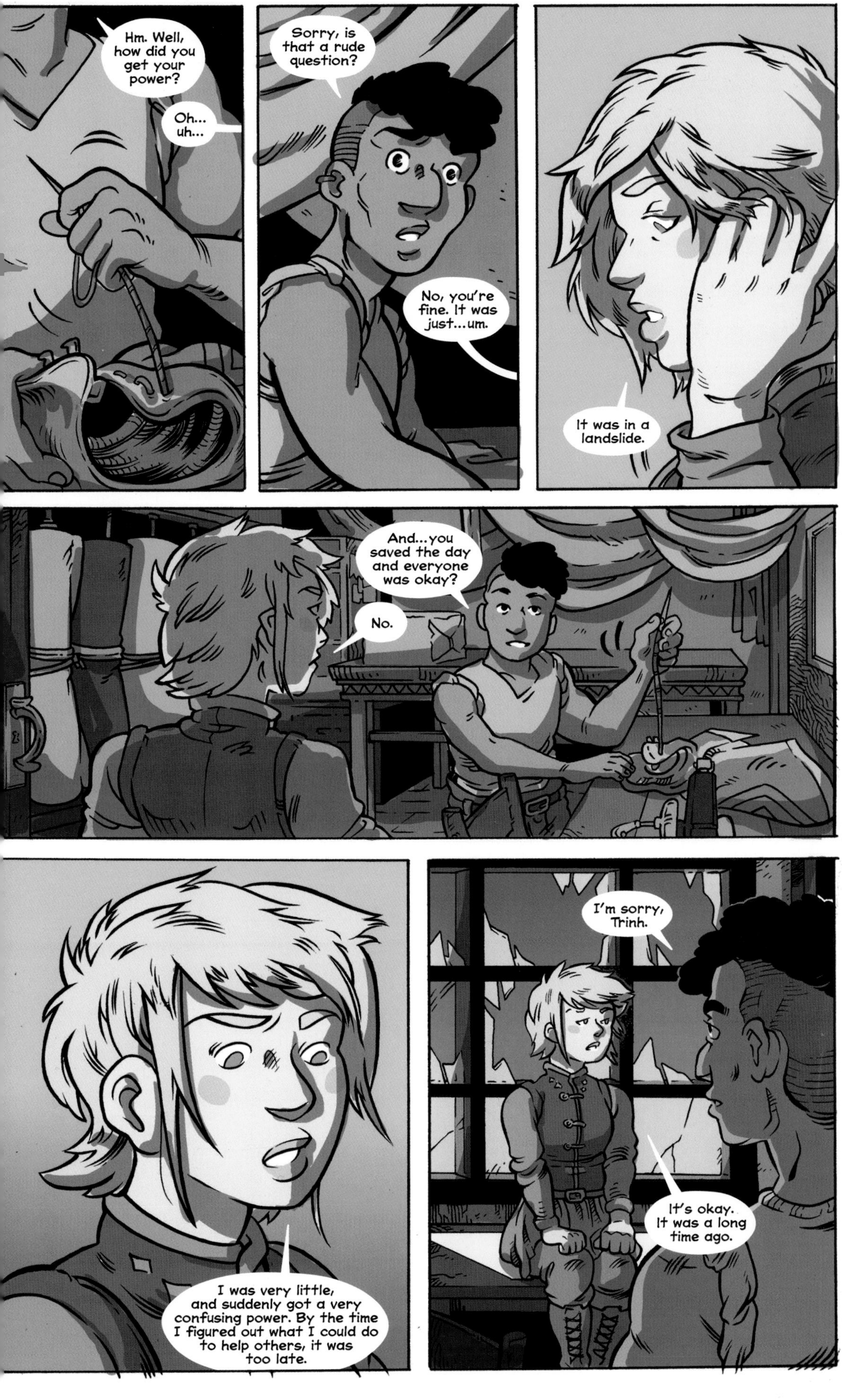
Hm. Well, how did you get your power?
Oh... uh...
Sorry, is that a rude question?
No, you're fine. It was just...um.
It was in a landslide.
And...you saved the day and everyone was okay?
No.
I was very little, and suddenly got a very confusing power. By the time I figured out what I could do to help others, it was too late.
I'm sorry, Trinh.
It's okay. It was a long time ago.

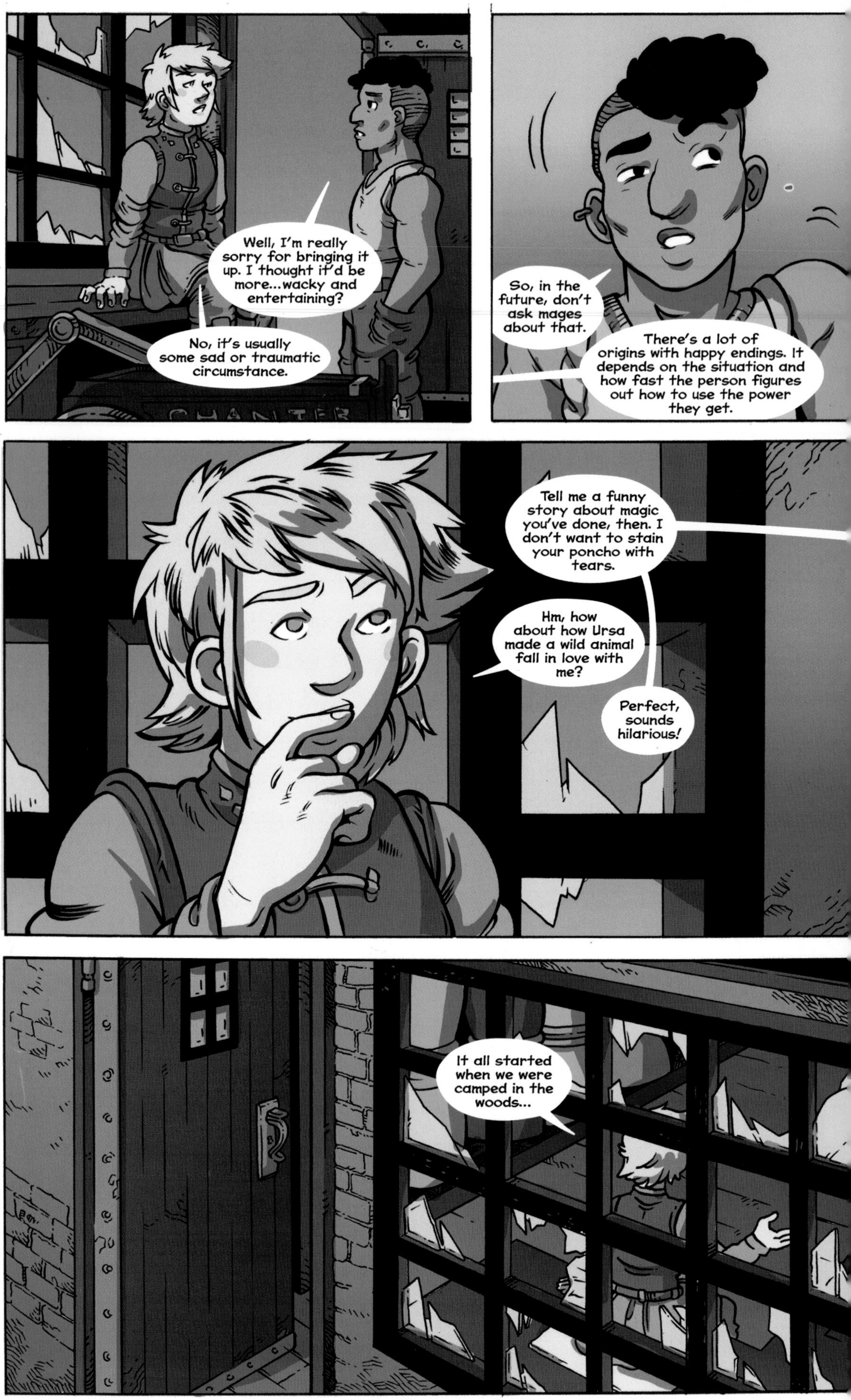

Well, I'm really sorry for bringing it up. I thought it'd be more...wacky and entertaining?
No, it's usually some sad or traumatic circumstance.
So, in the future, don't ask mages about that.
There's a lot of origins with happy endings. It depends on the situation and how fast the person figures out how to use the power they get.
Tell me a funny story about magic you've done, then. I don't want to stain your poncho with tears.
Hm, how about how Ursa made a wild animal fall in love with me?
Perfect, sounds hilarious!
It all started when we were camped in the woods...

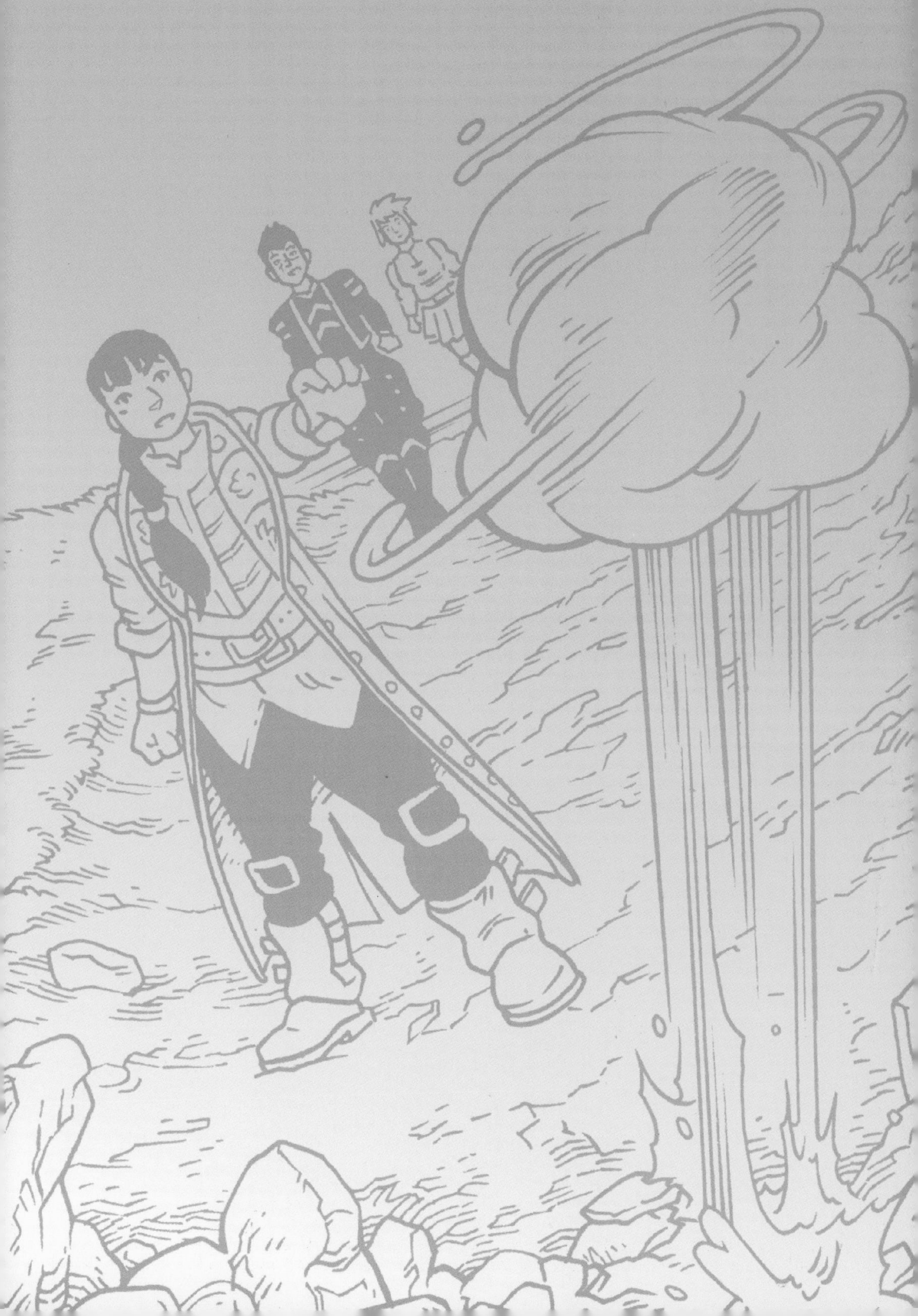

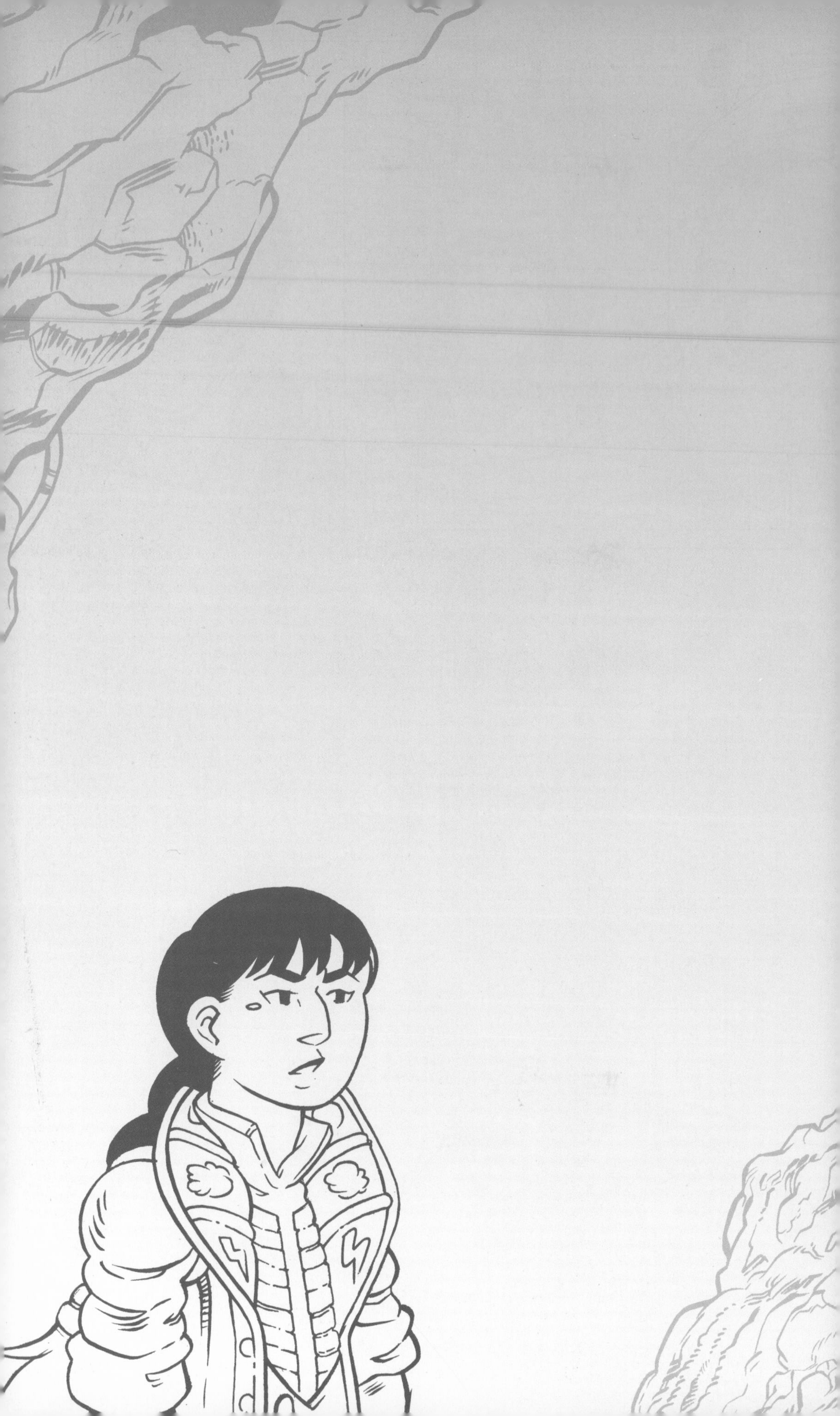

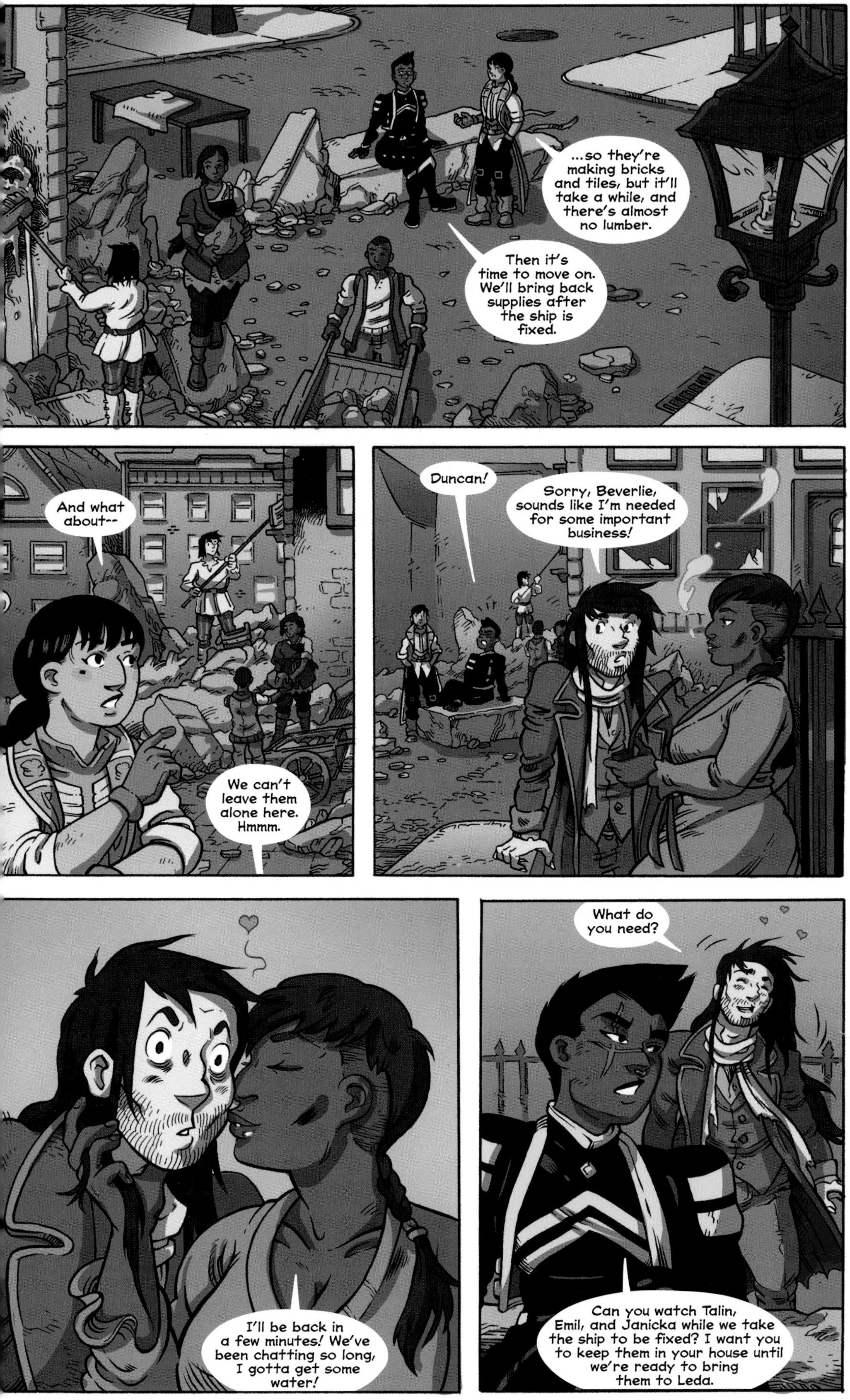
...so they're making bricks and tiles, but it'll take a while, and there's almost no lumber.
Then it's time to move on. We'll bring back supplies after the ship is fixed.
And what about--
We can't leave them alone here. Hmmm.
Duncan!
Sorry, Beverlie, sounds like I'm needed for some important business!
I'll be back in a few minutes! We've been chatting so long, I gotta get some water!
What do you need?
Can you watch Talin, Emil, and Janicka while we take the ship to be fixed? I want you to keep them in your house until we're ready to bring them to Leda.

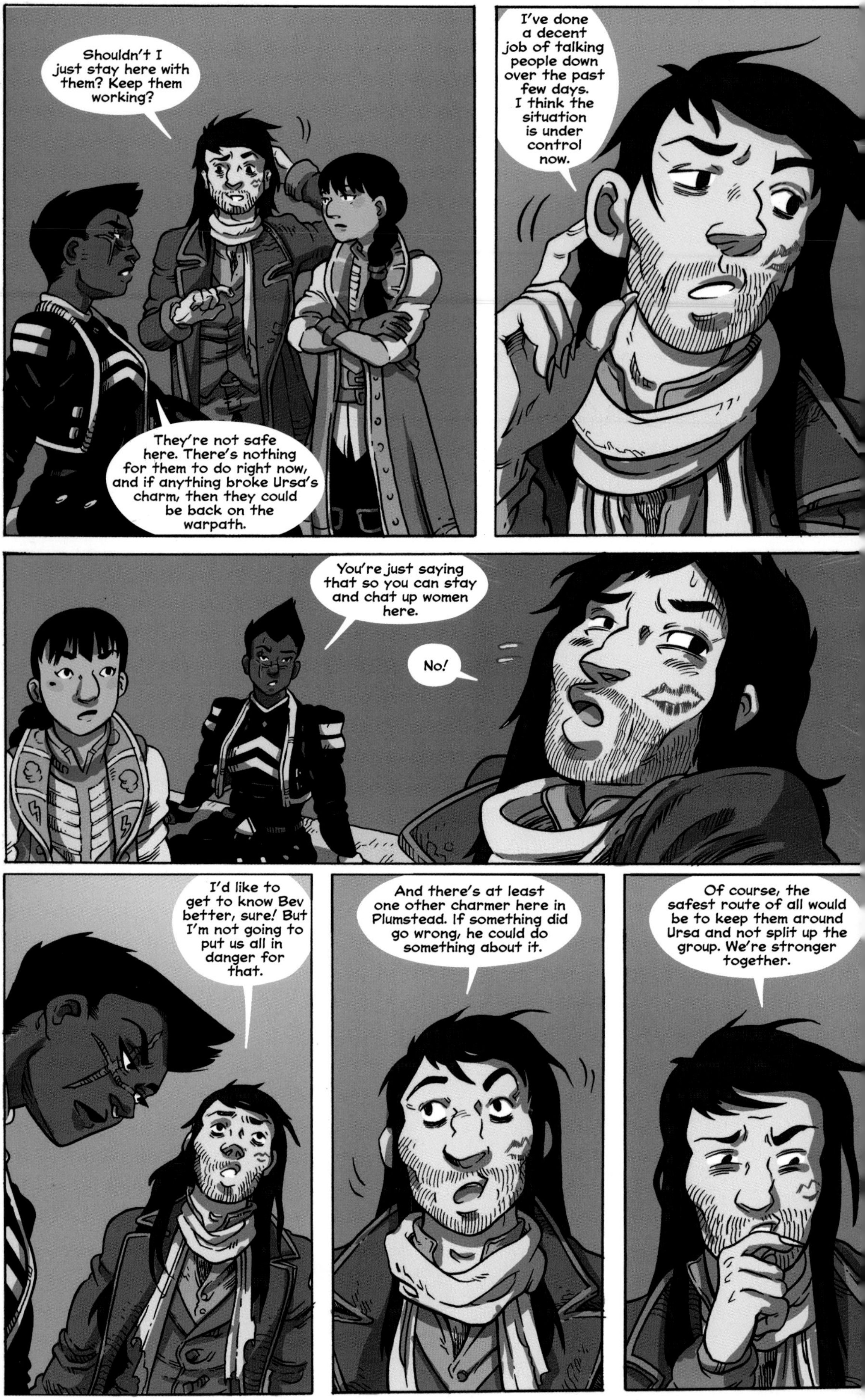

Shouldn't I just stay here with them? Keep them working?
They're not safe here. There's nothing for them to do right now, and if anything broke Ursa's charm, then they could be back on the warpath.
I've done a decent job of talking people down over the past few days. I think the situation is under control now.
You're just saying that so you can stay and chat up women here.
No!
I'd like to get to know Bev better, sure! But I'm not going to put us all in danger for that.
And there's at least one other charmer here in Plumstead. If something did go wrong, he could do something about it.
Of course, the safest route of all would be to keep them around Ursa and not split up the group. We're stronger together.

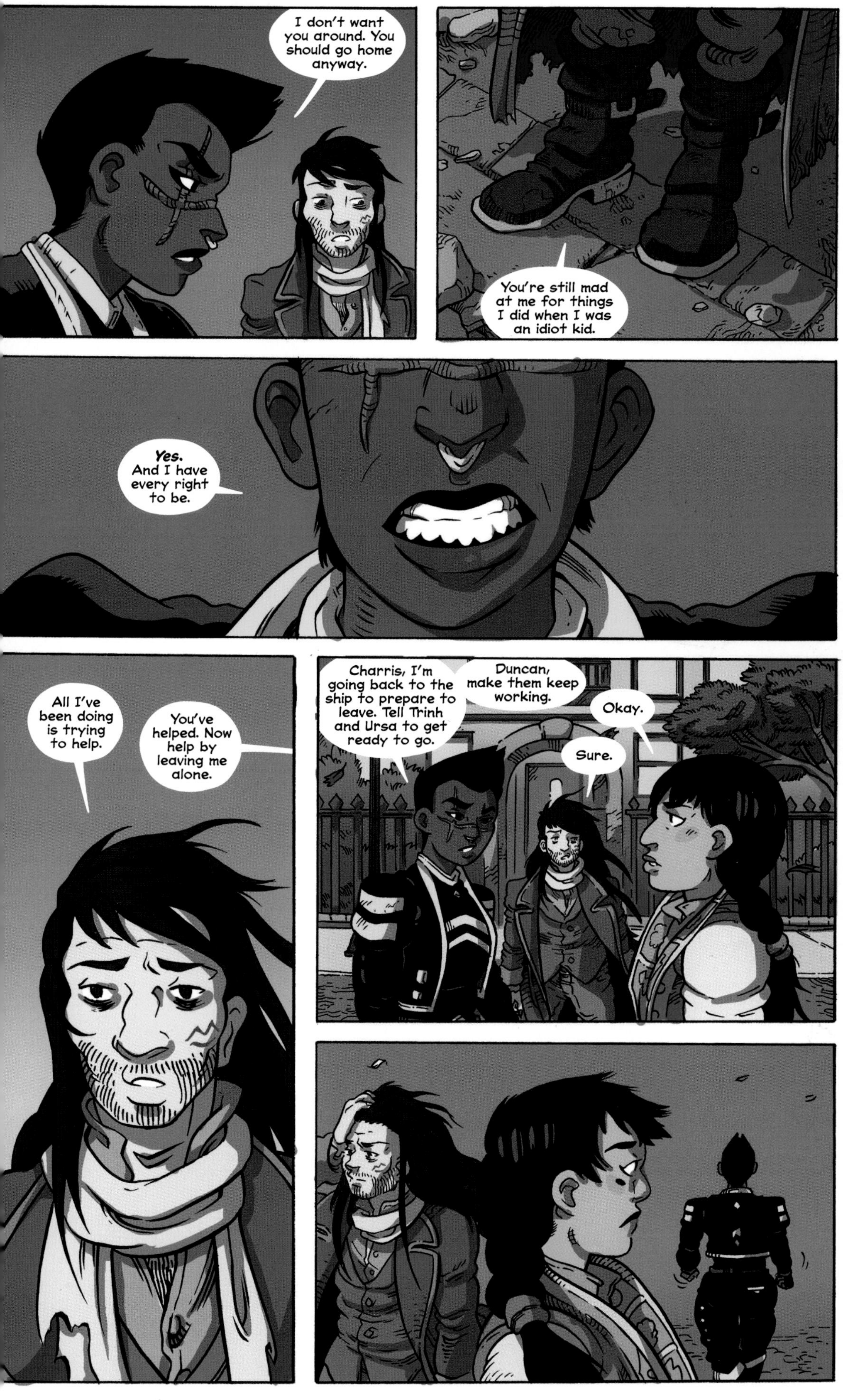
I don't want you around. You should go home anyway.
You're still mad at me for things I did when I was an idiot kid.
Yes. And I have every right to be.
All I've been doing is trying to help.
You've helped. Now help by leaving me alone.
Charris, I'm going back to the ship to prepare to leave. Tell Trinh and Ursa to get ready to go.
Duncan, make them keep working.
Okay.
Sure.

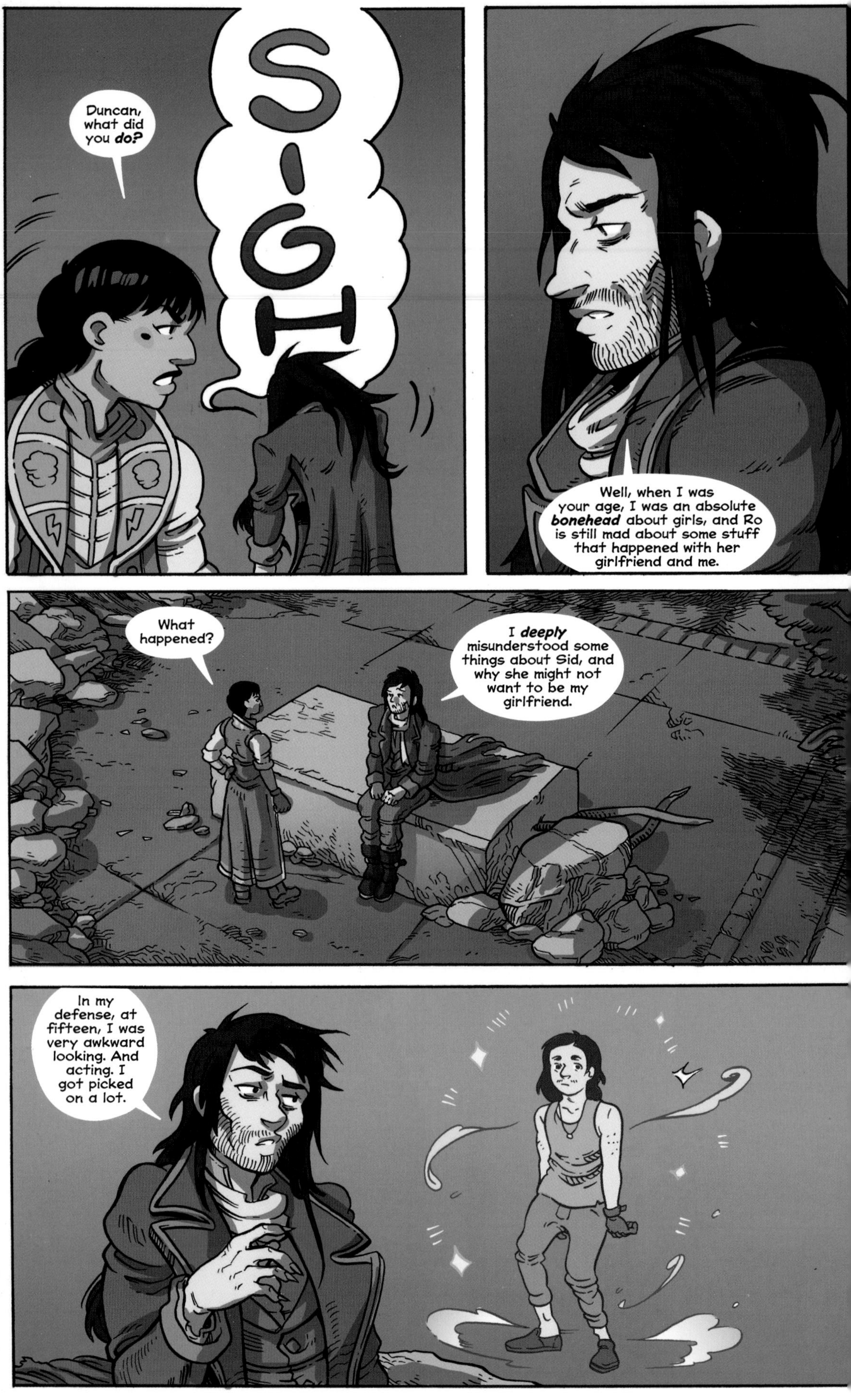

Duncan, what did you *do?*
SIGH
Well, when I was your age, I was an absolute *bonehead* about girls, and Ro is still mad about some stuff that happened with her girlfriend and me.
What happened?
I *deeply* misunderstood some things about Sid, and why she might not want to be my girlfriend.
In my defense, at fifteen, I was very awkward looking. And acting. I got picked on a lot.

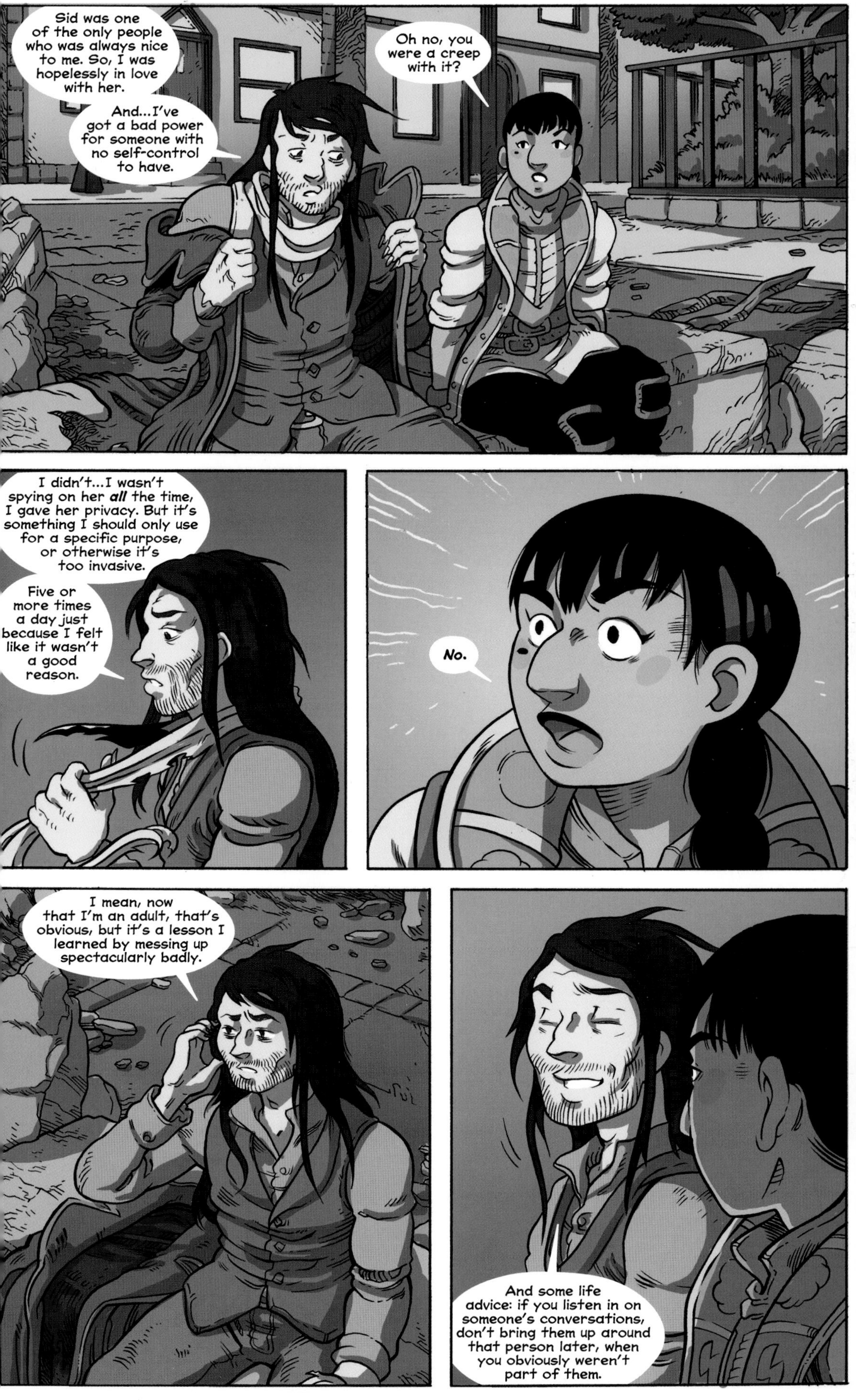
Sid was one of the only people who was always nice to me. So, I was hopelessly in love with her.
And...I've got a bad power for someone with no self-control to have.
Oh no, you were a creep with it?
I didn't...I wasn't spying on her *all* the time, I gave her privacy. But it's something I should only use for a specific purpose, or otherwise it's too invasive.
Five or more times a day just because I felt like it wasn't a good reason.
No.
I mean, now that I'm an adult, that's obvious, but it's a lesson I learned by messing up spectacularly badly.
And some life advice: if you listen in on someone's conversations, don't bring them up around that person later, when you obviously weren't part of them.

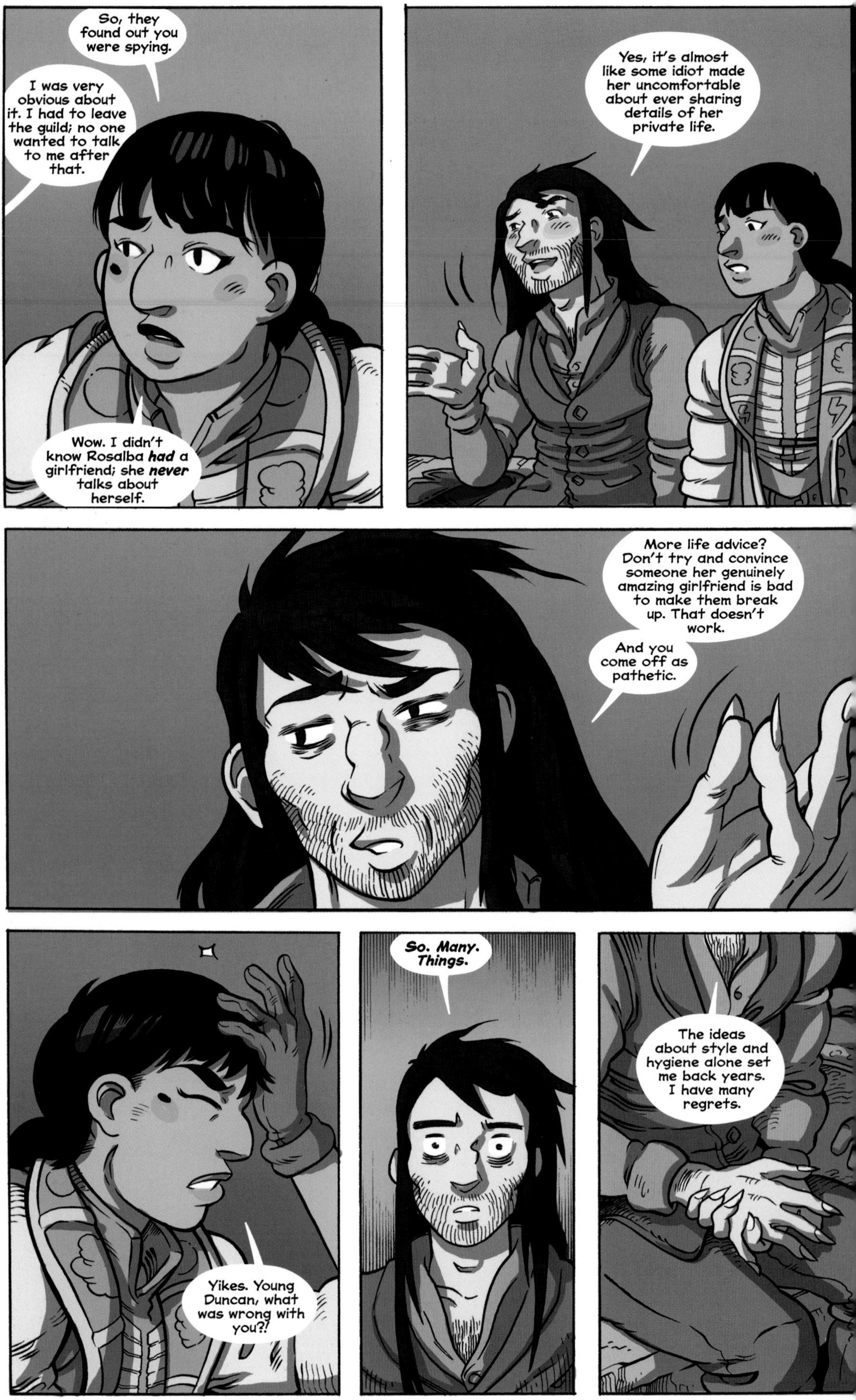
So, they found out you were spying.
I was very obvious about it. I had to leave the guild; no one wanted to talk to me after that.
Wow. I didn't know Rosalba *had* a girlfriend; she *never* talks about herself.
Yes, it's almost like some idiot made her uncomfortable about ever sharing details of her private life.
More life advice? Don't try and convince someone her genuinely amazing girlfriend is bad to make them break up. That doesn't work.
And you come off as pathetic.
Yikes. Young Duncan, what was wrong with you?!
So. Many. Things.
The ideas about style and hygiene alone set me back years. I have many regrets.

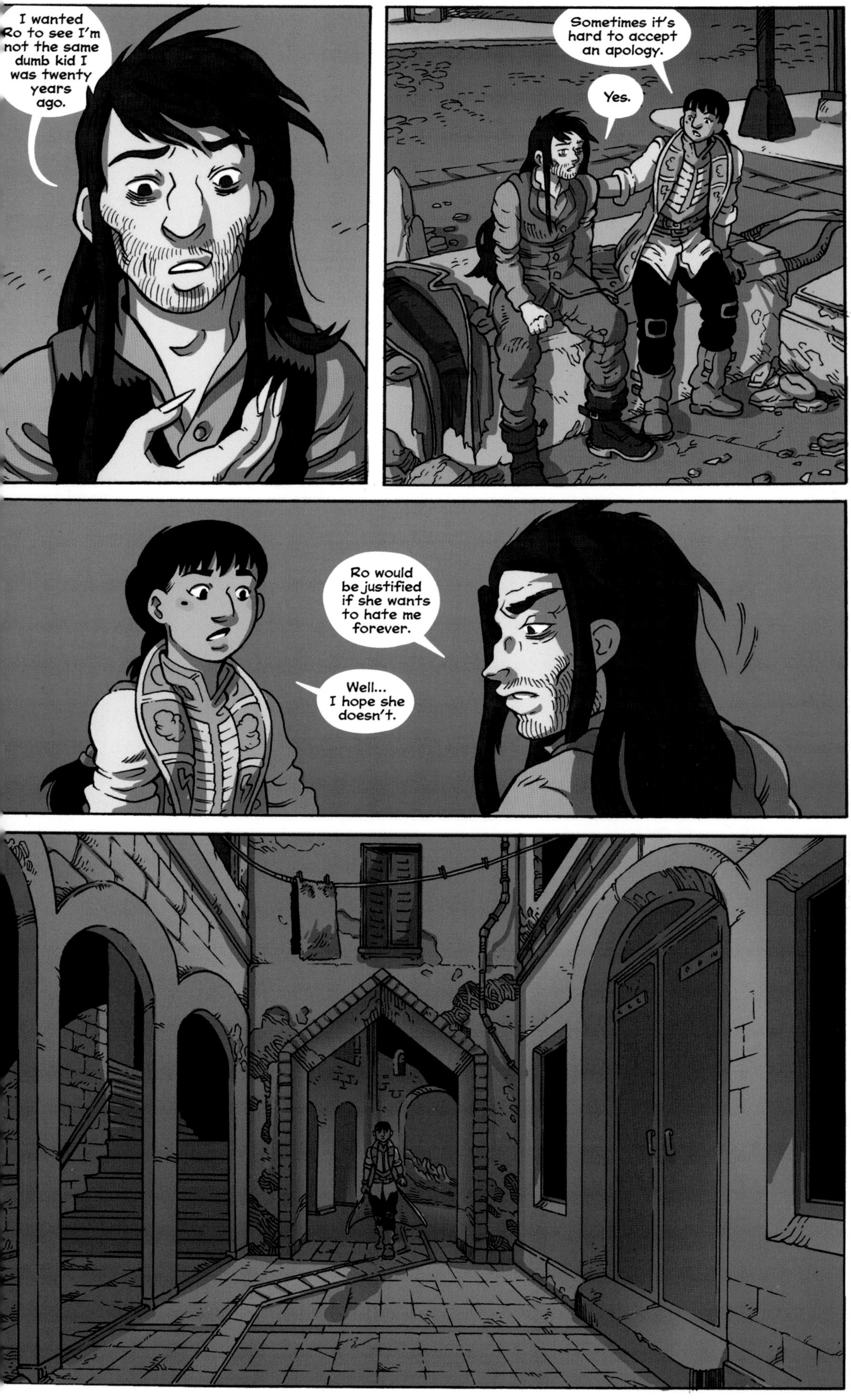

I wanted Ro to see I'm not the same dumb kid I was twenty years ago.
Sometimes it's hard to accept an apology.
Yes.
Ro would be justified if she wants to hate me forever.
Well... I hope she doesn't.

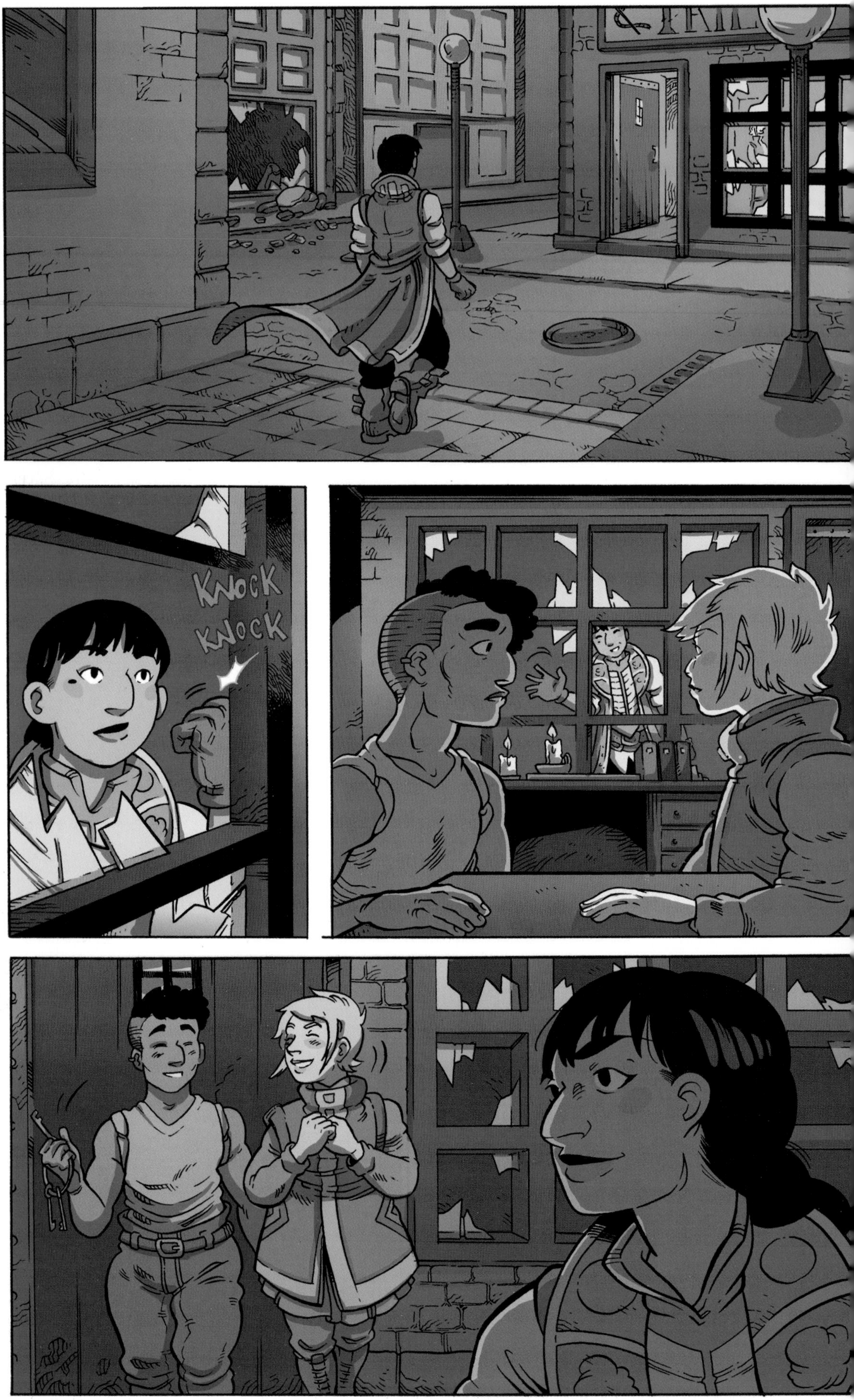
KNOCK
KNOCK

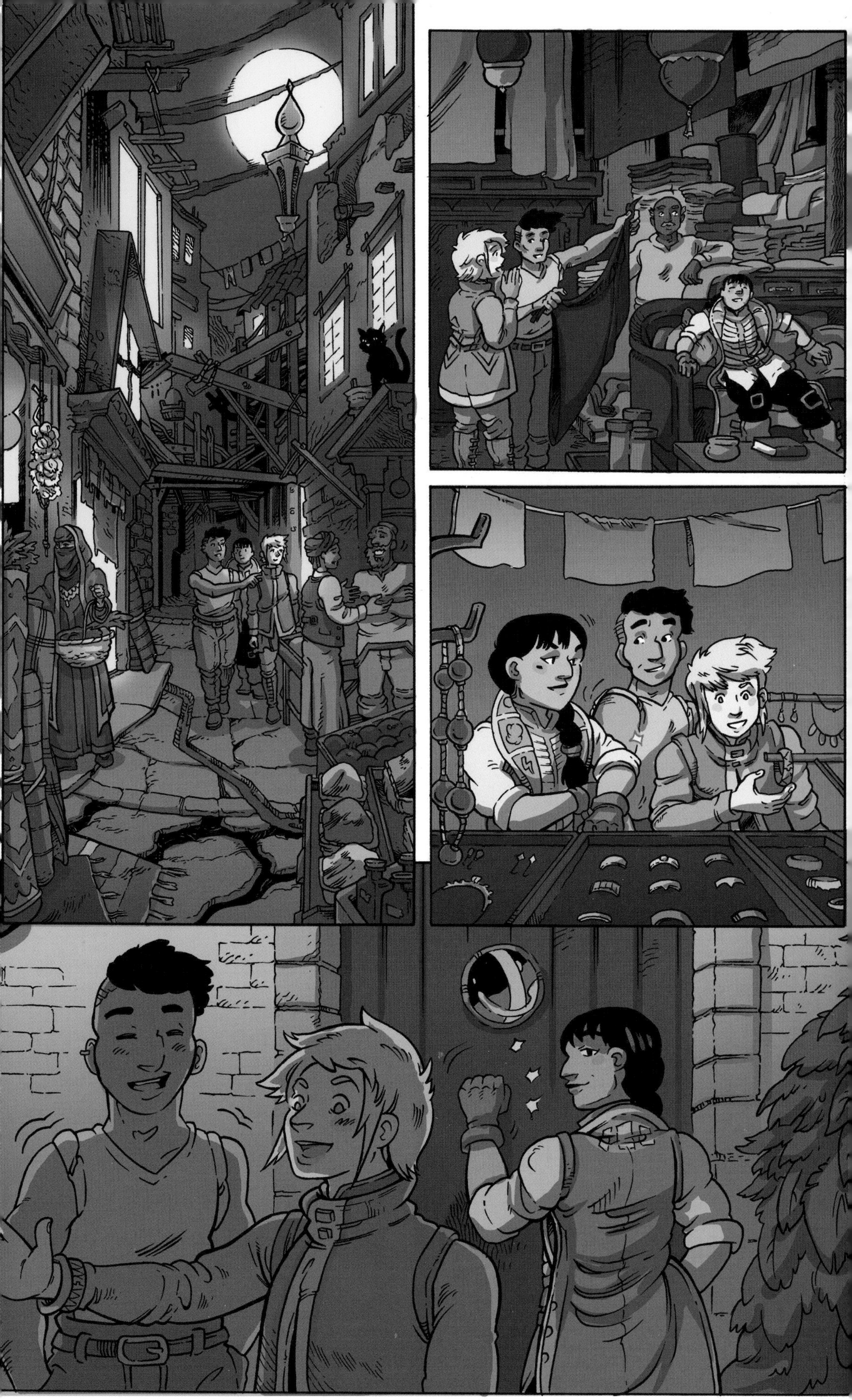

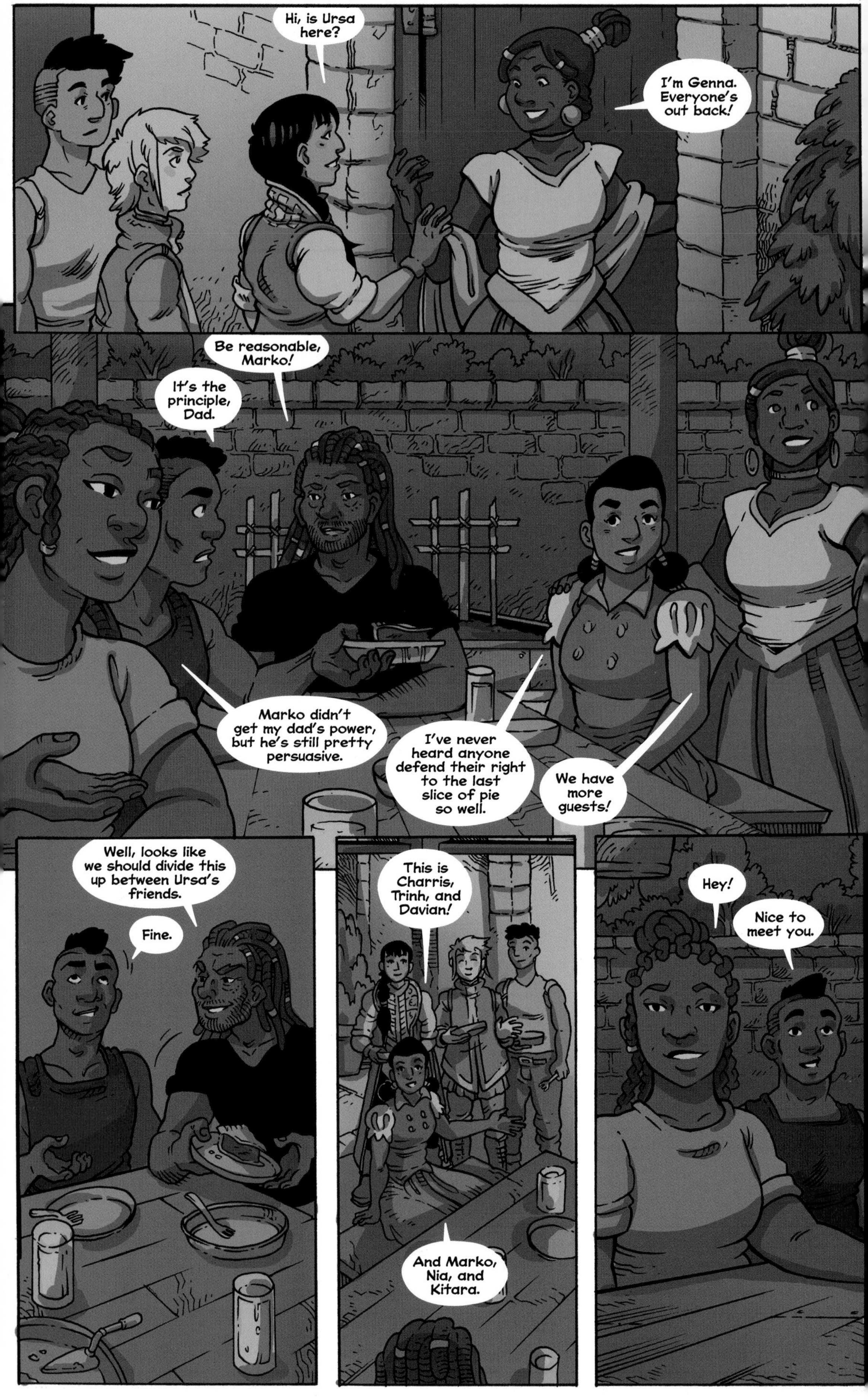
Hi, is Ursa here?
I'm Genna. Everyone's out back!
Be reasonable, Marko!
It's the principle, Dad.
Marko didn't get my dad's power, but he's still pretty persuasive.
I've never heard anyone defend their right to the last slice of pie so well.
We have more guests!
Well, looks like we should divide this up between Ursa's friends.
Fine.
This is Charris, Trinh, and Davian!
And Marko, Nia, and Kitara.
Hey!
Nice to meet you.

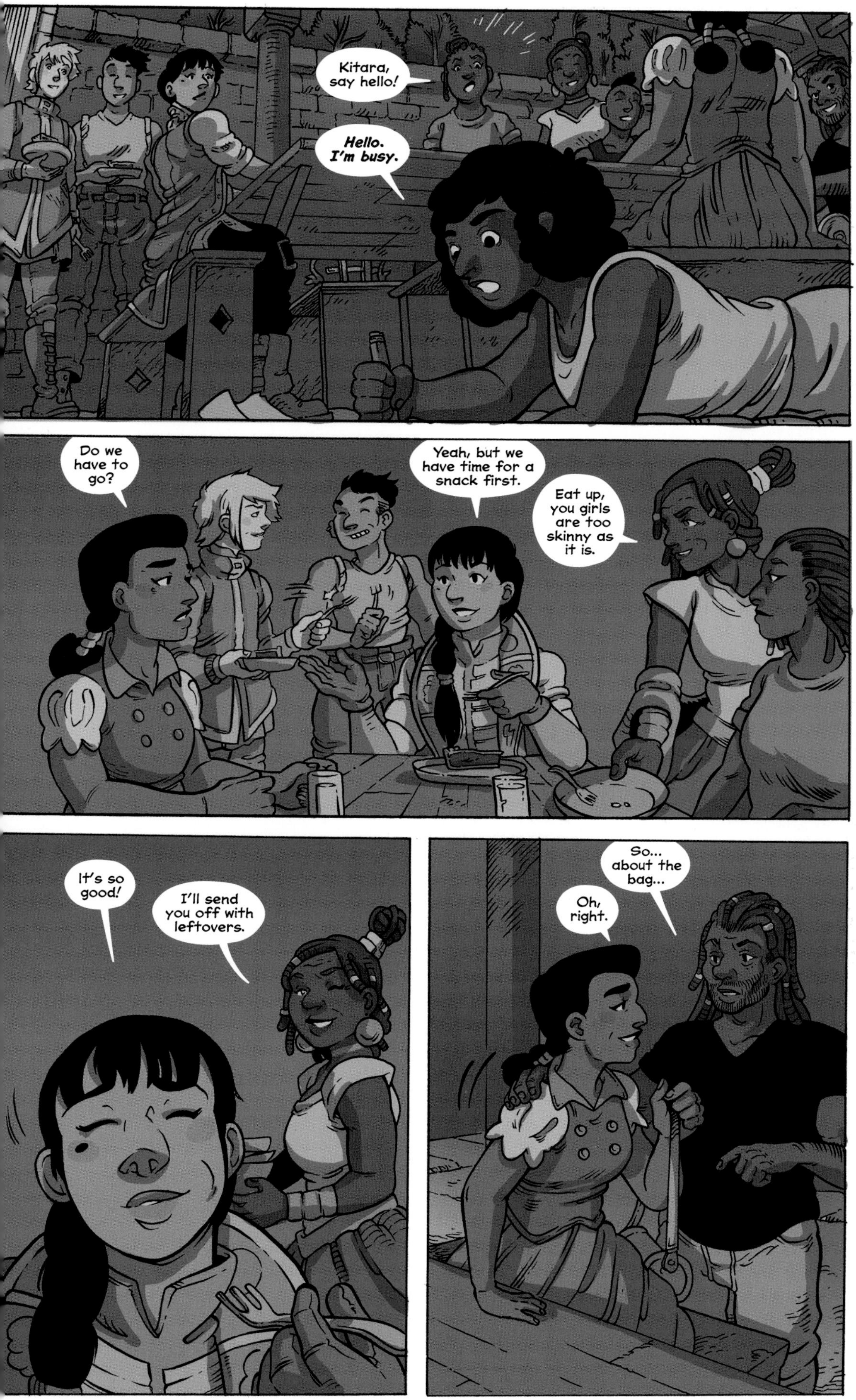
Kitara, say hello!
Hello. I'm busy.
Do we have to go?
Yeah, but we have time for a snack first.
Eat up, you girls are too skinny as it is.
It's so good!
I'll send you off with leftovers.
So... about the bag...
Oh, right.

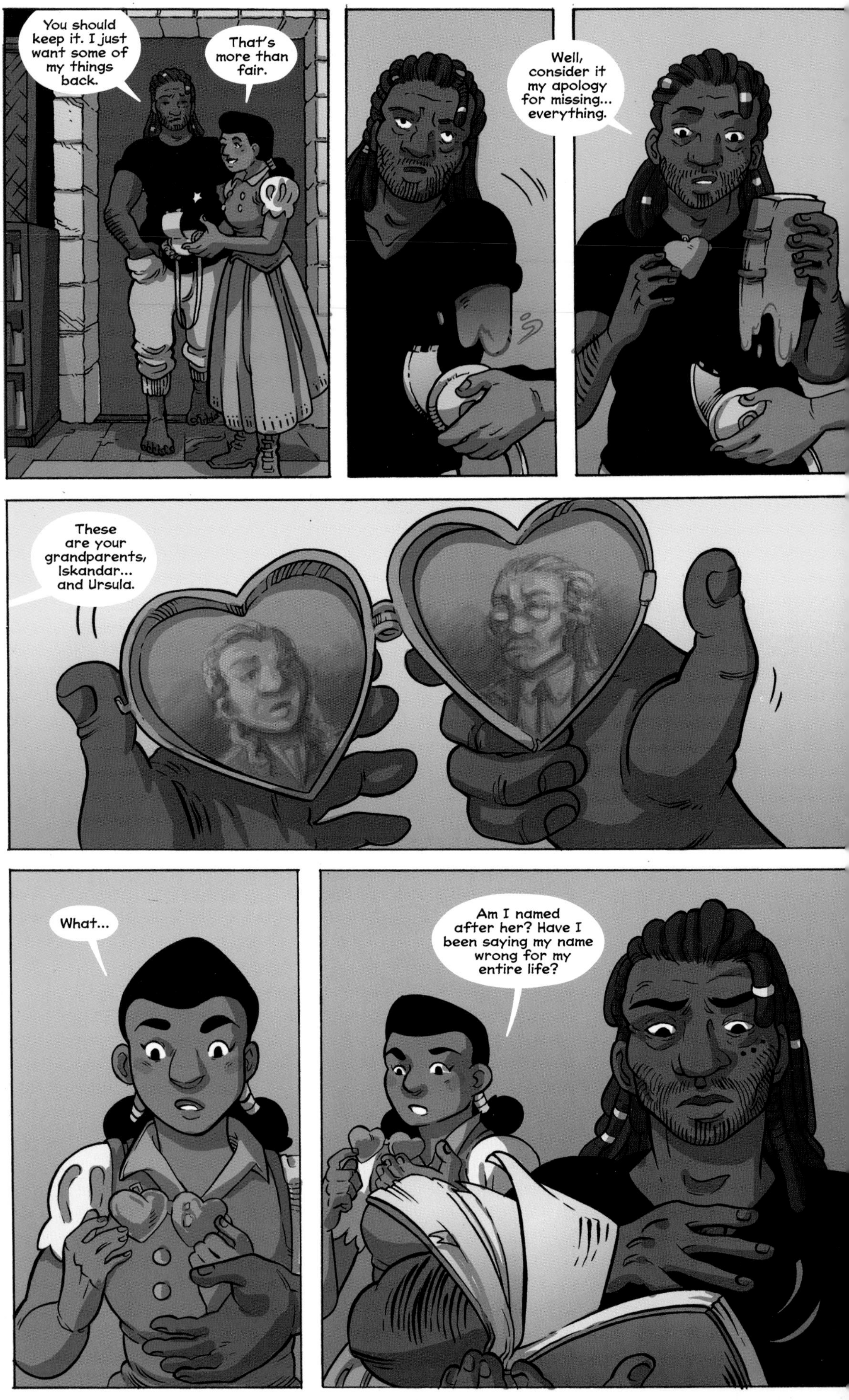

You should keep it. I just want some of my things back.
That's more than fair.
Well, consider it my apology for missing... everything.
These are your grandparents, Iskandar... and Ursula.
What...
Am I named after her? Have I been saying my name wrong for my entire life?

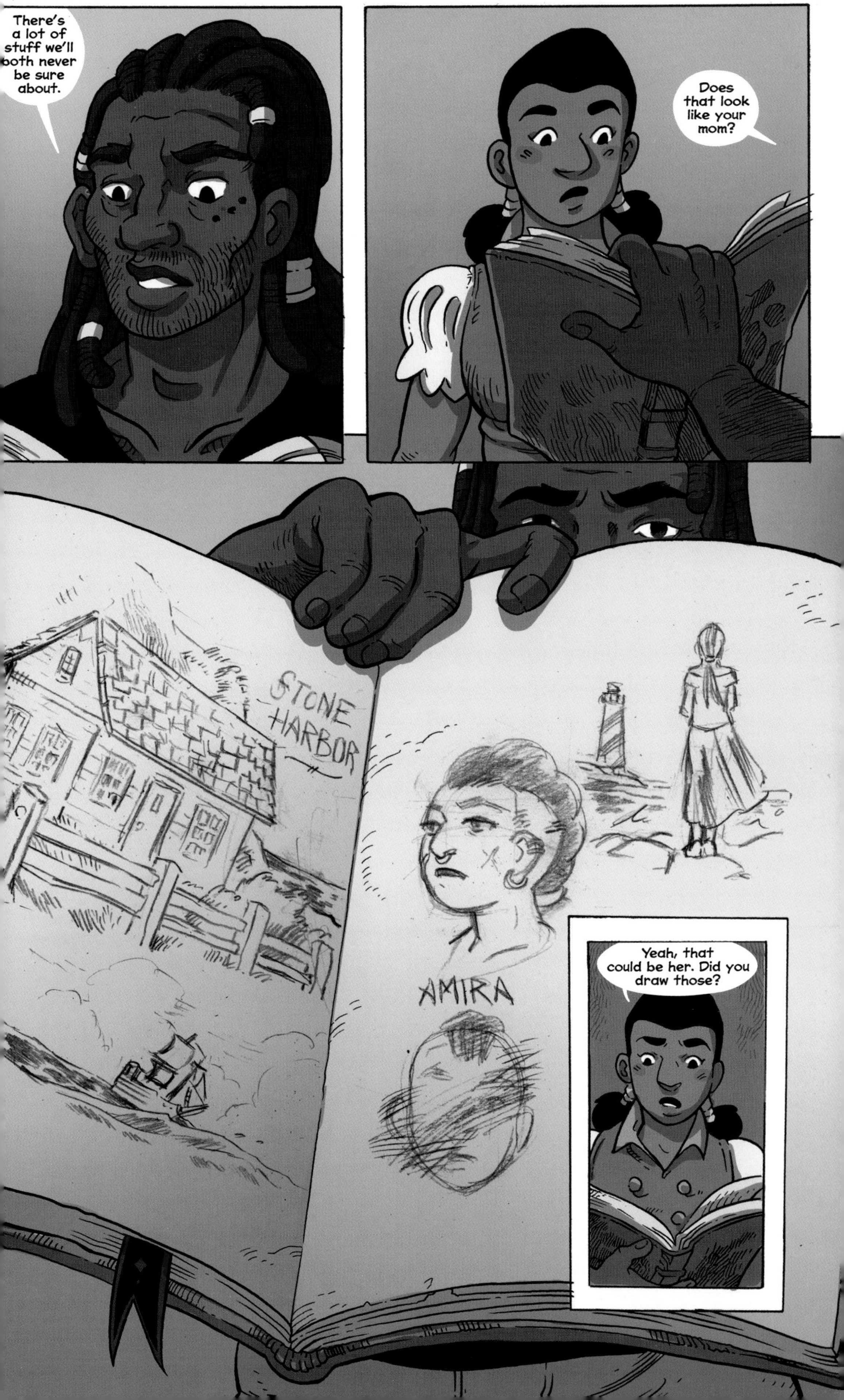

There's a lot of stuff we'll both never be sure about.
Does that look like your mom?
STONE HARBOR
AMIRA
Yeah, that could be her. Did you draw those?

It's my sketchbook, and it's how I used to draw... but I still don't remember any of this.

Um.

Well, anyway. Let me get the last of it out of there.

Effects of the Lunar Cycle On The Growth Of Lichens -or- MOSS & THE MOON BY M.G. Tselva

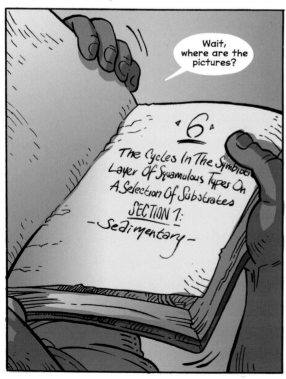

Wait, where are the pictures?

6

The Cycles In The Symbiotic Layer Of Squamulous Types On A Selection Of Substrates SECTION 1: -Sedimentary-

Either I need to hold it, or you need to know the phrase to see what I wrote.

Is it full of secrets?

What's the phrase?

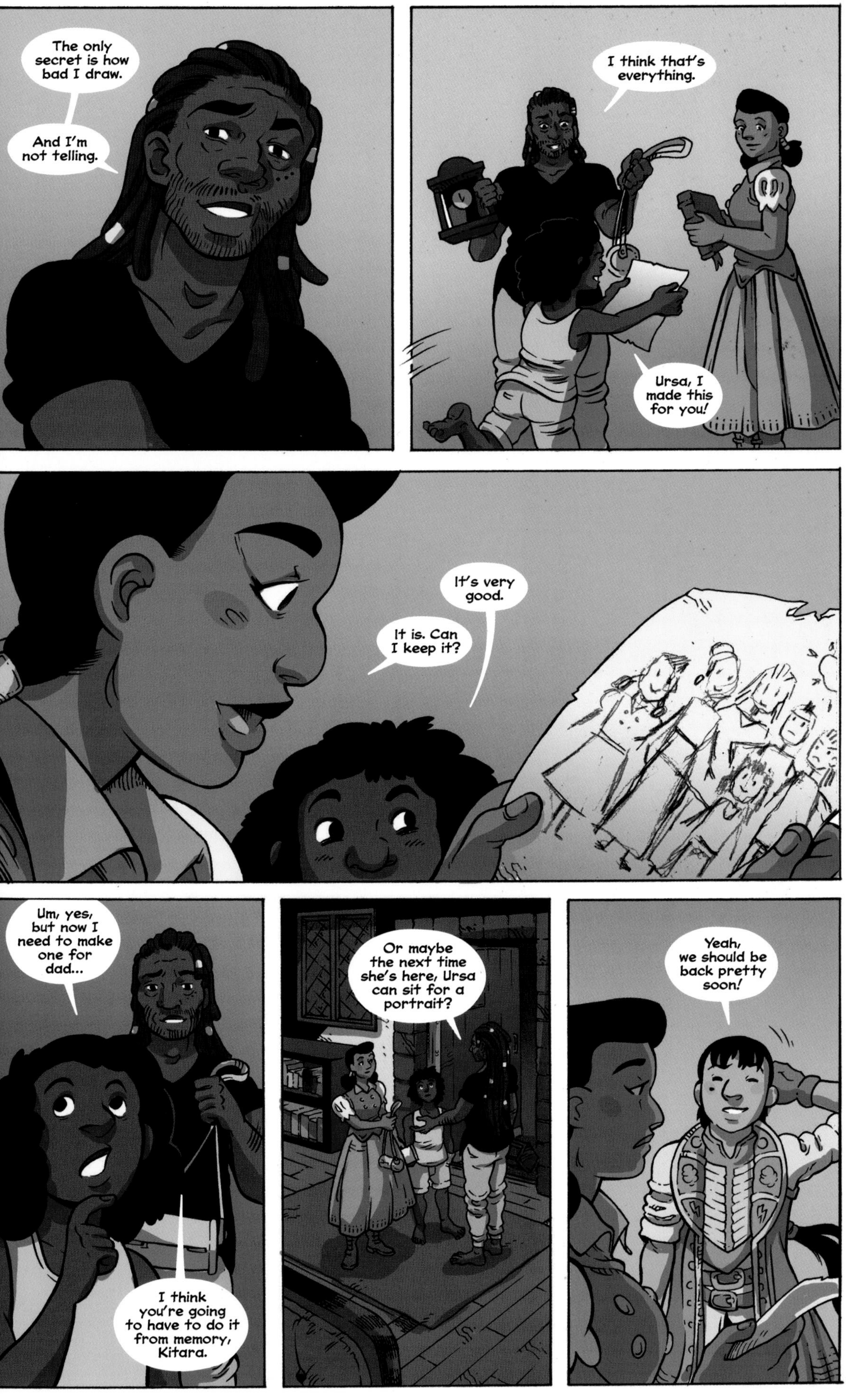
The only secret is how bad I draw.
And I'm not telling.
I think that's everything.
Ursa, I made this for you!
It's very good.
It is. Can I keep it?
Um, yes, but now I need to make one for dad...
I think you're going to have to do it from memory, Kitara.
Or maybe the next time she's here, Ursa can sit for a portrait?
Yeah, we should be back pretty soon!

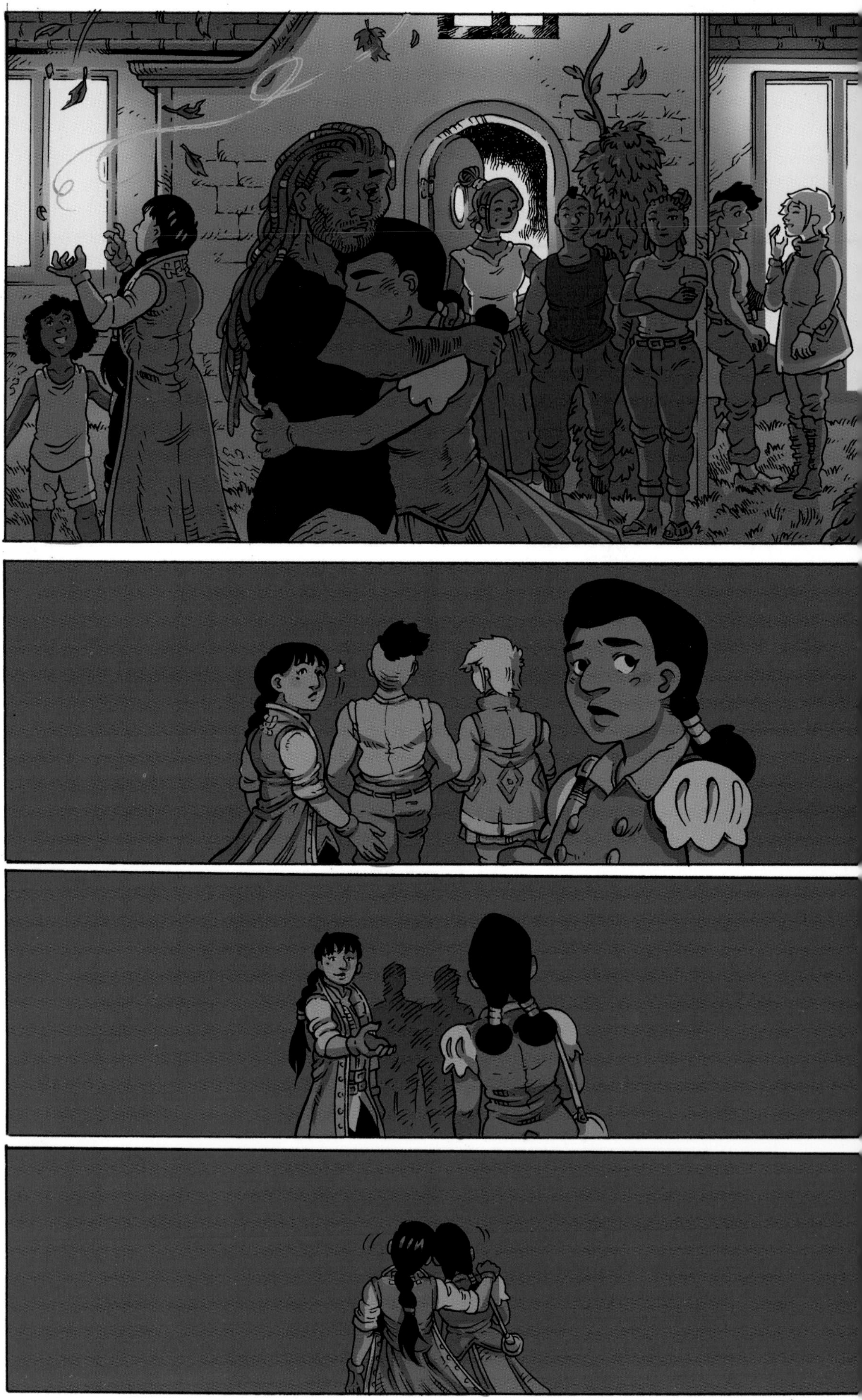

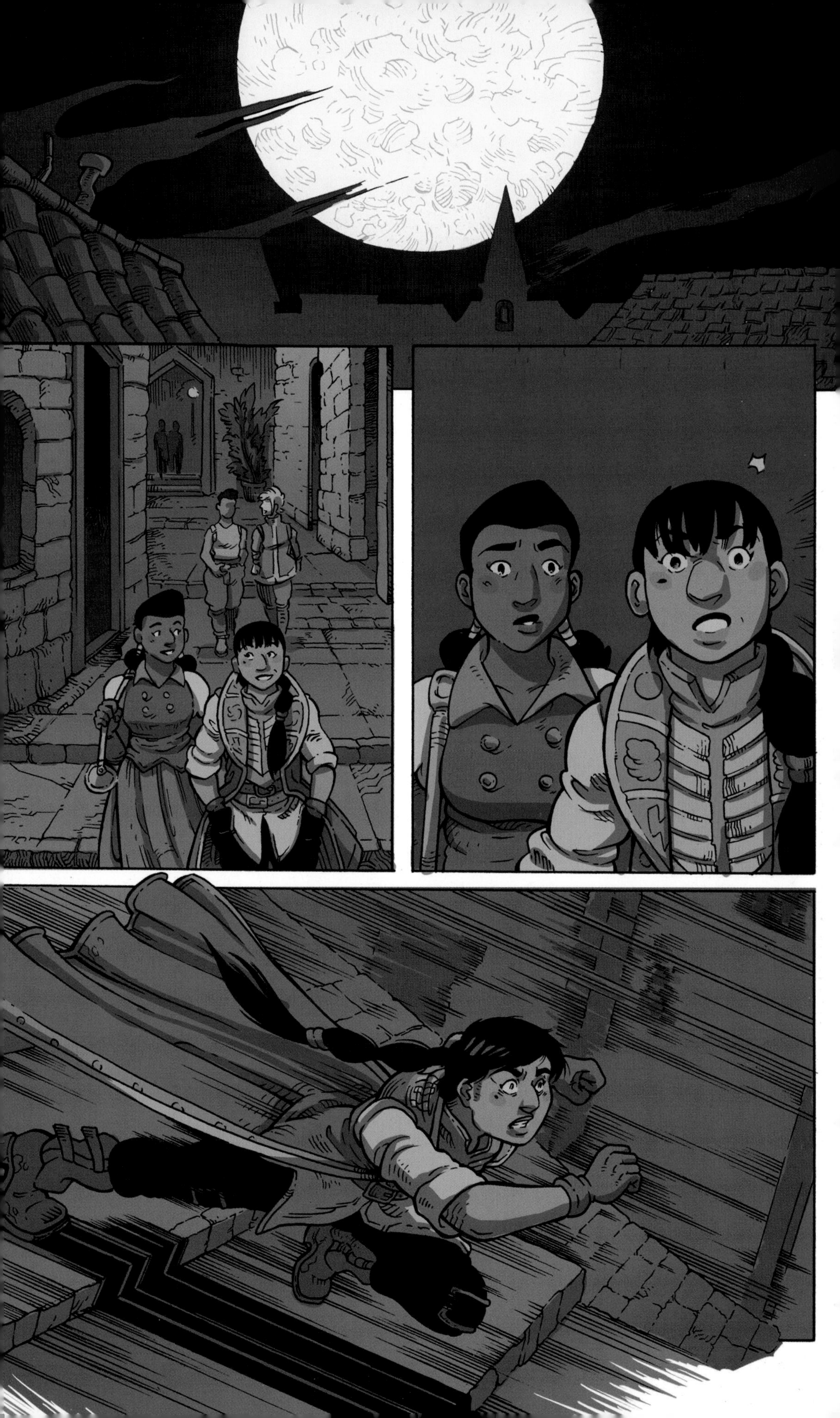

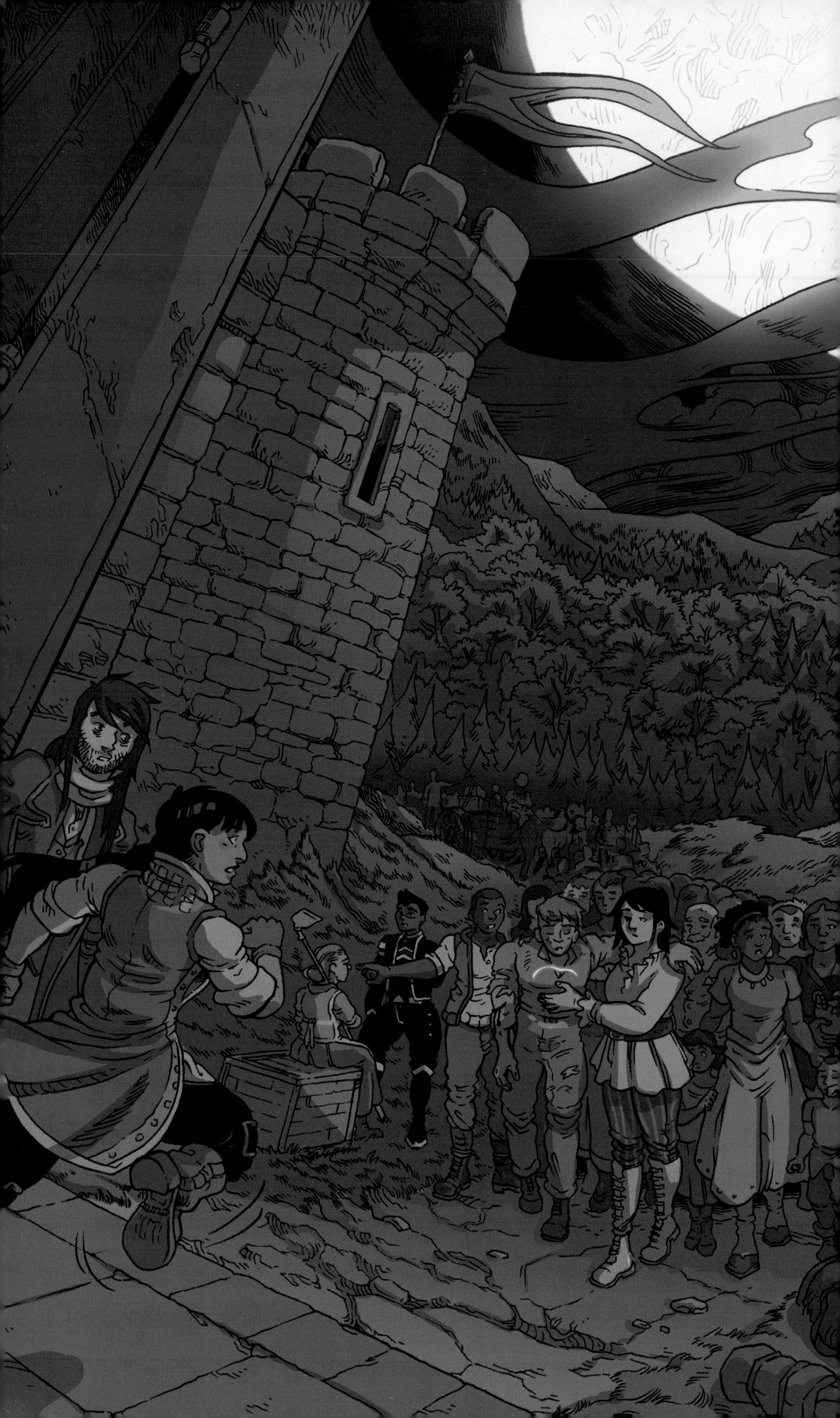

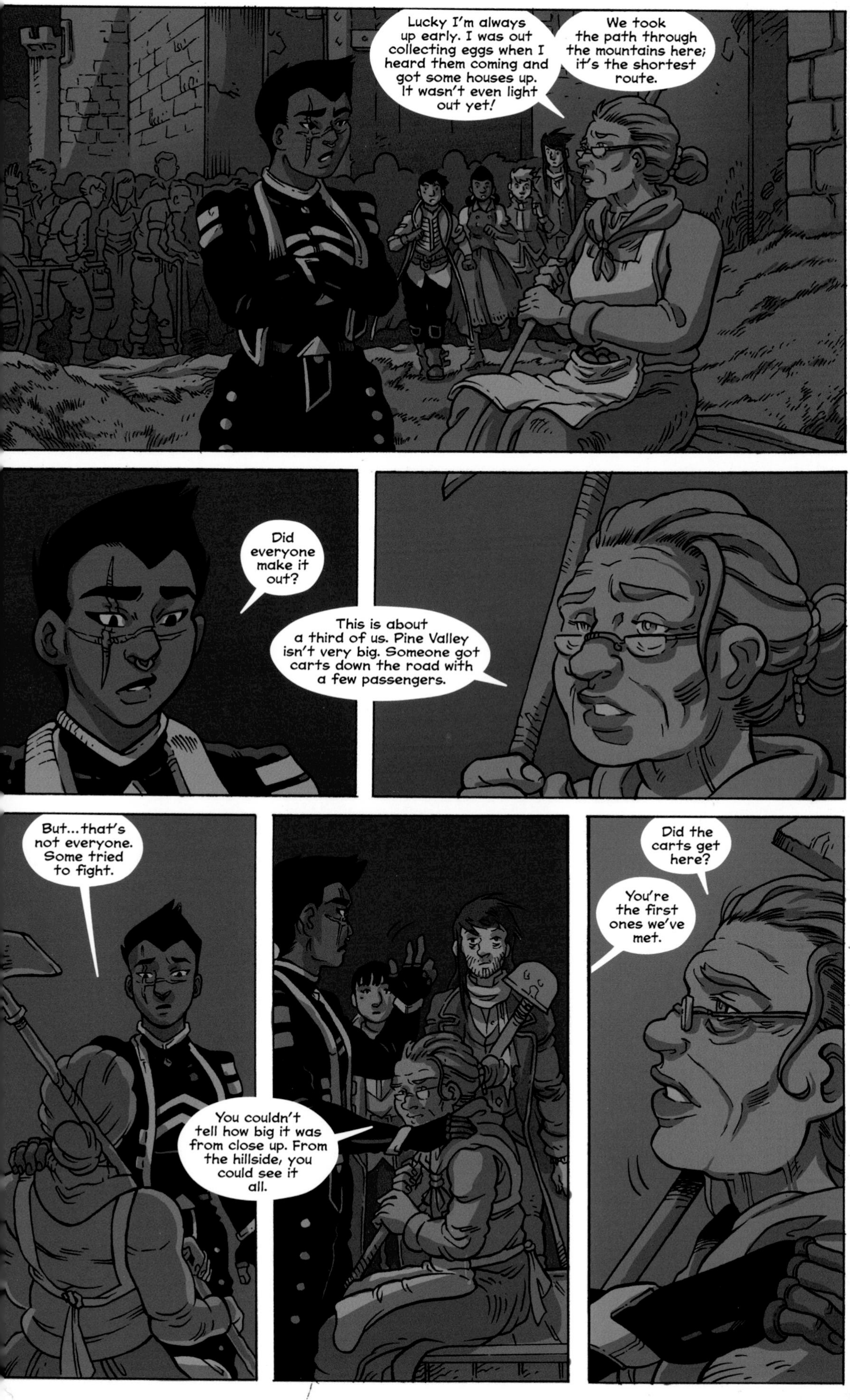
Lucky I'm always up early. I was out collecting eggs when I heard them coming and got some houses up. It wasn't even light out yet!
We took the path through the mountains here; it's the shortest route.
Did everyone make it out?
This is about a third of us. Pine Valley isn't very big. Someone got carts down the road with a few passengers.
But...that's not everyone. Some tried to fight.
You couldn't tell how big it was from close up. From the hillside, you could see it all.
Did the carts get here?
You're the first ones we've met.

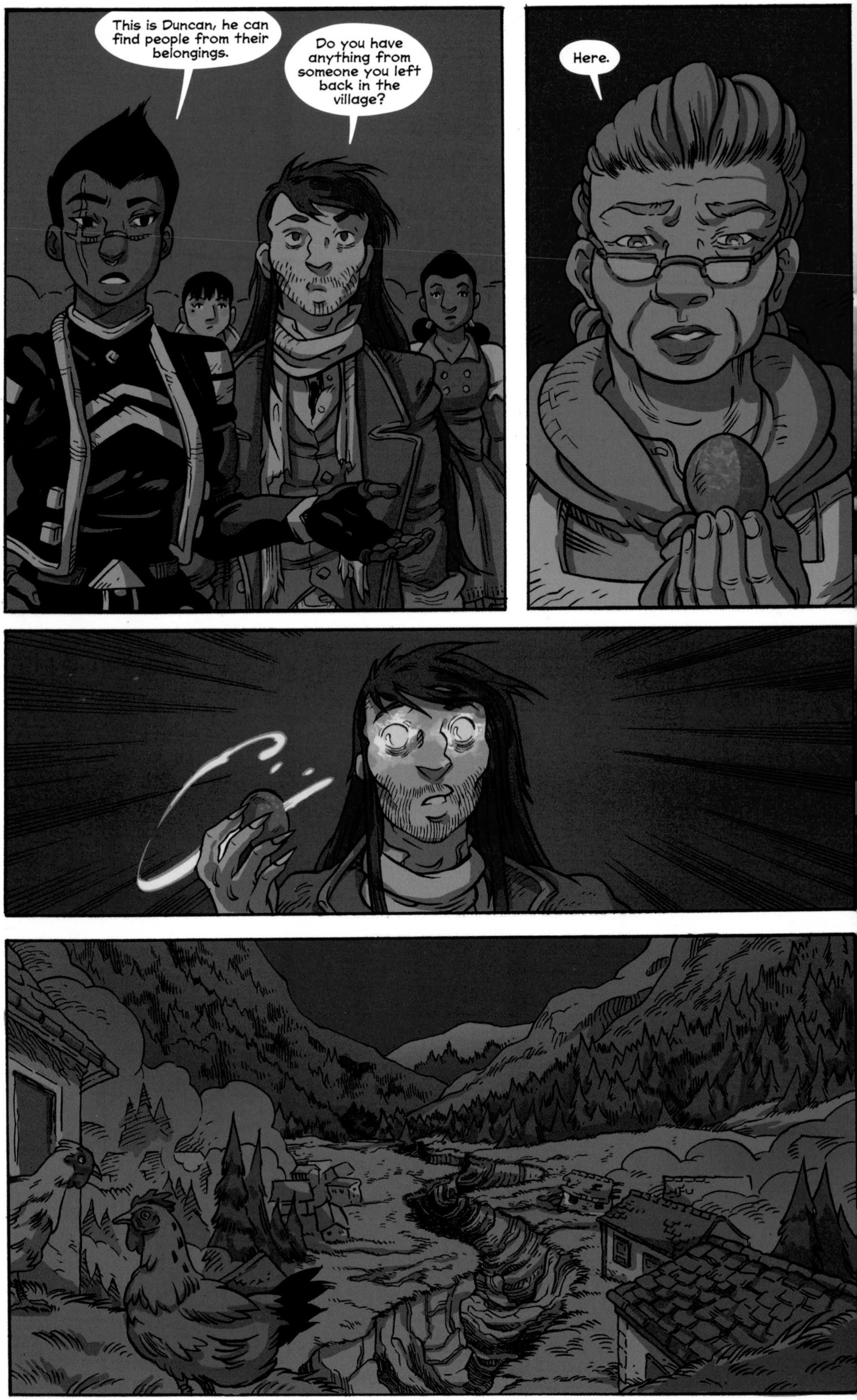
This is Duncan, he can find people from their belongings.
Do you have anything from someone you left back in the village?
Here.

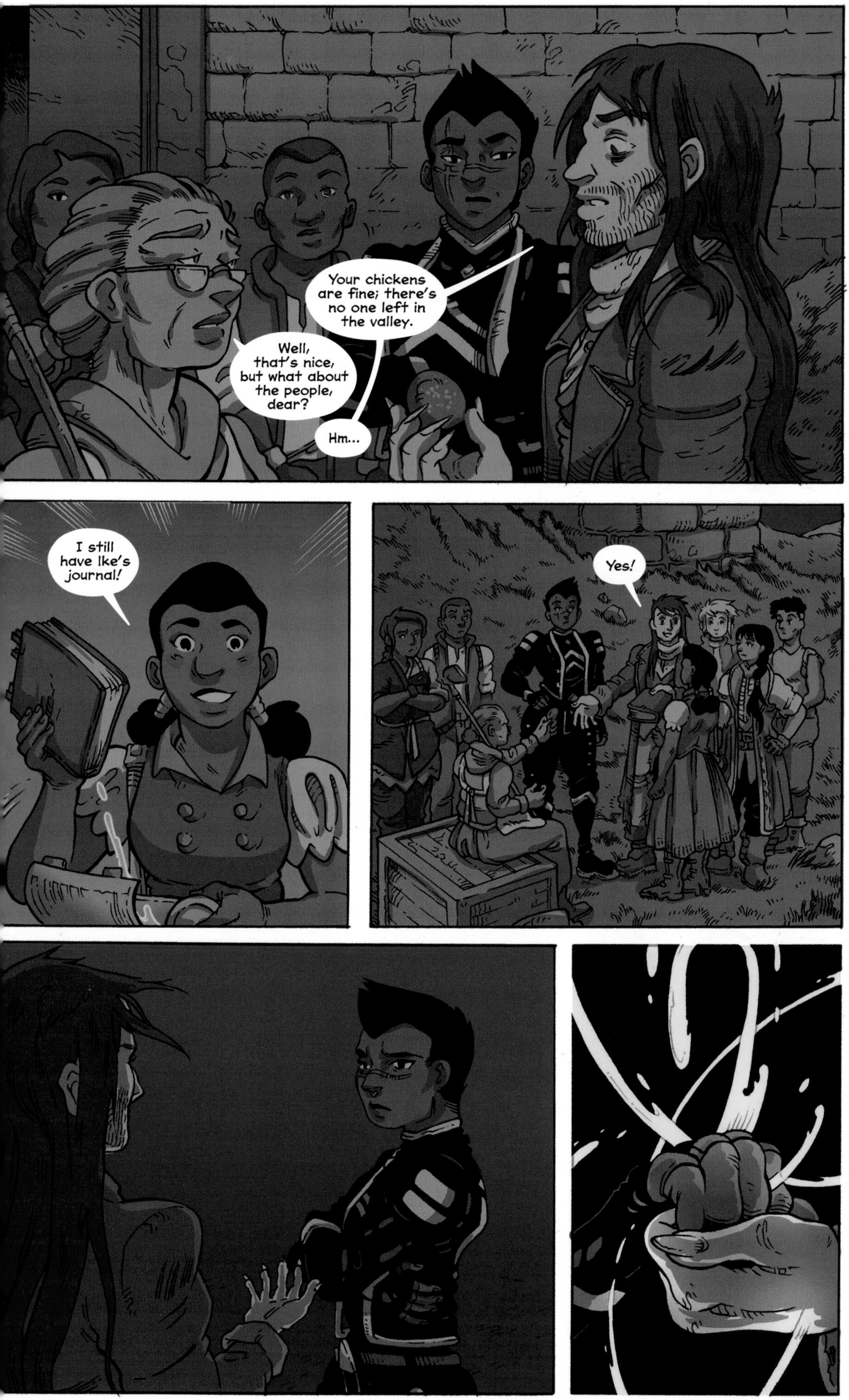
Your chickens are fine; there's no one left in the valley.
Well, that's nice, but what about the people, dear?
Hm...
I still have Ike's journal!
Yes!

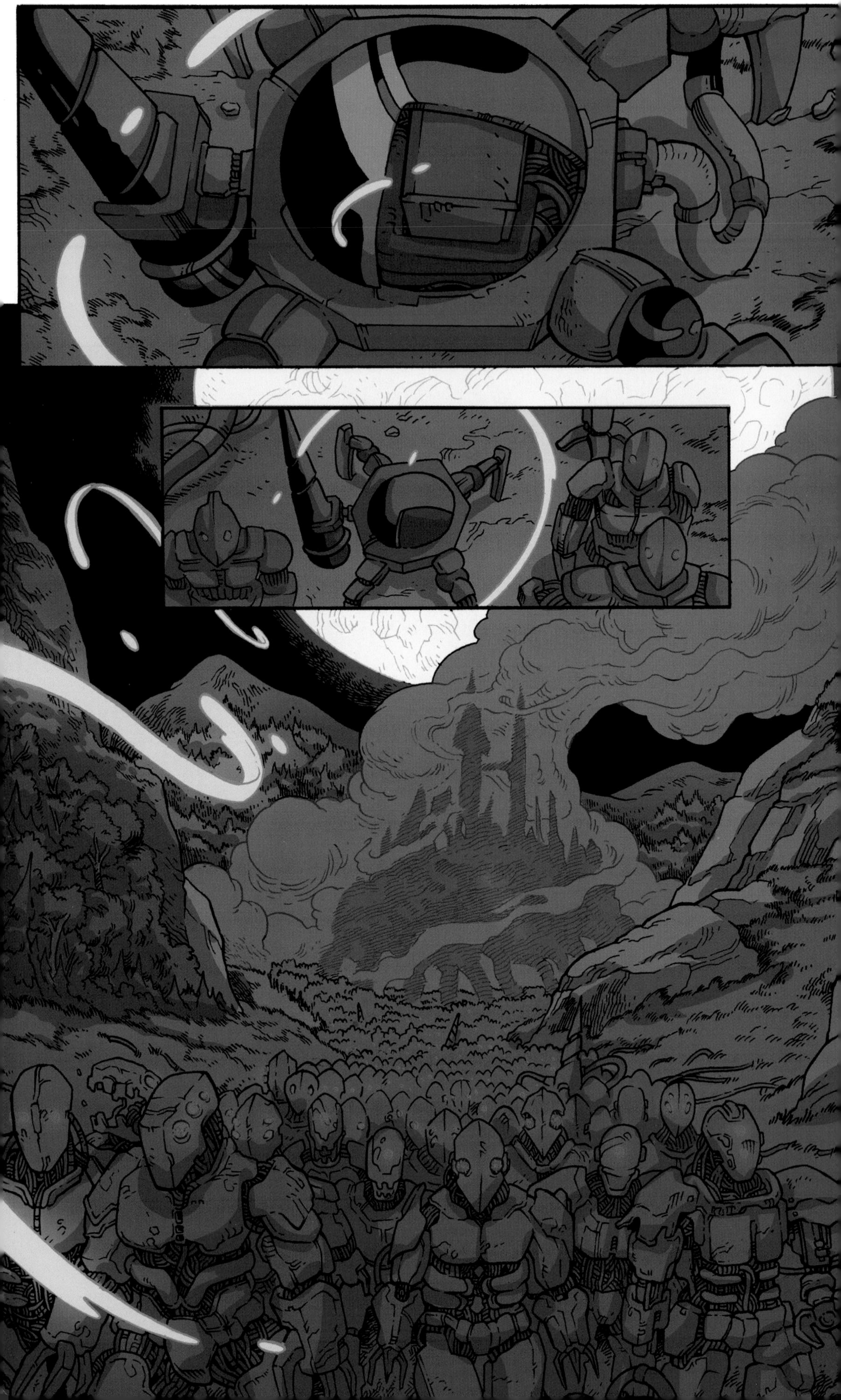

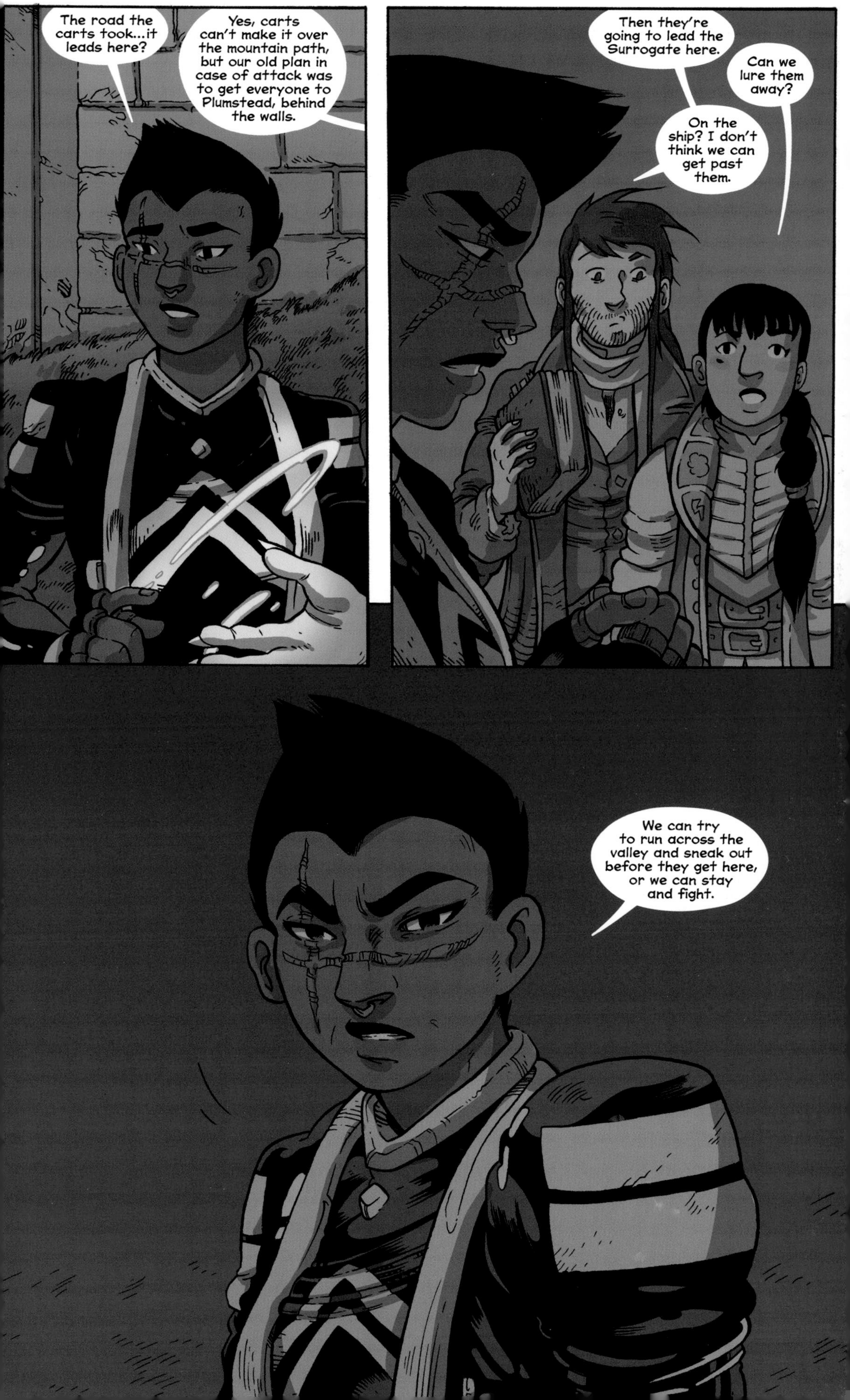
The road the carts took...it leads here?
Yes, carts can't make it over the mountain path, but our old plan in case of attack was to get everyone to Plumstead, behind the walls.
Then they're going to lead the Surrogate here.
Can we lure them away?
On the ship? I don't think we can get past them.
We can try to run across the valley and sneak out before they get here, or we can stay and fight.

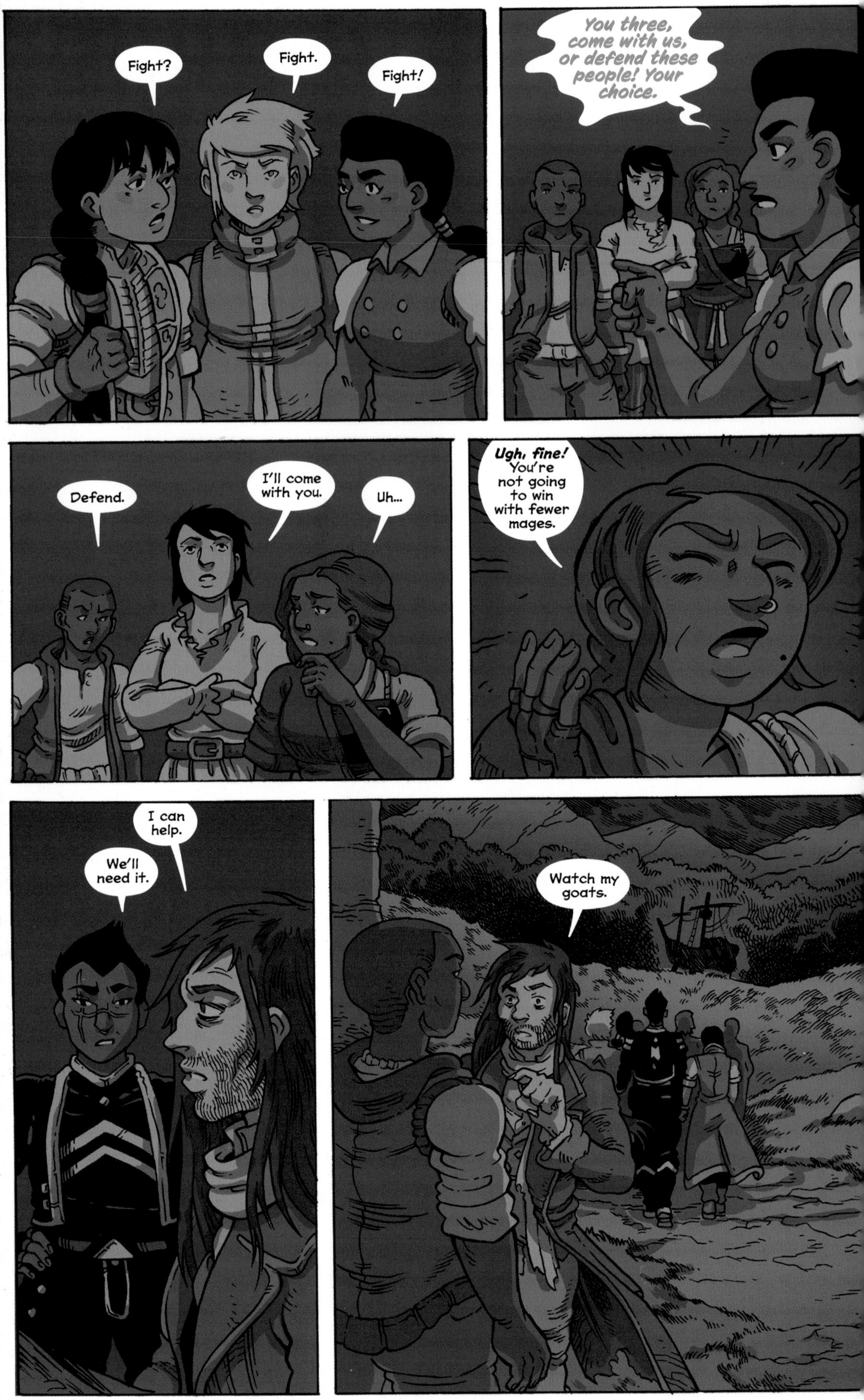
Fight?
Fight.
Fight!
You three, come with us, or defend these people! Your choice.
Defend.
I'll come with you.
Uh...
Ugh, fine! You're not going to win with fewer mages.
I can help.
We'll need it.
Watch my goats.

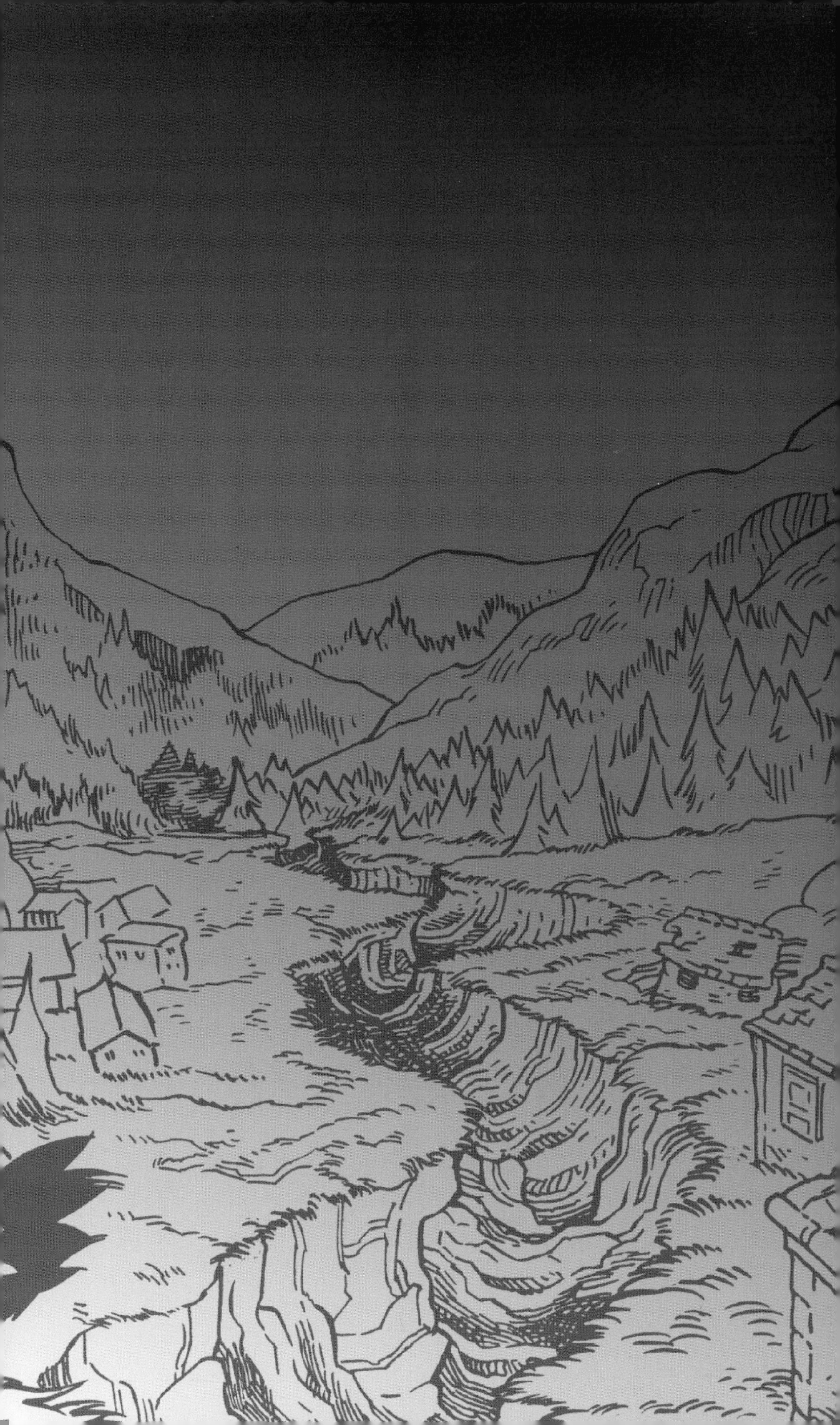

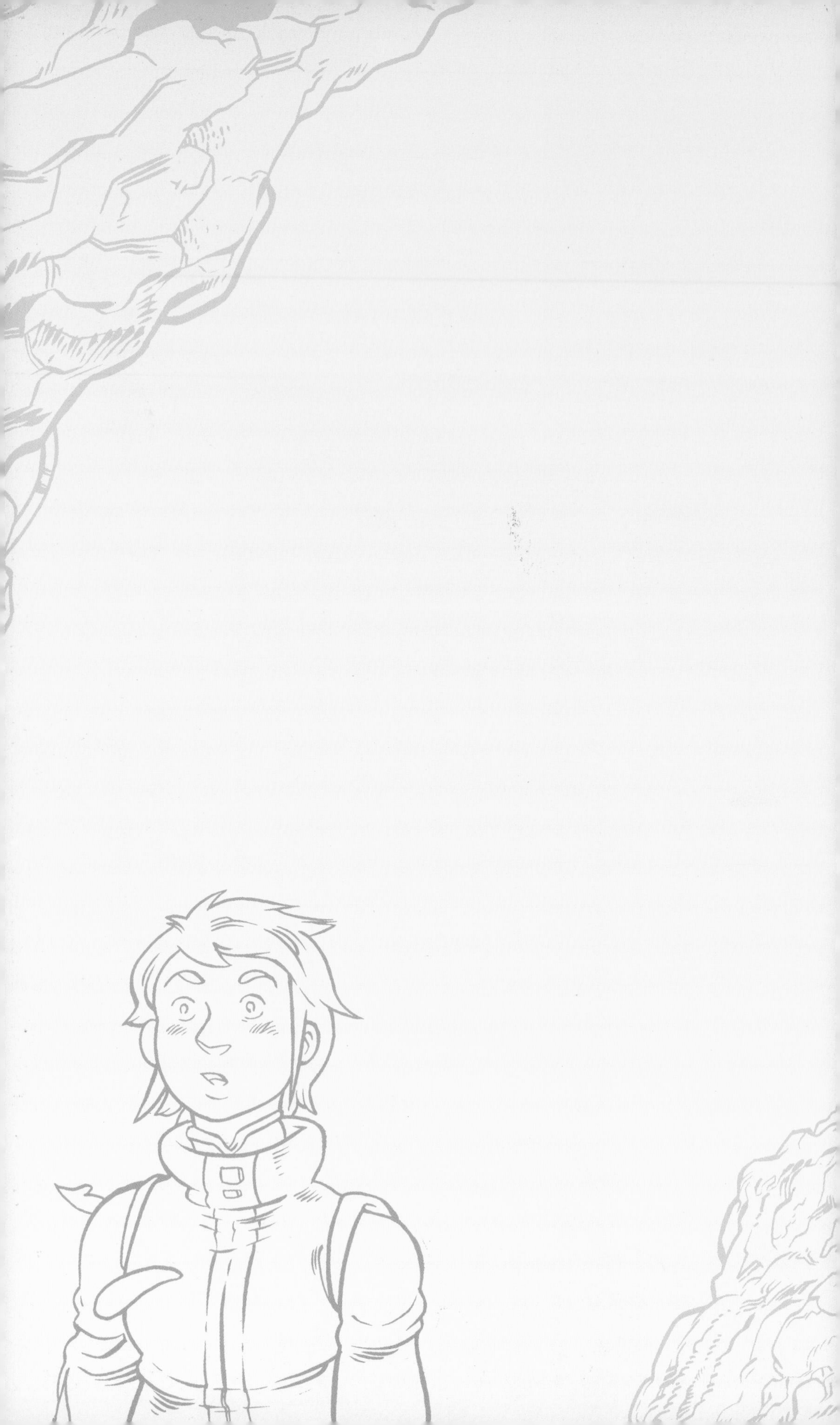

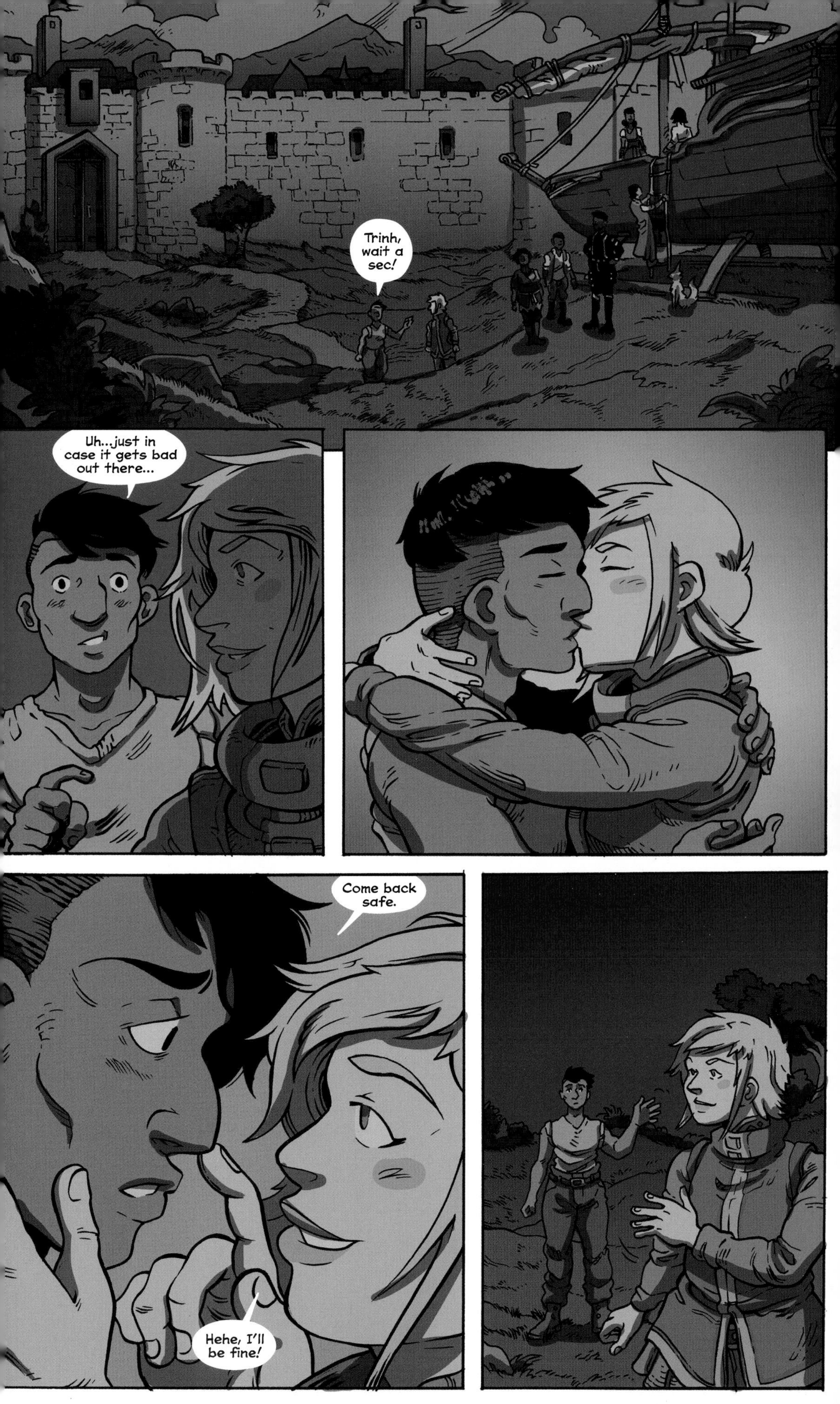
Trinh, wait a sec!
Uh...just in case it gets bad out there...
Come back safe.
Hehe, I'll be fine!

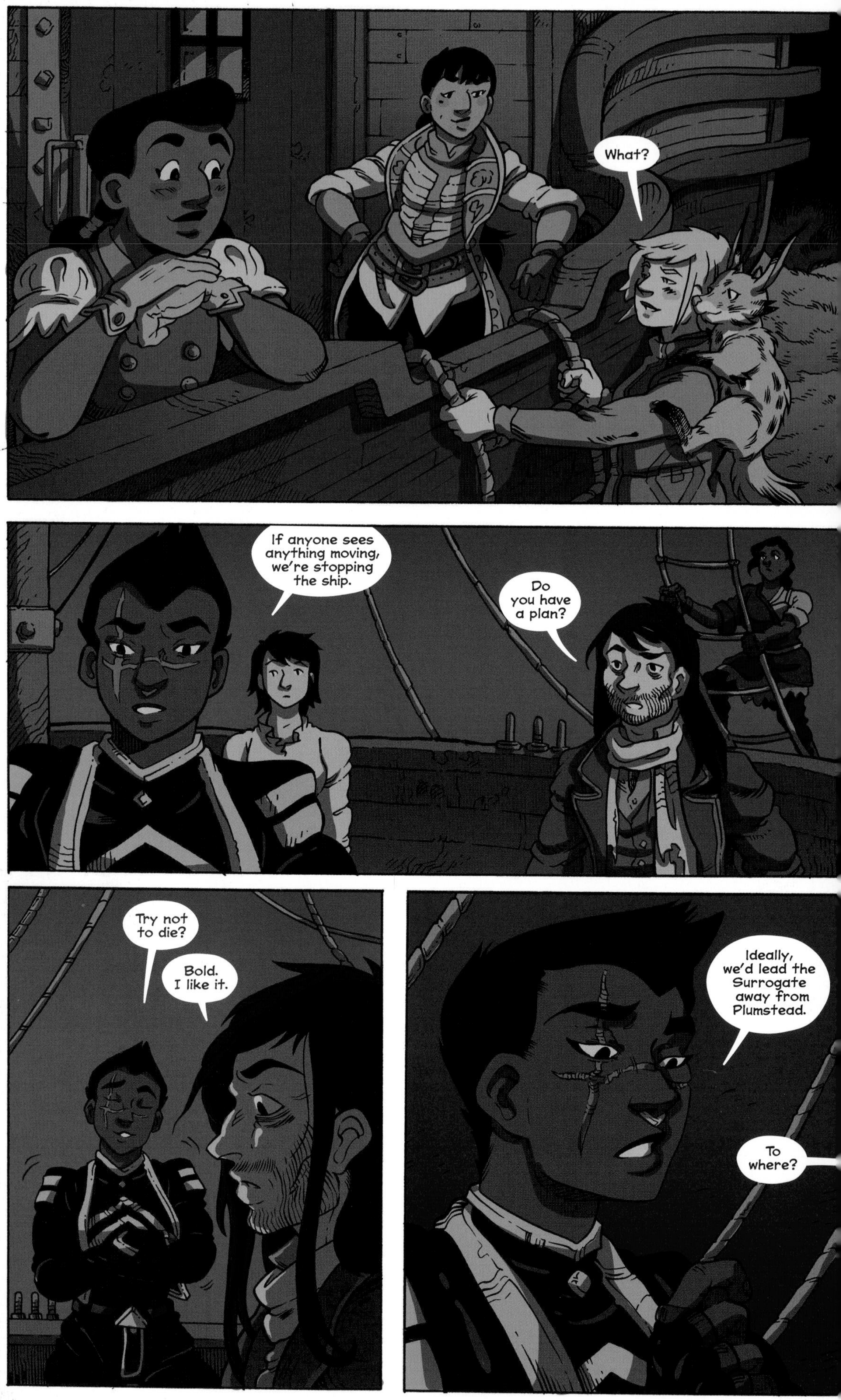
What?
If anyone sees anything moving, we're stopping the ship.
Do you have a plan?
Try not to die?
Bold. I like it.
Ideally, we'd lead the Surrogate away from Plumstead.
To where?

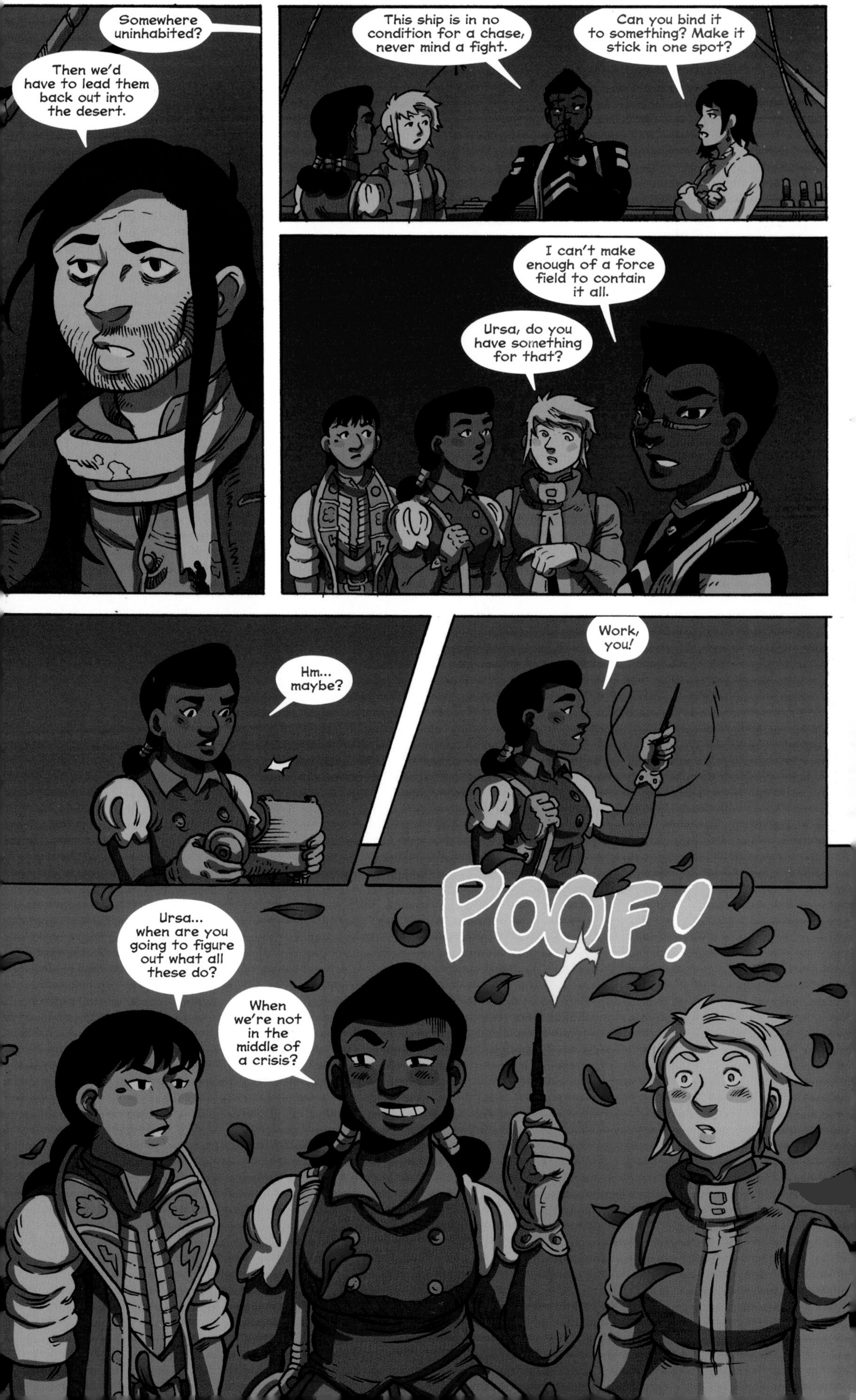

Somewhere uninhabited?
Then we'd have to lead them back out into the desert.
This ship is in no condition for a chase, never mind a fight.
Can you bind it to something? Make it stick in one spot?
I can't make enough of a force field to contain it all.
Ursa, do you have something for that?
Hm... maybe?
Work, you!
POOF!
Ursa... when are you going to figure out what all these do?
When we're not in the middle of a crisis?

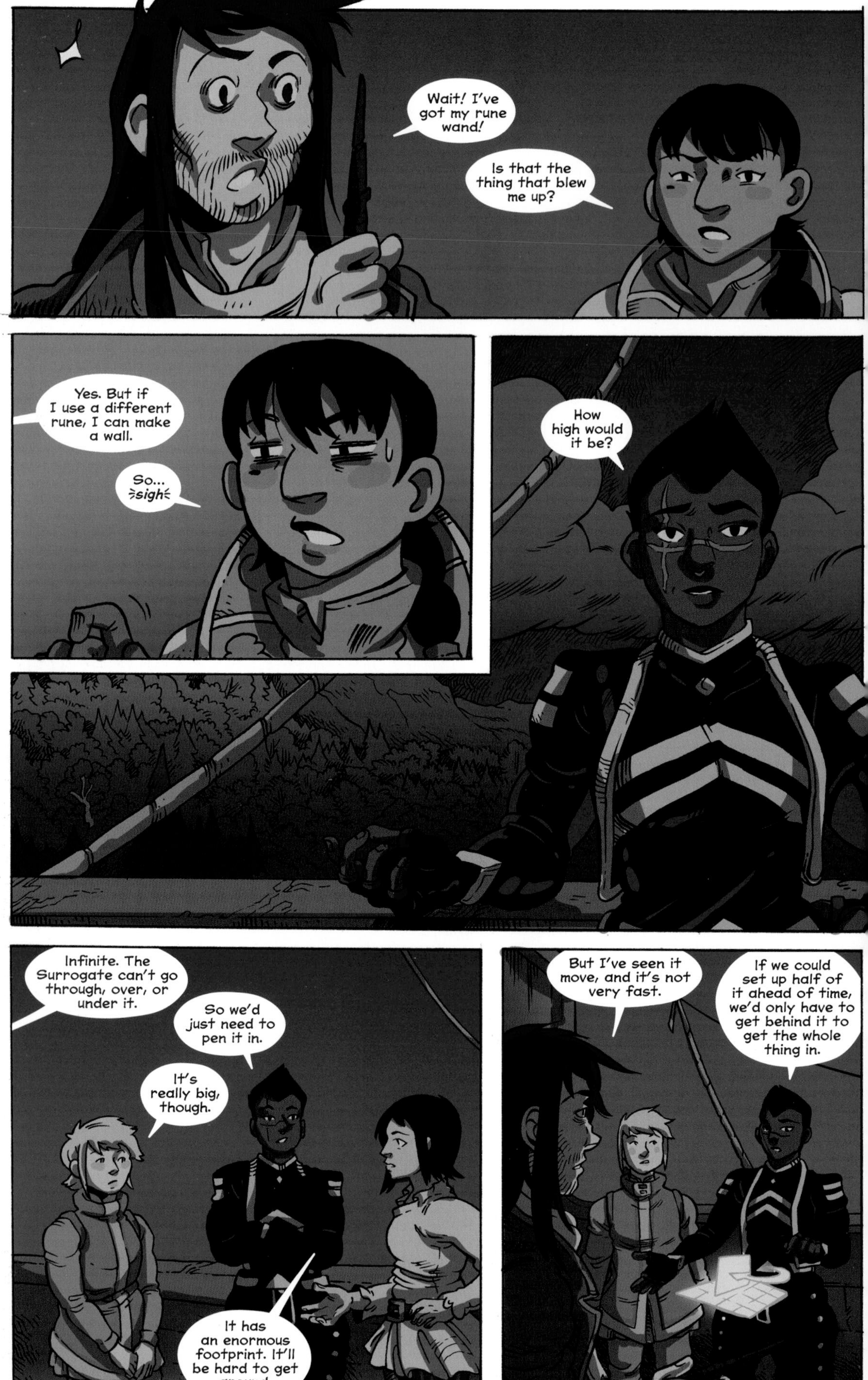
Wait! I've got my rune wand!
Is that the thing that blew me up?
Yes. But if I use a different rune, I can make a wall.
So... ⩩sigh⩩
How high would it be?
Infinite. The Surrogate can't go through, over, or under it.
So we'd just need to pen it in.
It's really big, though.
It has an enormous footprint. It'll be hard to get around.
But I've seen it move, and it's not very fast.
If we could set up half of it ahead of time, we'd only have to get behind it to get the whole thing in.

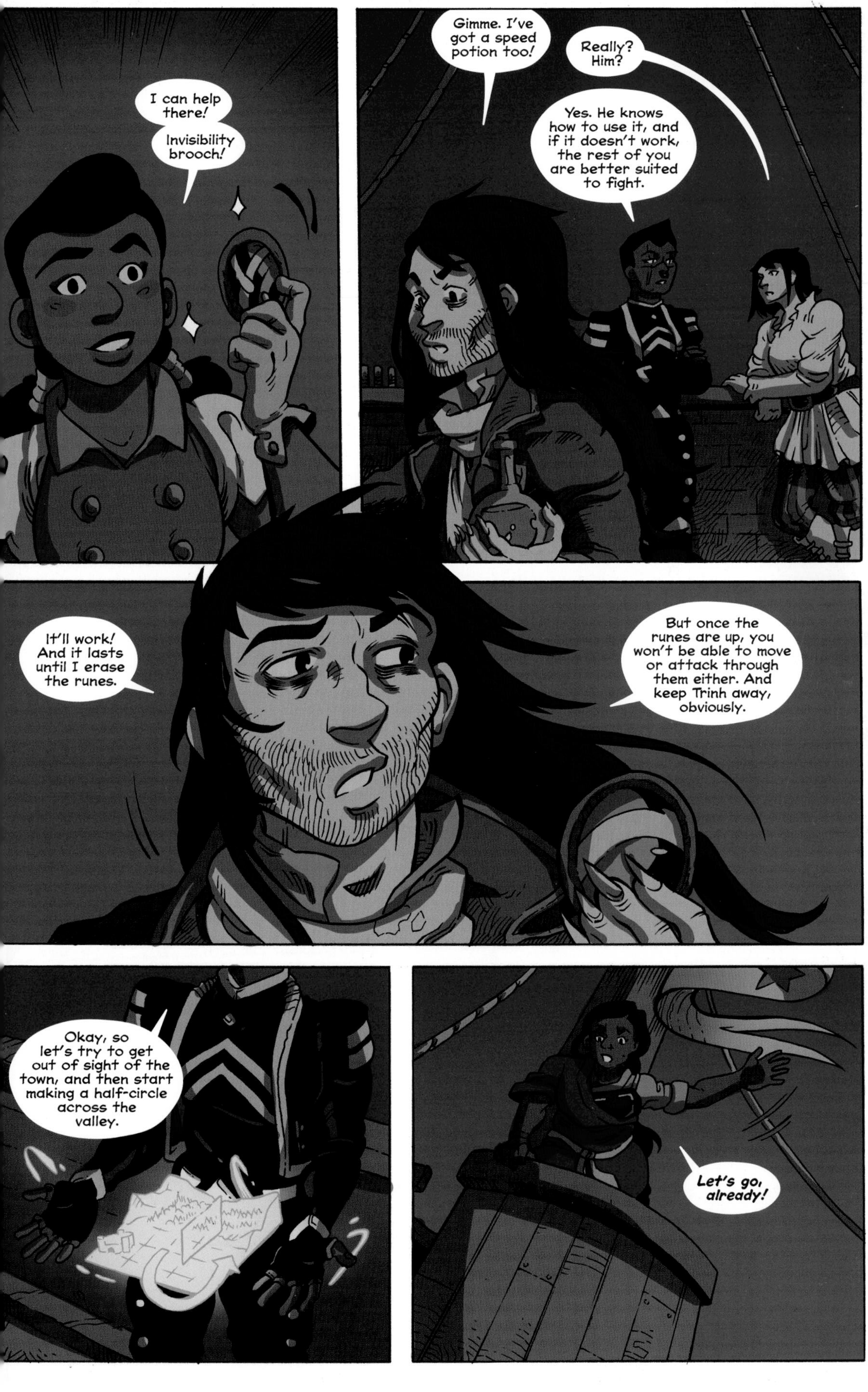
I can help there!
Invisibility brooch!
Gimme. I've got a speed potion too!
Really? Him?
Yes. He knows how to use it, and if it doesn't work, the rest of you are better suited to fight.
It'll work! And it lasts until I erase the runes.
But once the runes are up, you won't be able to move or attack through them either. And keep Trinh away, obviously.
Okay, so let's try to get out of sight of the town, and then start making a half-circle across the valley.
Let's go, already!

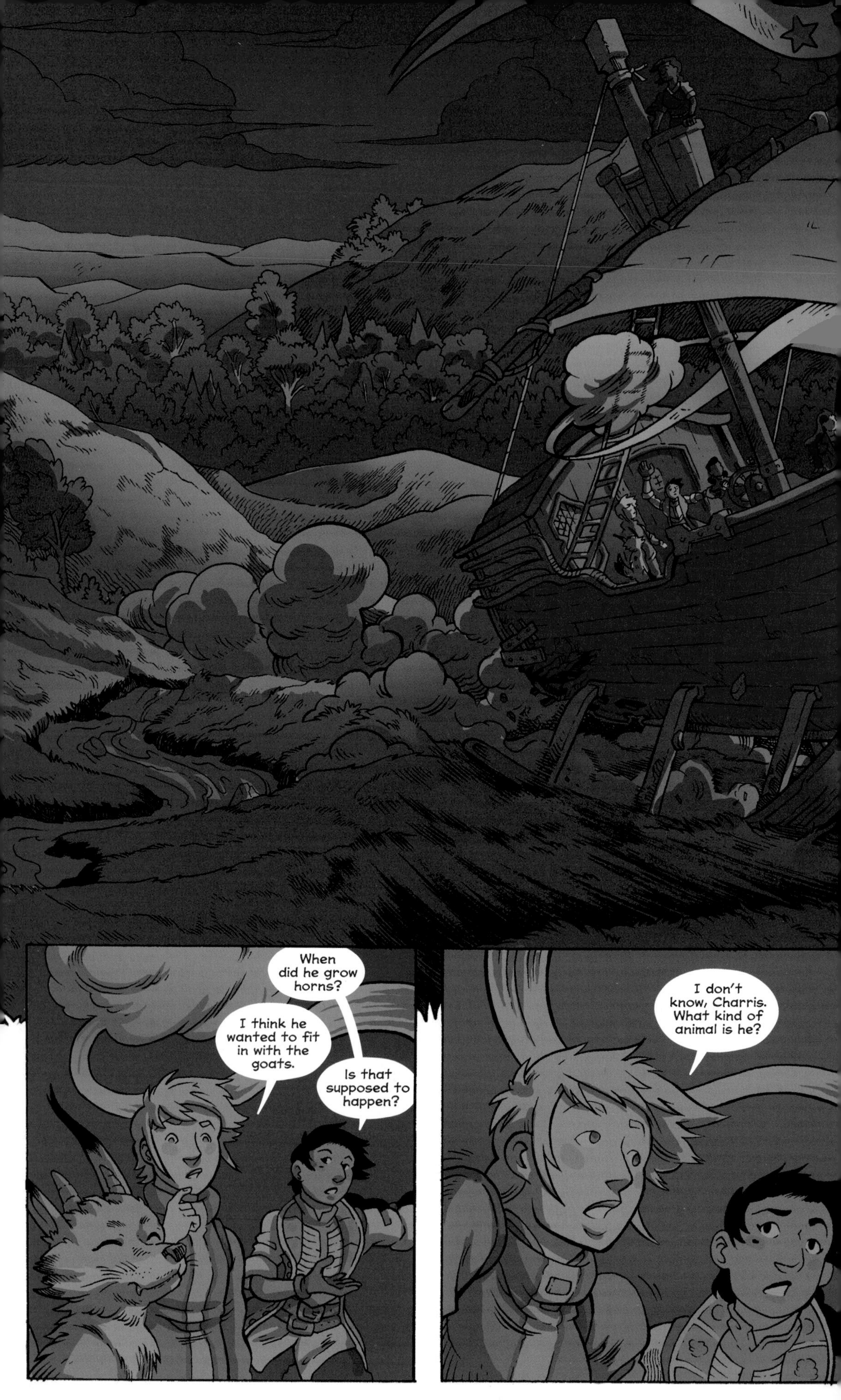
When did he grow horns?
I think he wanted to fit in with the goats.
Is that supposed to happen?
I don't know, Charris. What kind of animal is he?

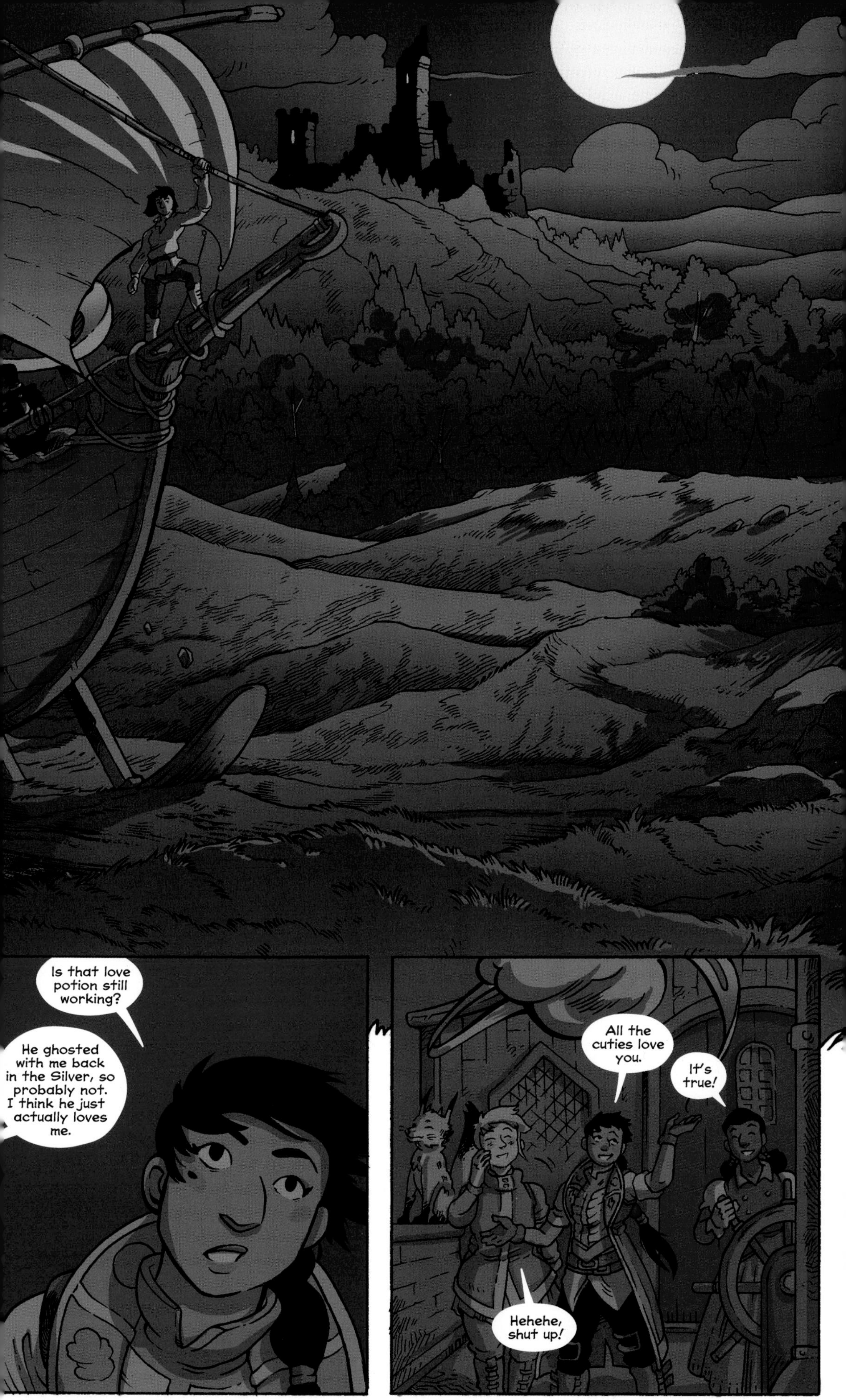
Is that love potion still working?
He ghosted with me back in the Silver, so probably not. I think he just actually loves me.
All the cuties love you.
It's true!
Hehehe, shut up!

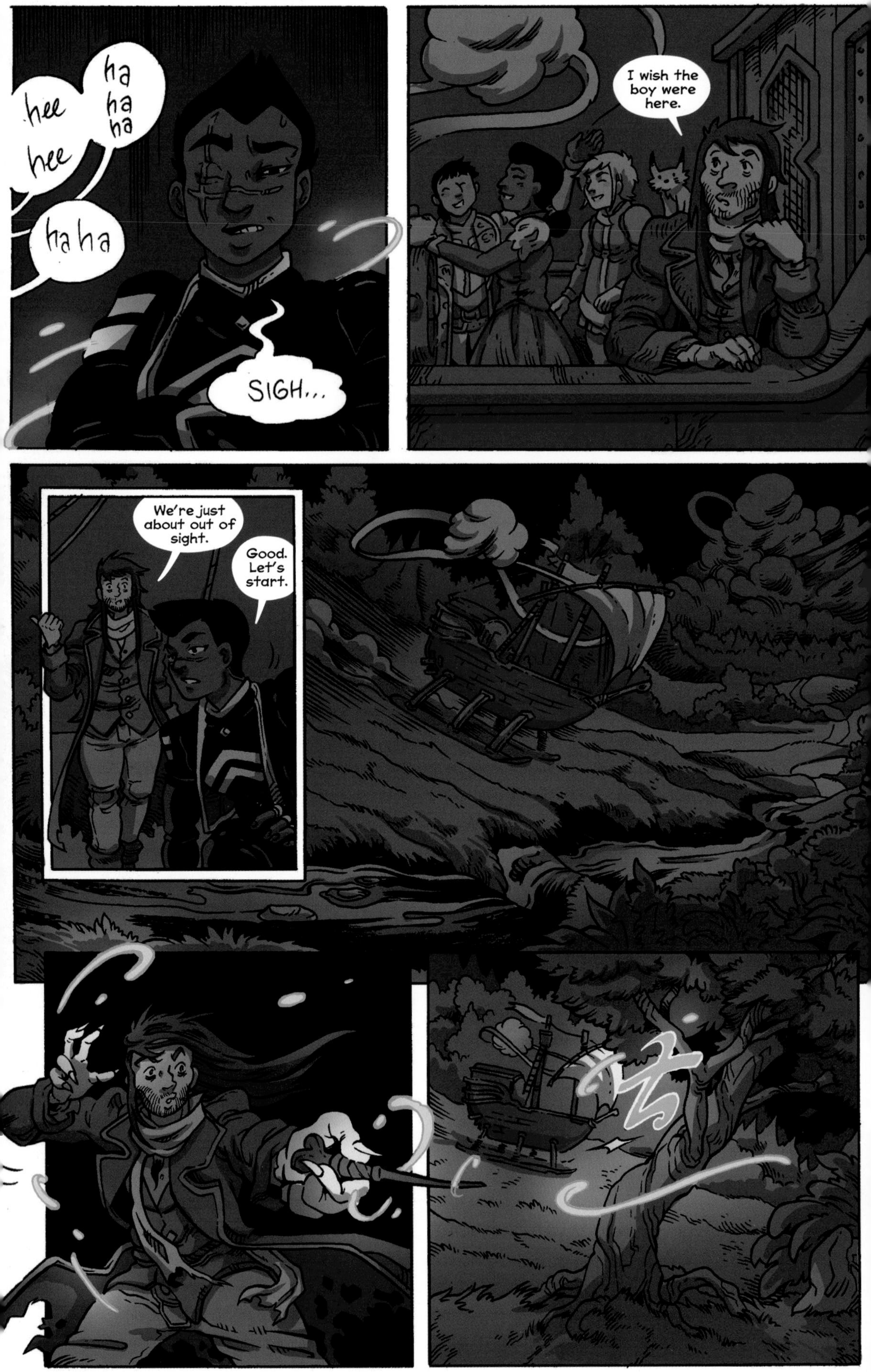
hee
hee
ha
ha
ha
ha ha
SIGH...
I wish the boy were here.
We're just about out of sight.
Good. Let's start.

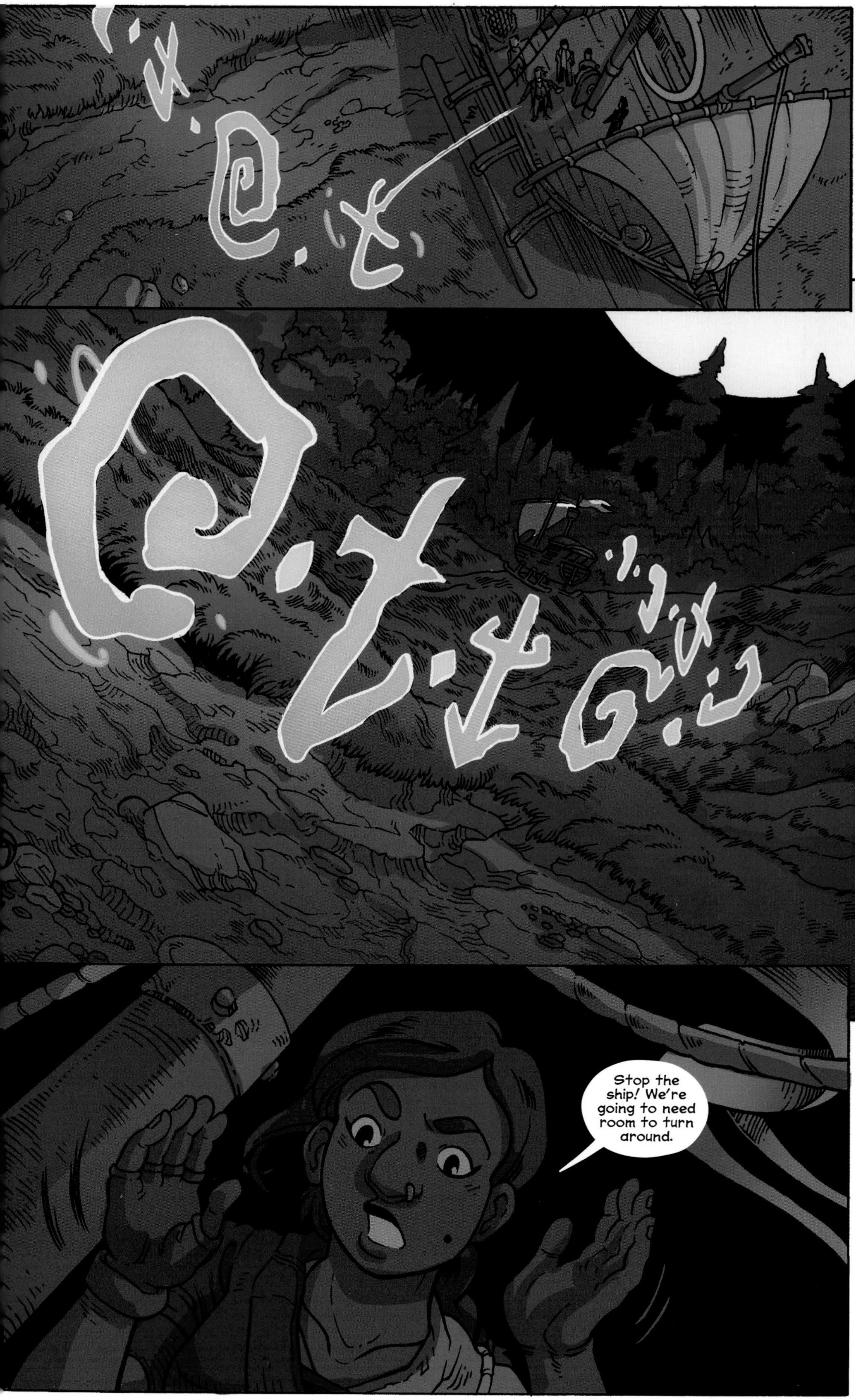
Stop the ship! We're going to need room to turn around.

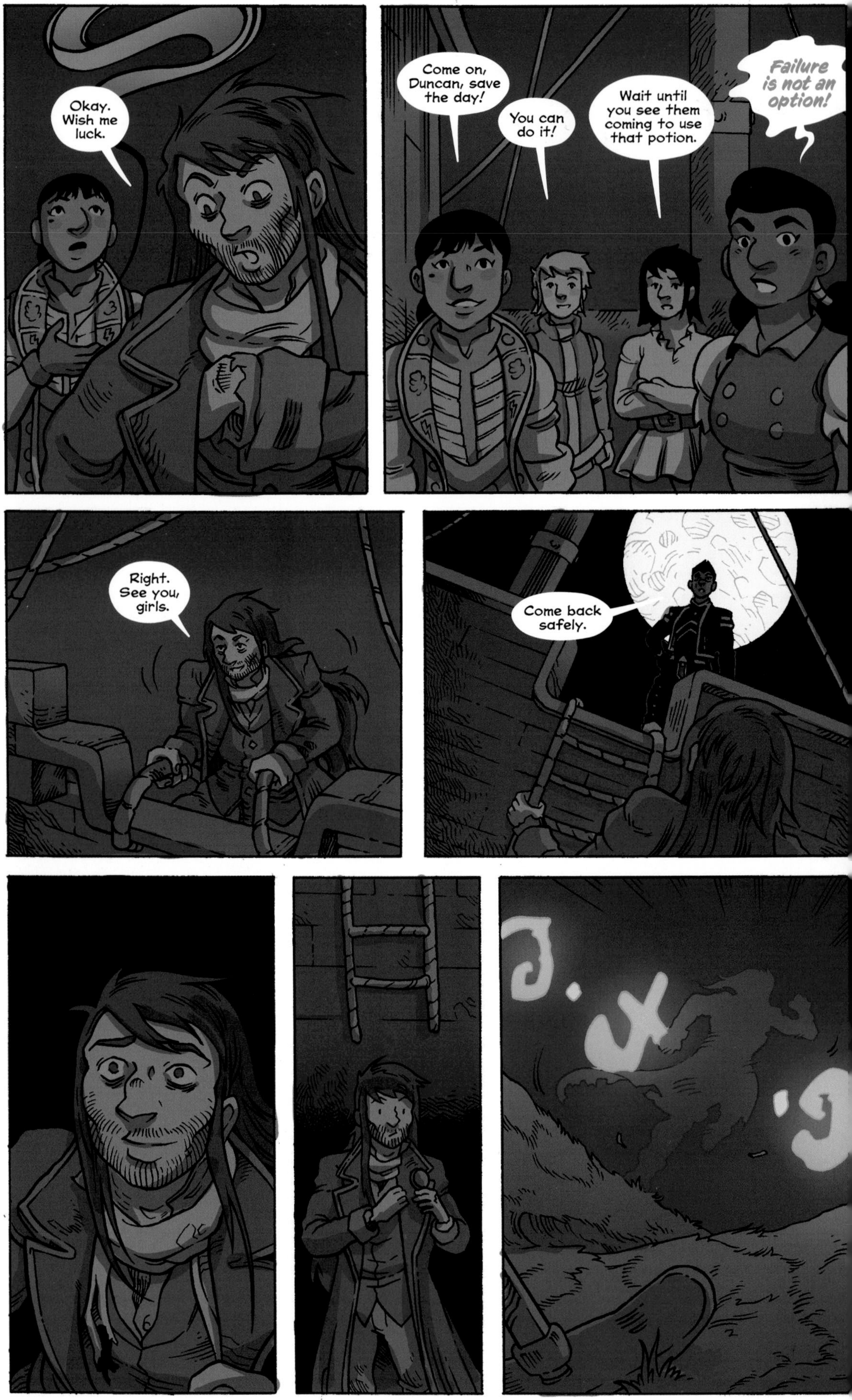
Okay. Wish me luck.
Come on, Duncan, save the day!
You can do it!
Wait until you see them coming to use that potion.
Failure is not an option!
Right. See you, girls.
Come back safely.

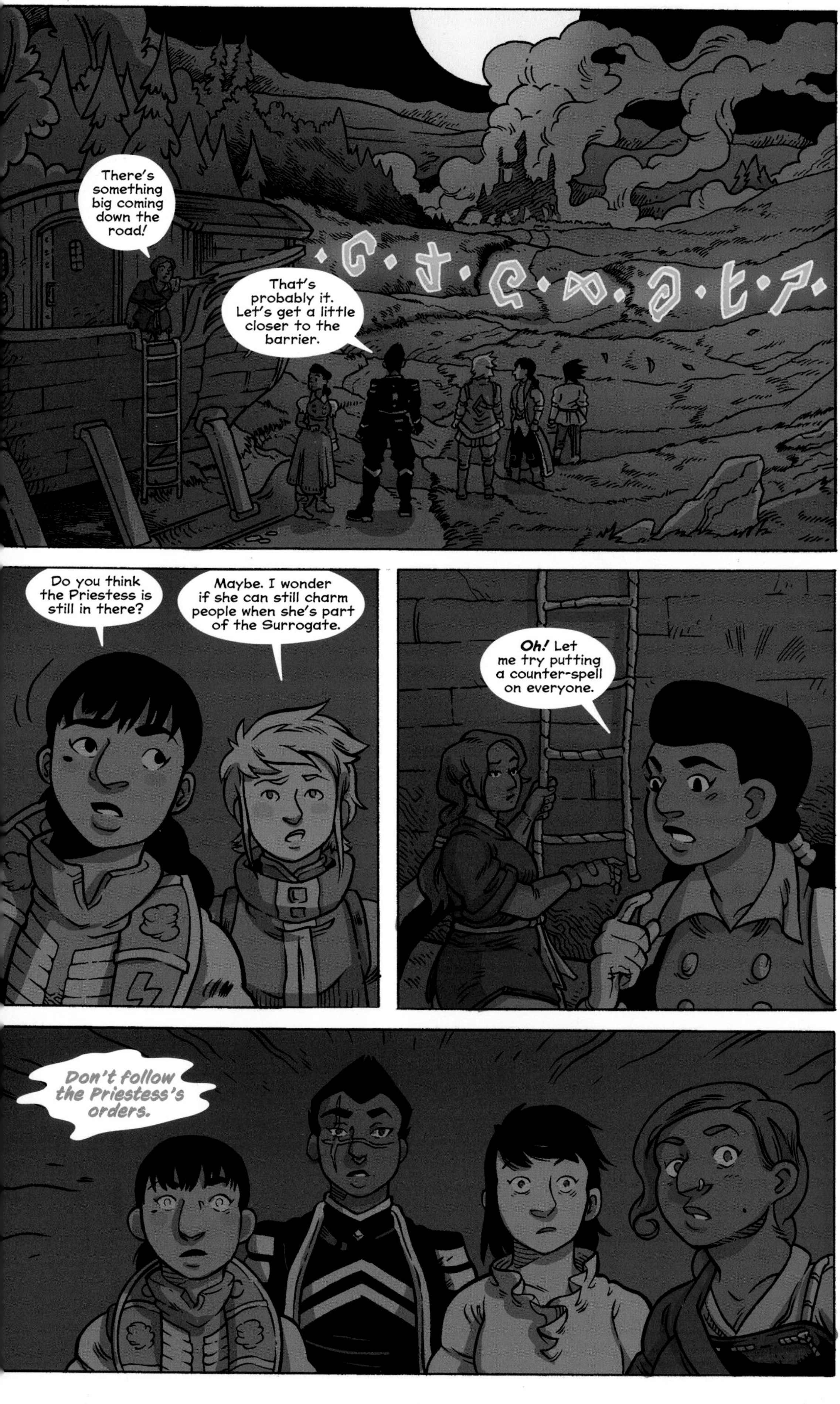
There's something big coming down the road!
That's probably it. Let's get a little closer to the barrier.
Do you think the Priestess is still in there?
Maybe. I wonder if she can still charm people when she's part of the Surrogate.
Oh! Let me try putting a counter-spell on everyone.
Don't follow the Priestess's orders.

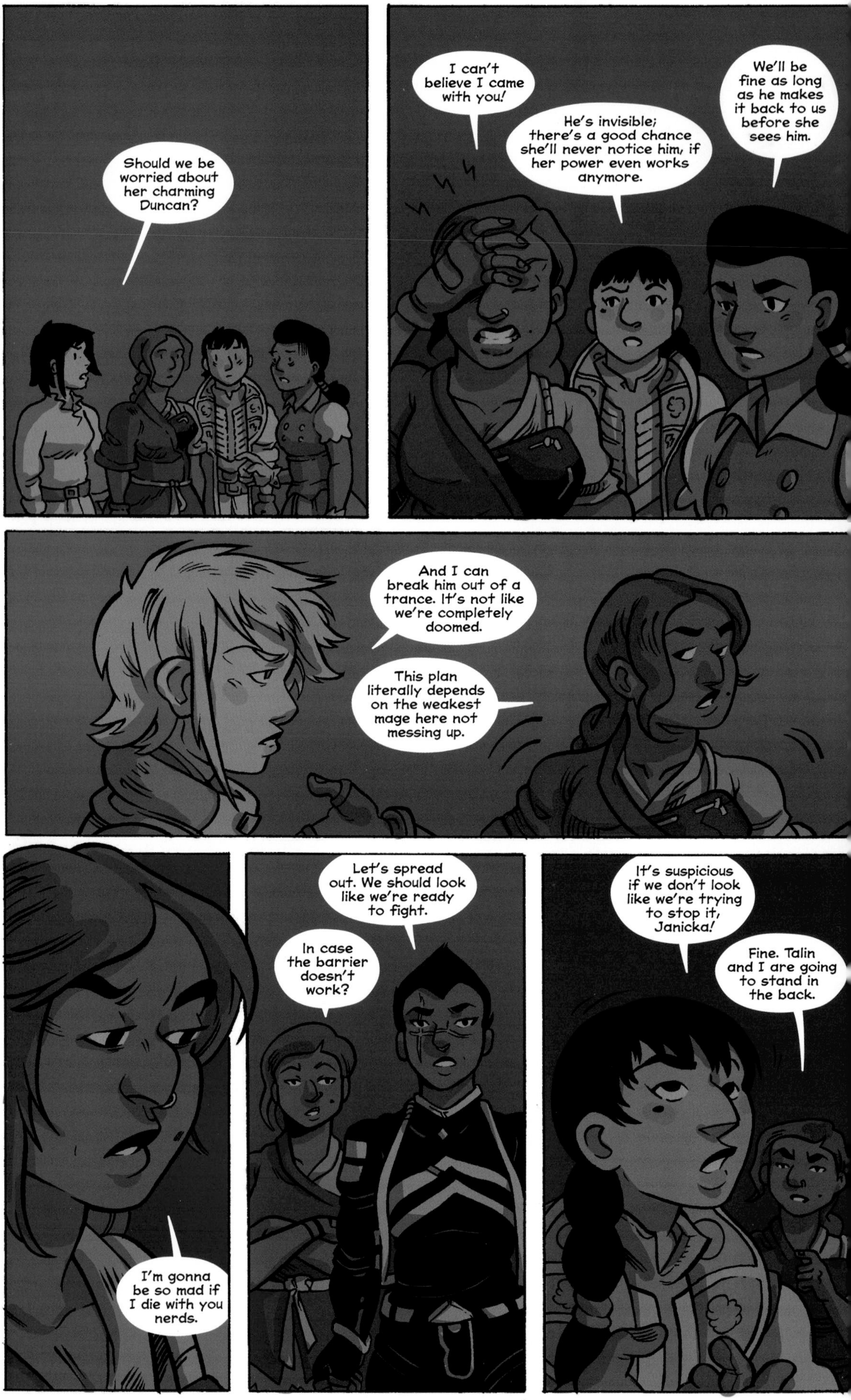
Should we be worried about her charming Duncan?
I can't believe I came with you!
He's invisible; there's a good chance she'll never notice him, if her power even works anymore.
We'll be fine as long as he makes it back to us before she sees him.
And I can break him out of a trance. It's not like we're completely doomed.
This plan literally depends on the weakest mage here not messing up.
I'm gonna be so mad if I die with you nerds.
Let's spread out. We should look like we're ready to fight.
In case the barrier doesn't work?
It's suspicious if we don't look like we're trying to stop it, Janicka!
Fine. Talin and I are going to stand in the back.

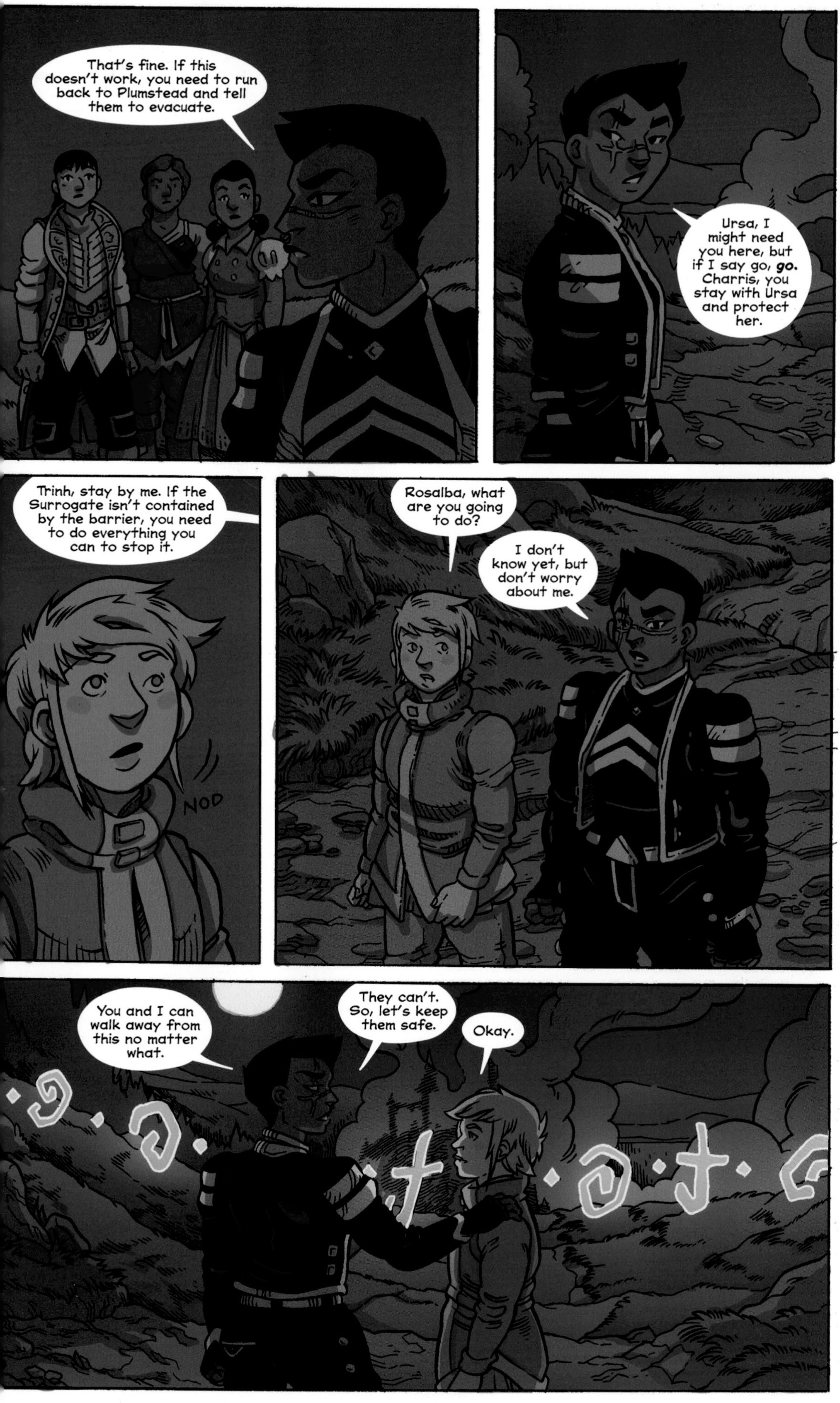
That's fine. If this doesn't work, you need to run back to Plumstead and tell them to evacuate.
Ursa, I might need you here, but if I say go, **go.** Charris, you stay with Ursa and protect her.
Trinh, stay by me. If the Surrogate isn't contained by the barrier, you need to do everything you can to stop it.
NOD
Rosalba, what are you going to do?
I don't know yet, but don't worry about me.
You and I can walk away from this no matter what.
They can't. So, let's keep them safe.
Okay.

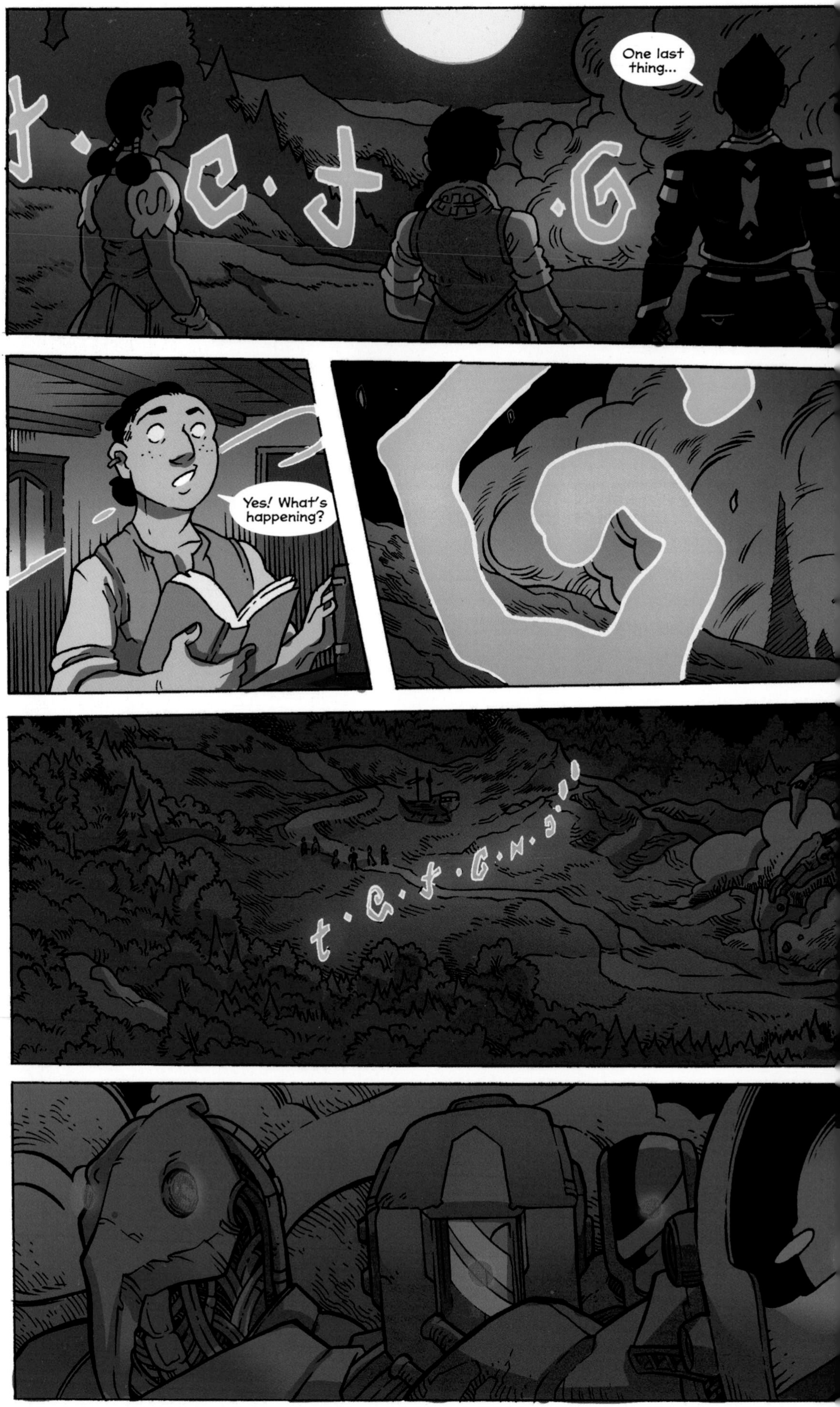
One last thing...
Yes! What's happening?

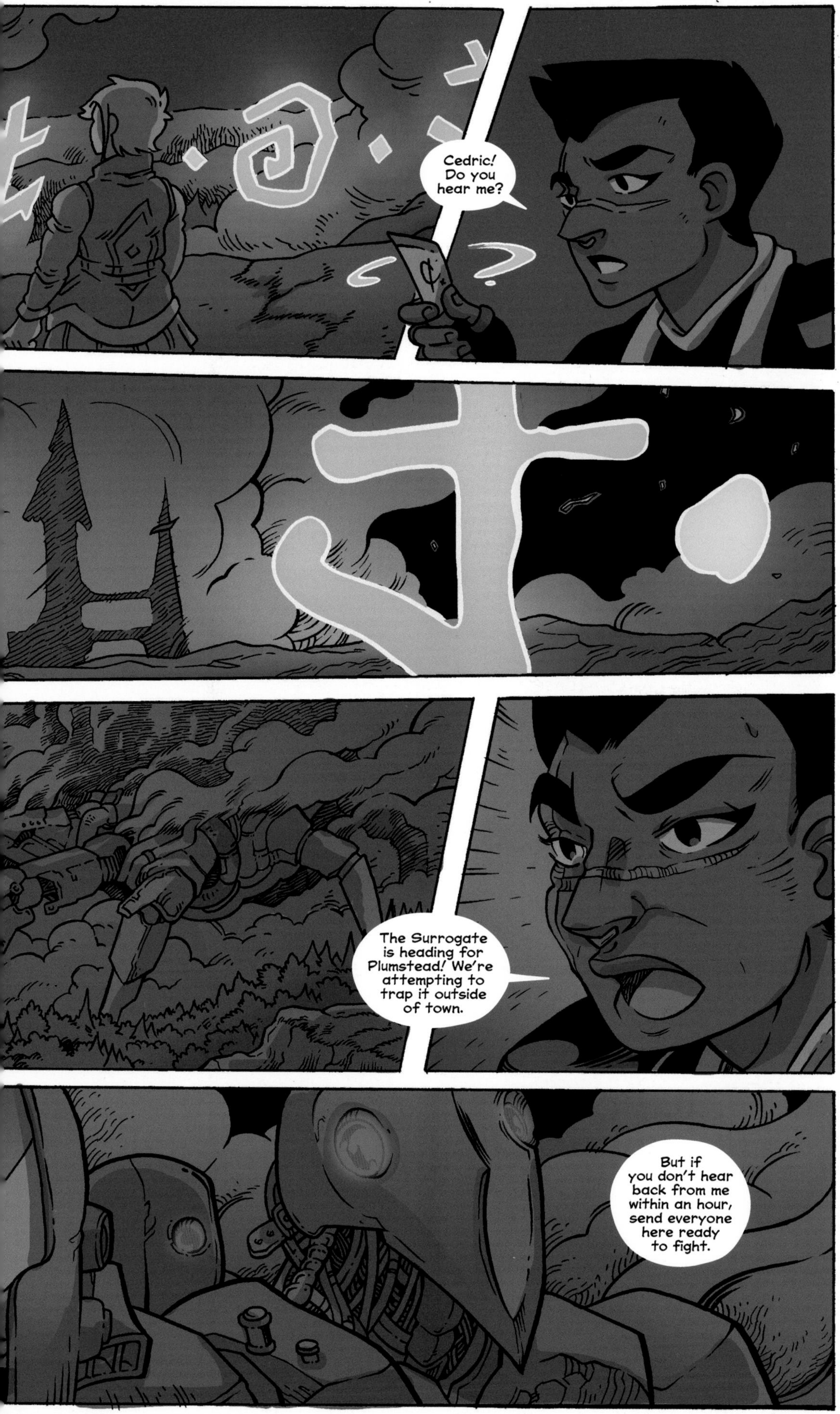
Cedric! Do you hear me?
The Surrogate is heading for Plumstead! We're attempting to trap it outside of town.
But if you don't hear back from me within an hour, send everyone here ready to fight.

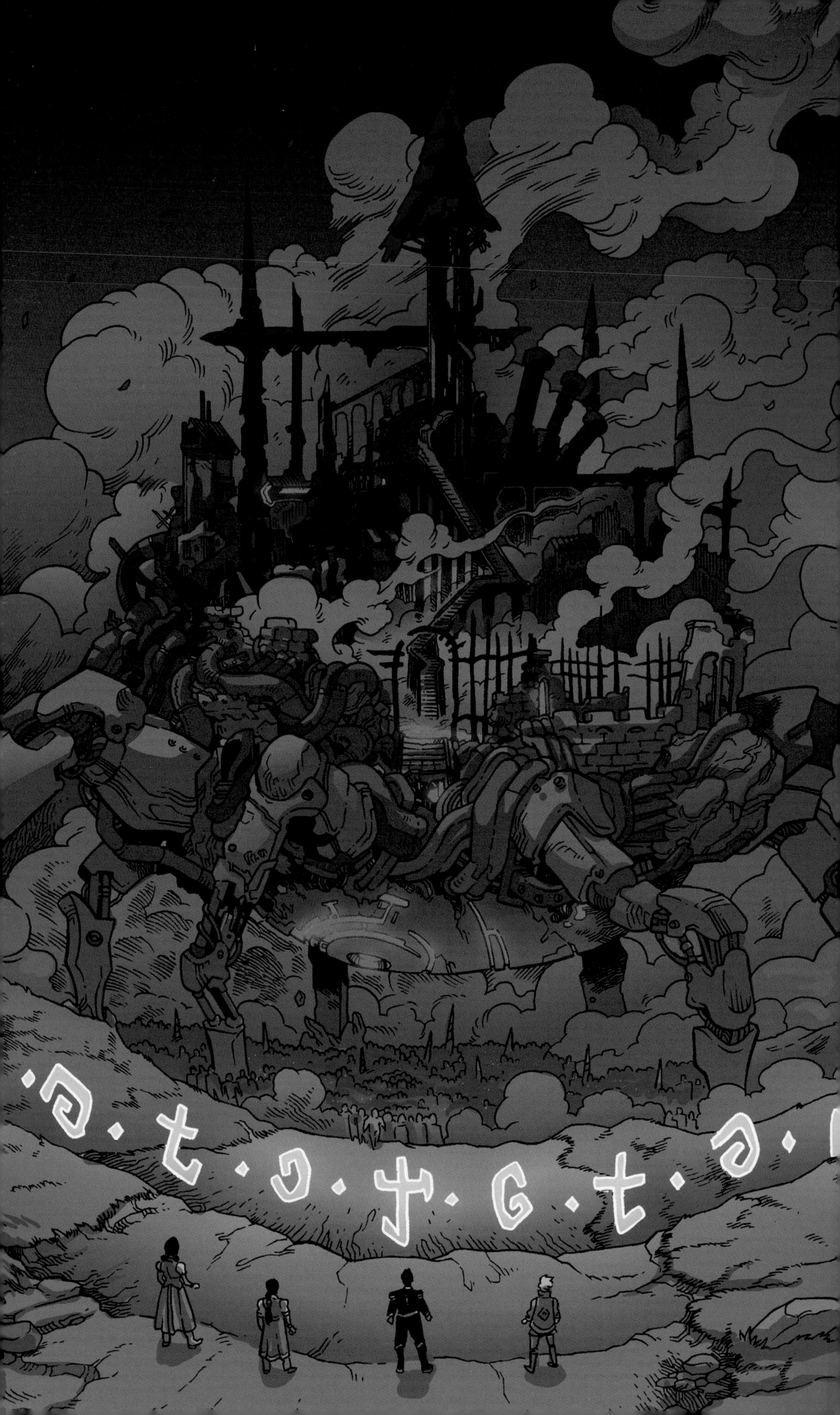

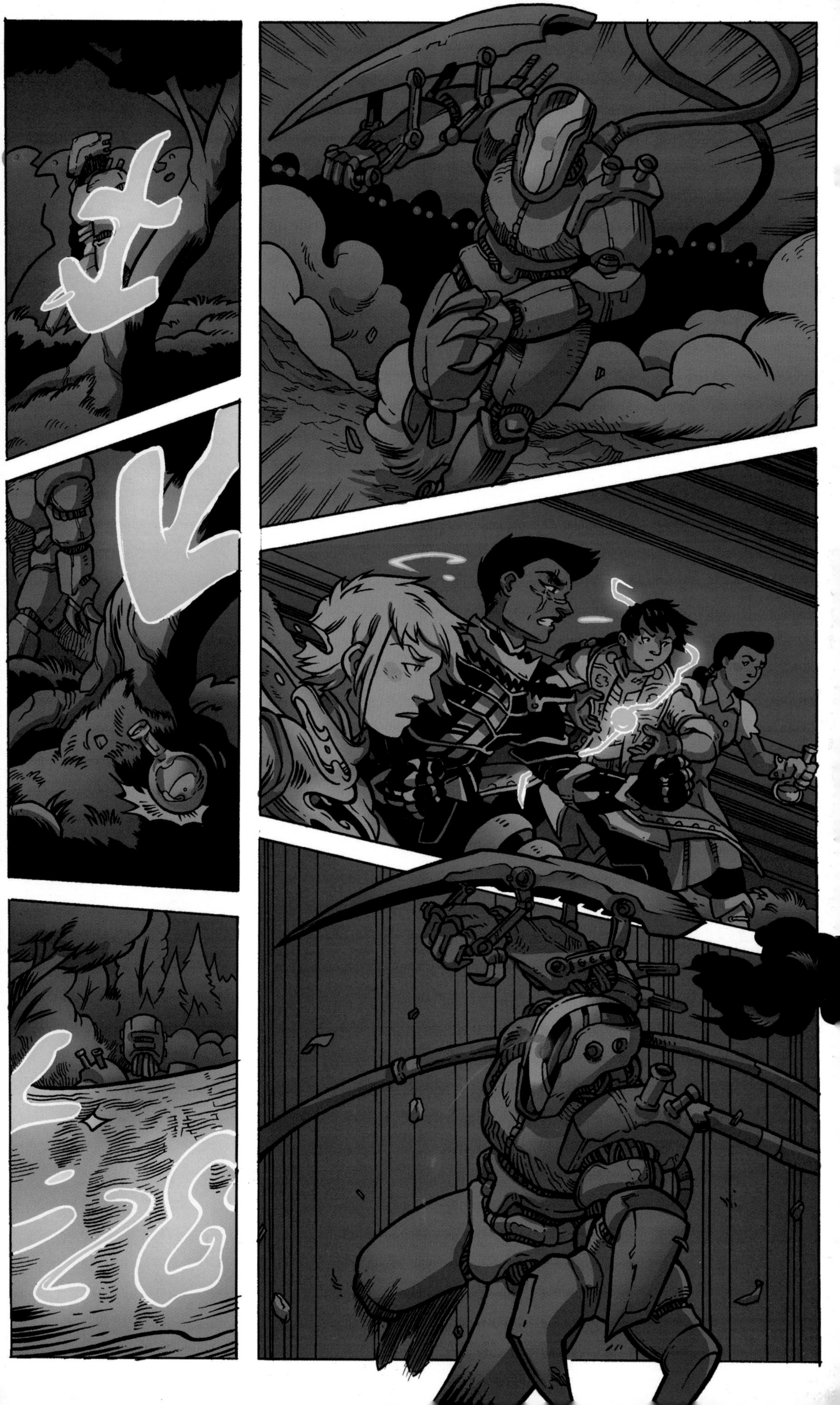

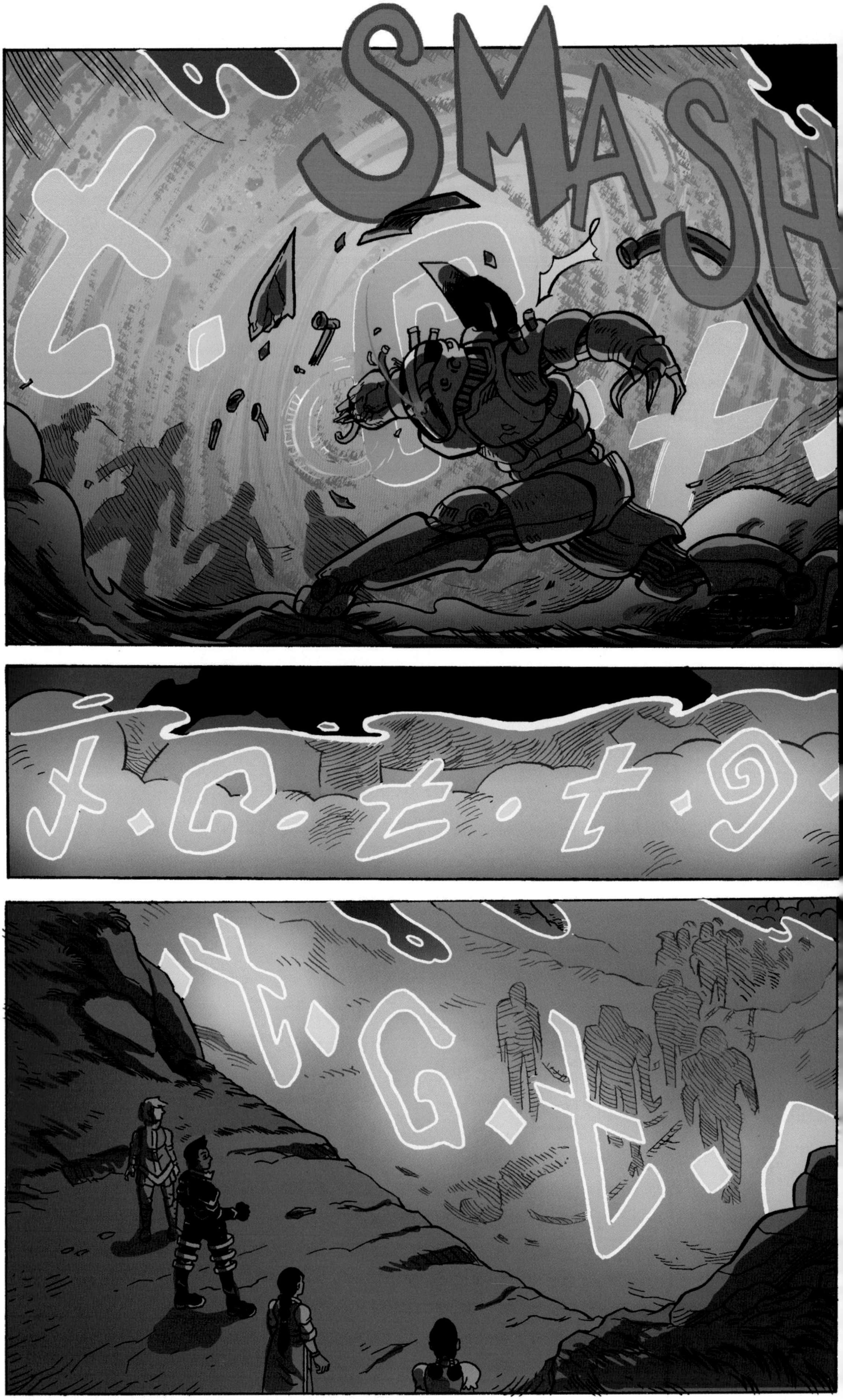
SMASH

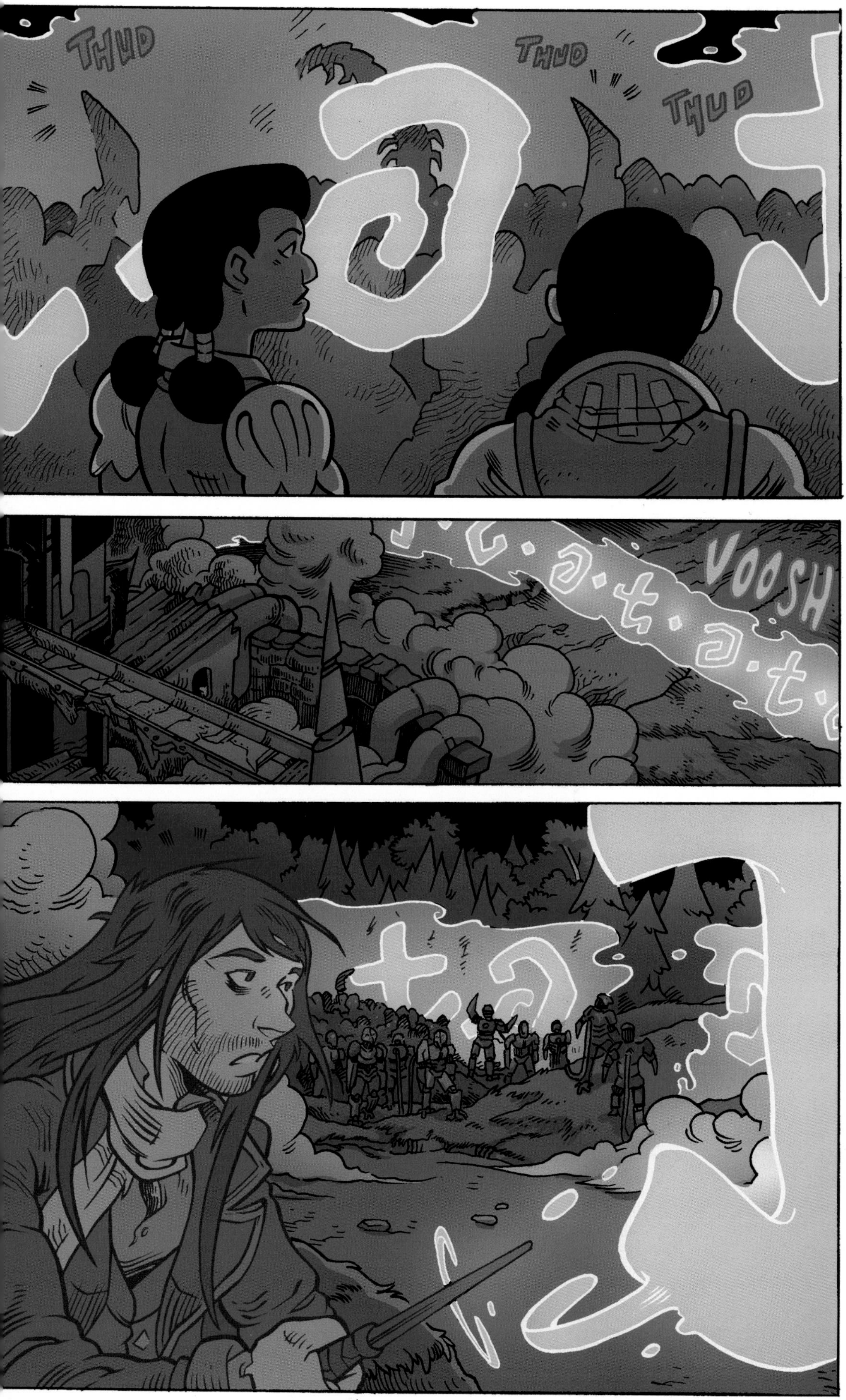
THUD
THUD
THUD
VOOSH

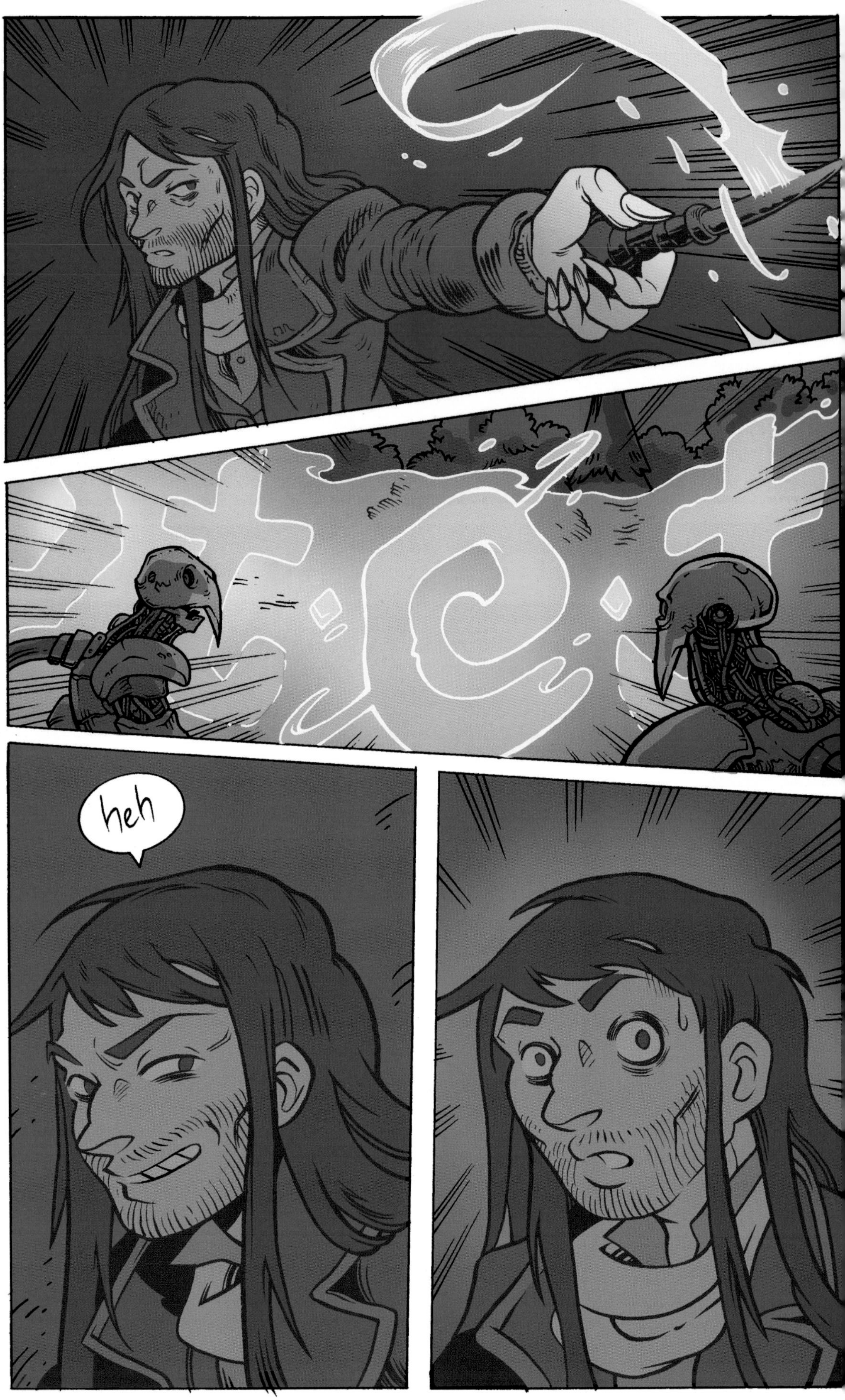
heh

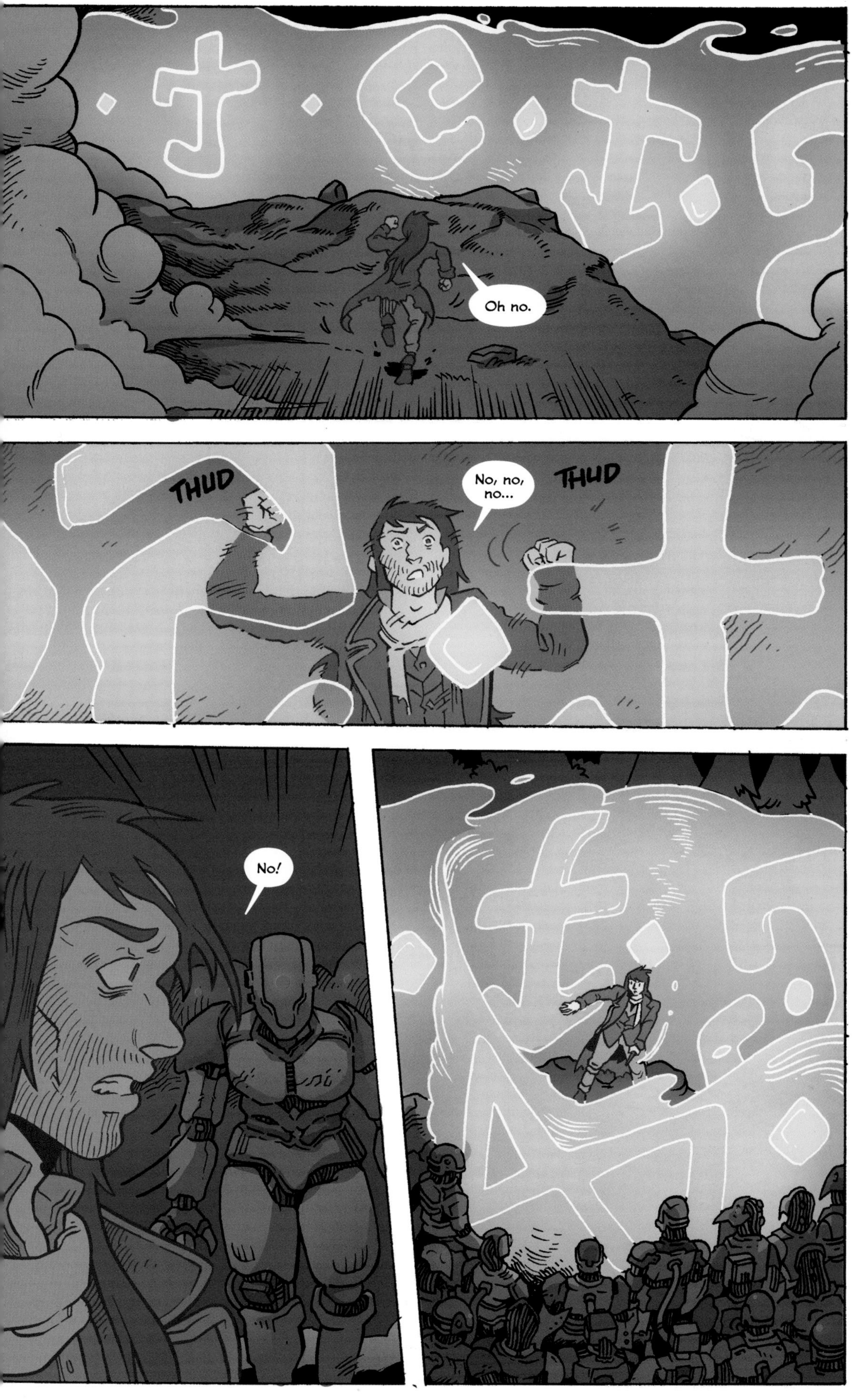
Oh no.
THUD
No, no, no...
THUD
No!

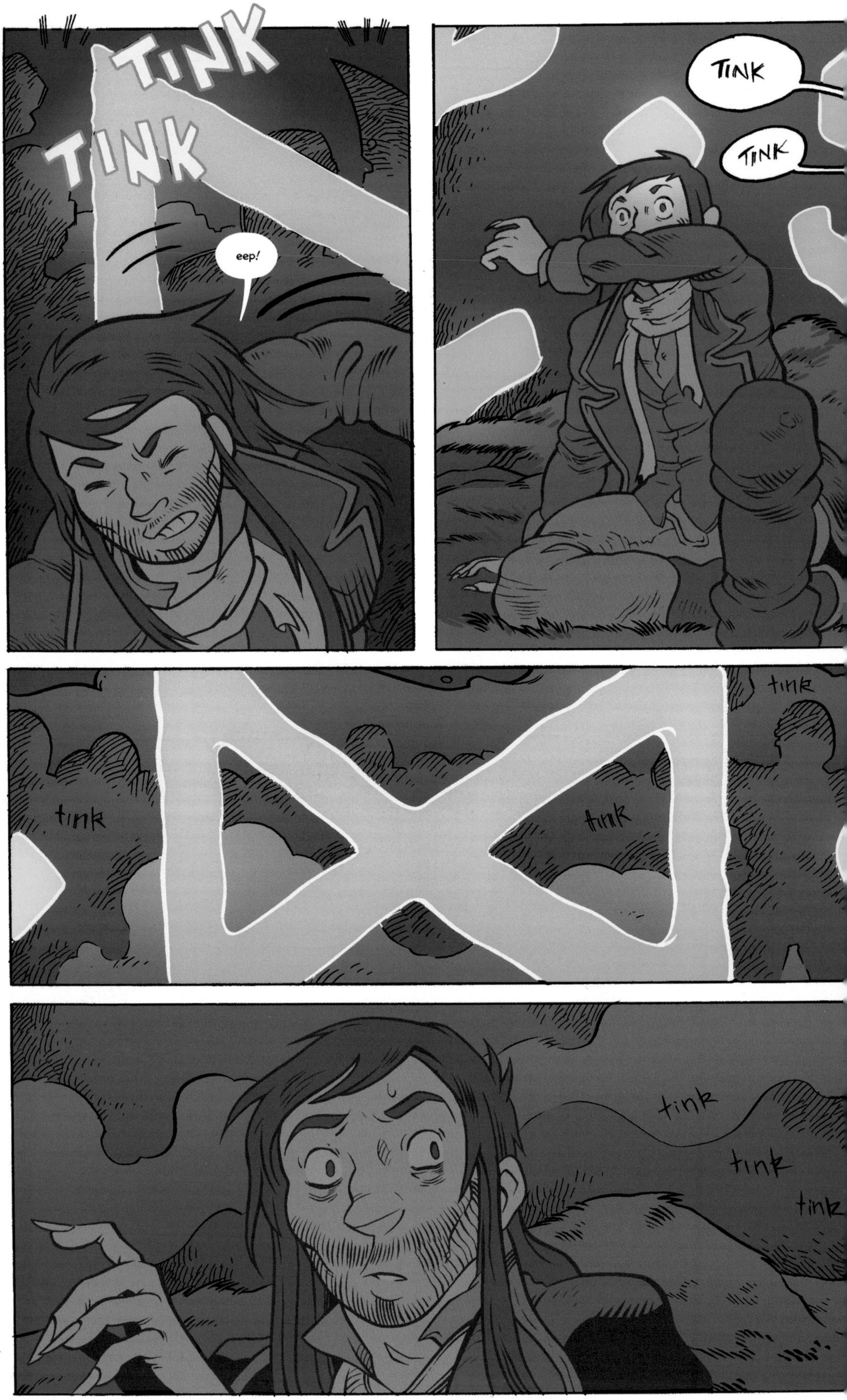
TINK
TINK
eep!
TINK
TINK
tink
tink
tink
tink
tink
tink

That's right, I'm invisible!

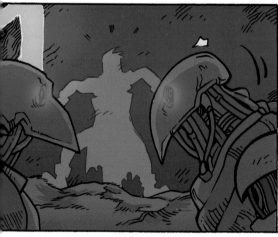

...

Stupid.

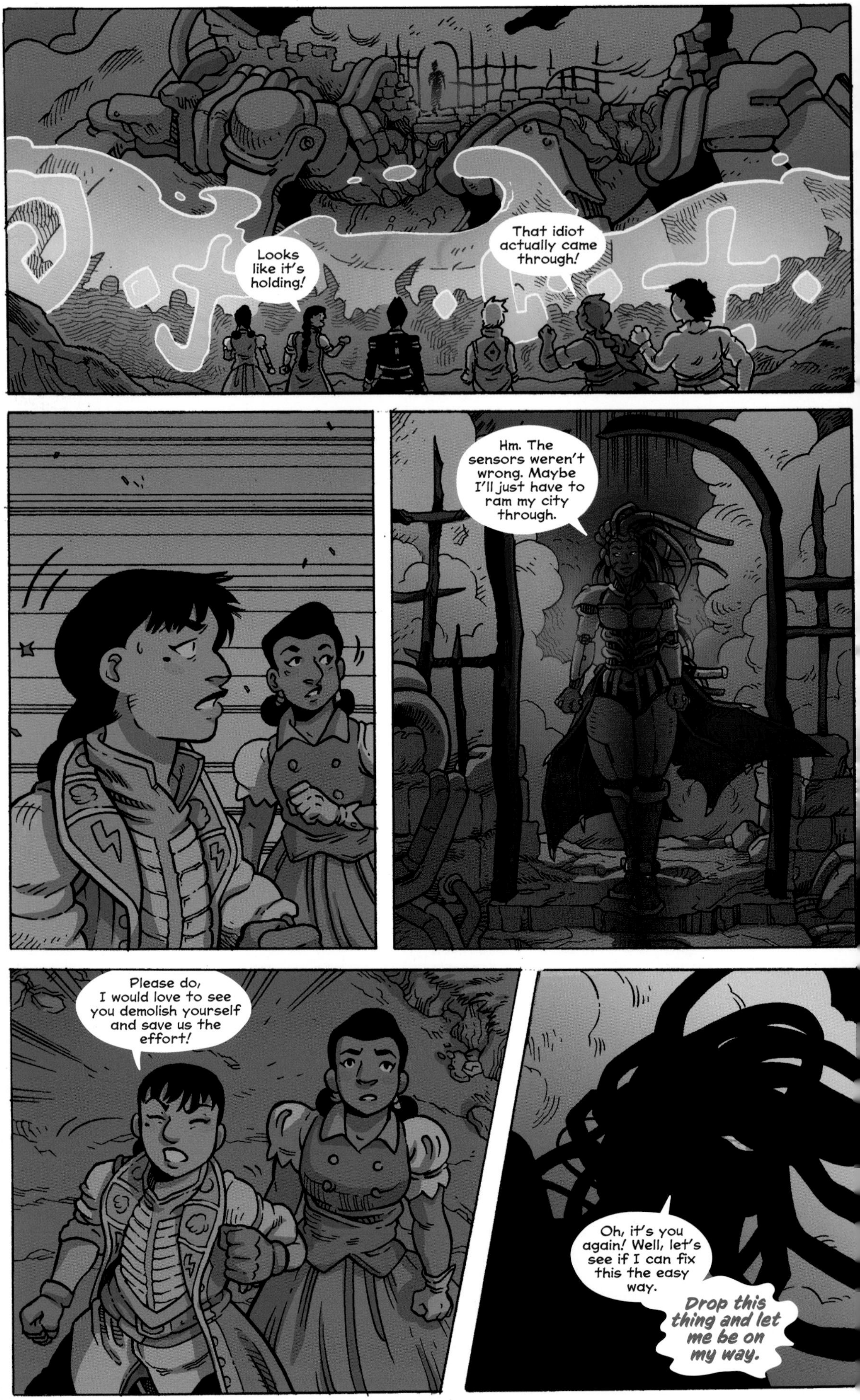
Looks like it's holding!
That idiot actually came through!
Hm. The sensors weren't wrong. Maybe I'll just have to ram my city through.
Please do, I would love to see you demolish yourself and save us the effort!
Oh, it's you again! Well, let's see if I can fix this the easy way.
Drop this thing and let me be on my way.

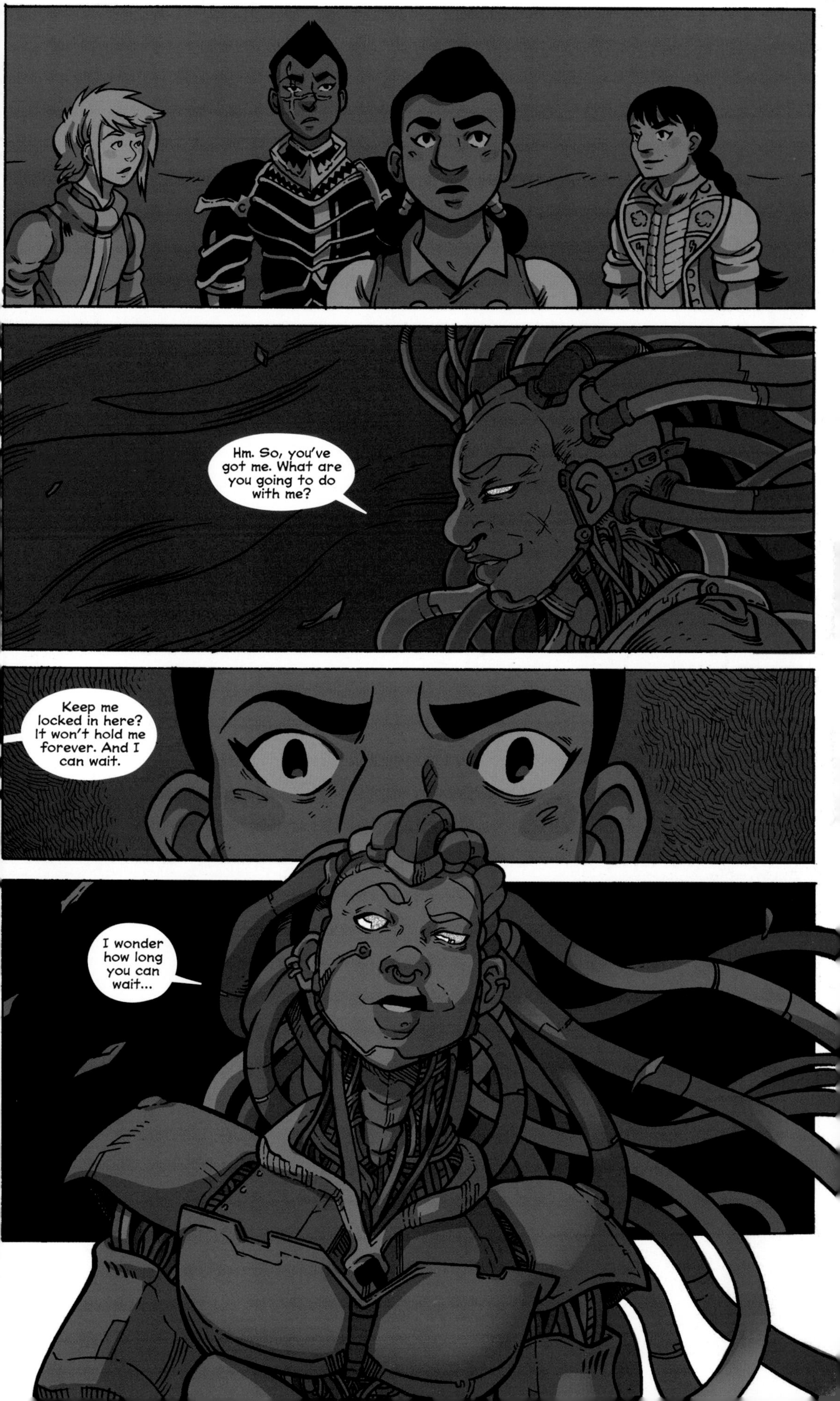
Hm. So, you've got me. What are you going to do with me?
Keep me locked in here? It won't hold me forever. And I can wait.
I wonder how long you can wait...

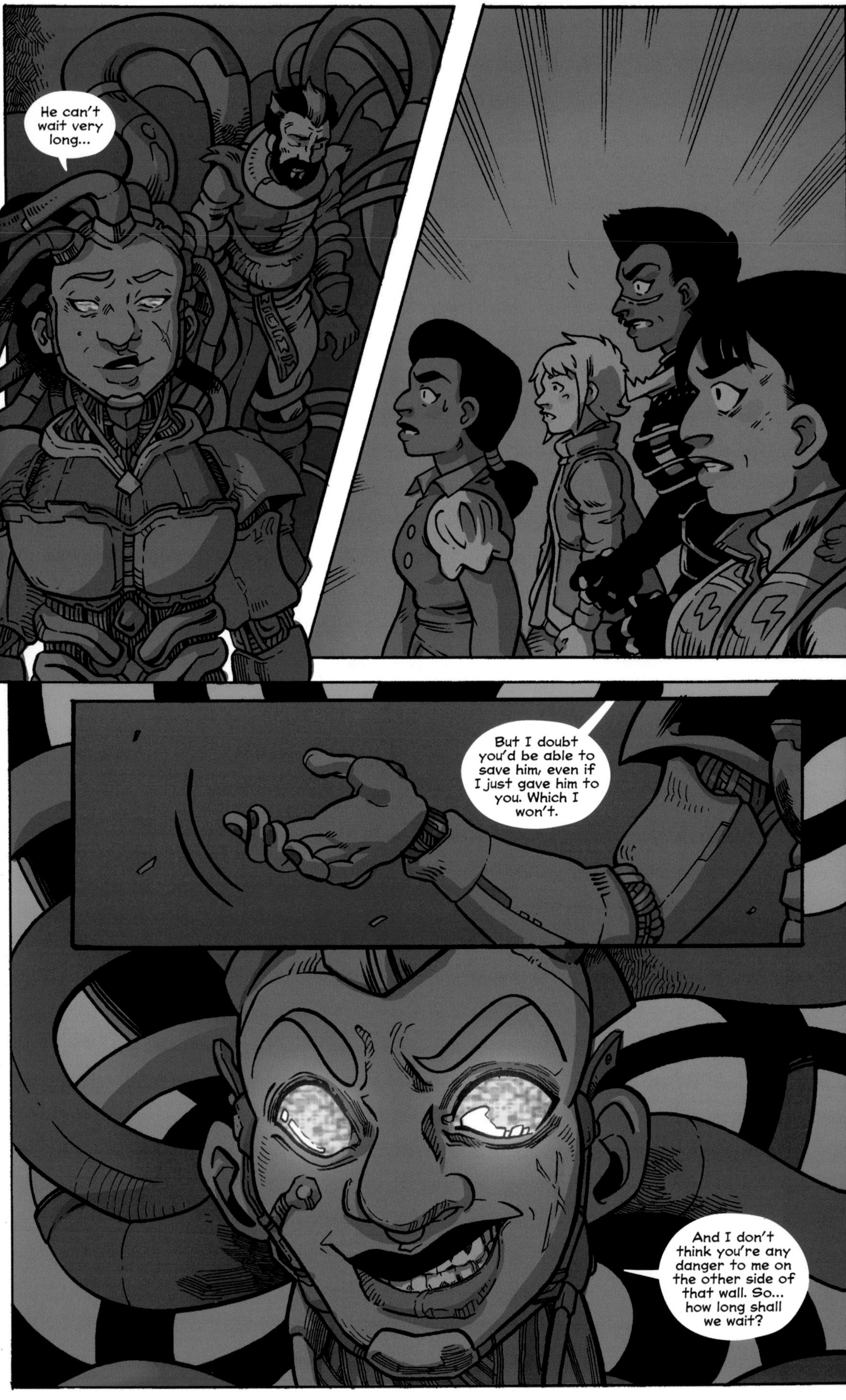
He can't wait very long...
But I doubt you'd be able to save him, even if I just gave him to you. Which I won't.
And I don't think you're any danger to me on the other side of that wall. So... how long shall we wait?

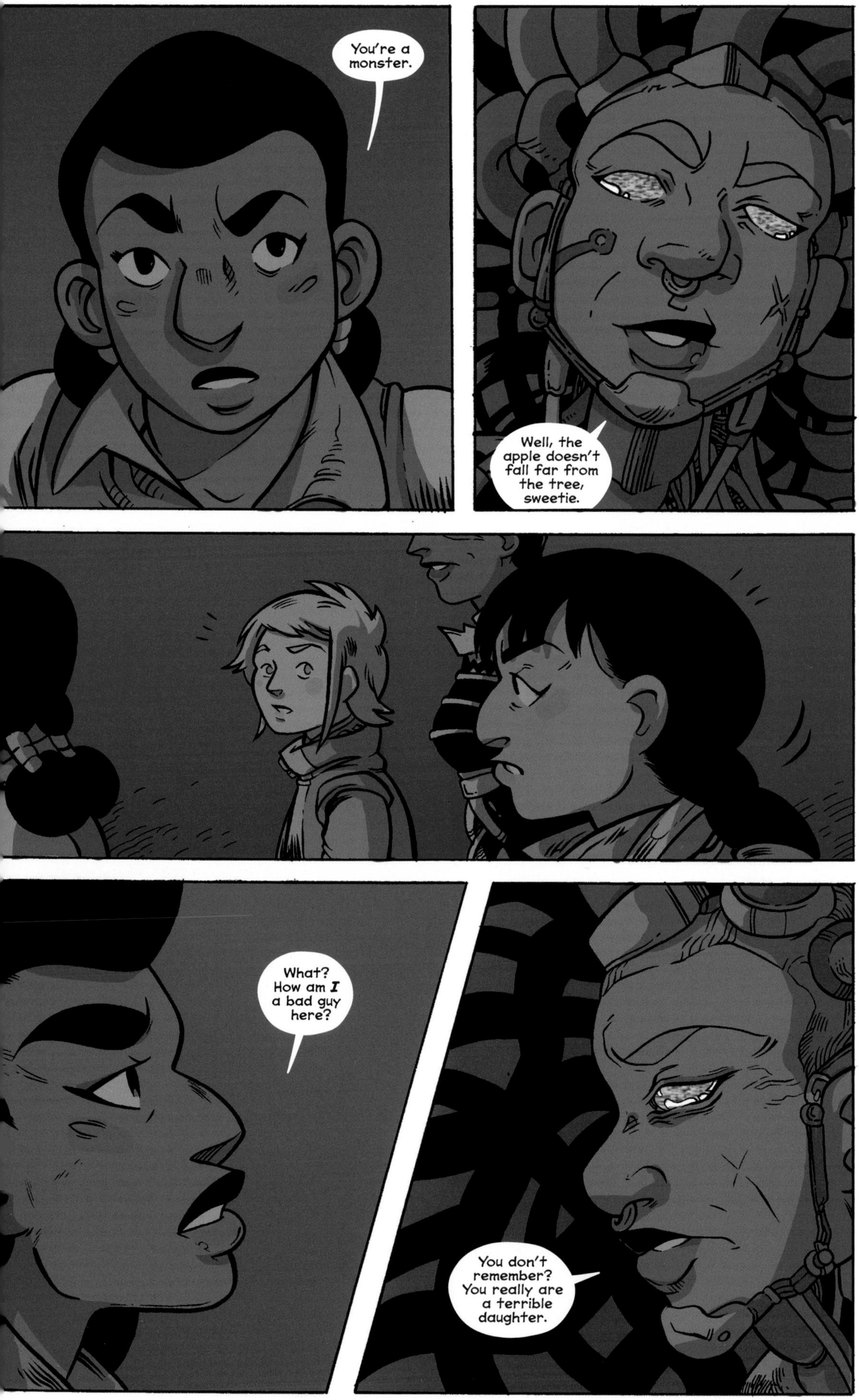
You're a monster.
Well, the apple doesn't fall far from the tree, sweetie.
What? How am *I* a bad guy here?
You don't remember? You really are a terrible daughter.

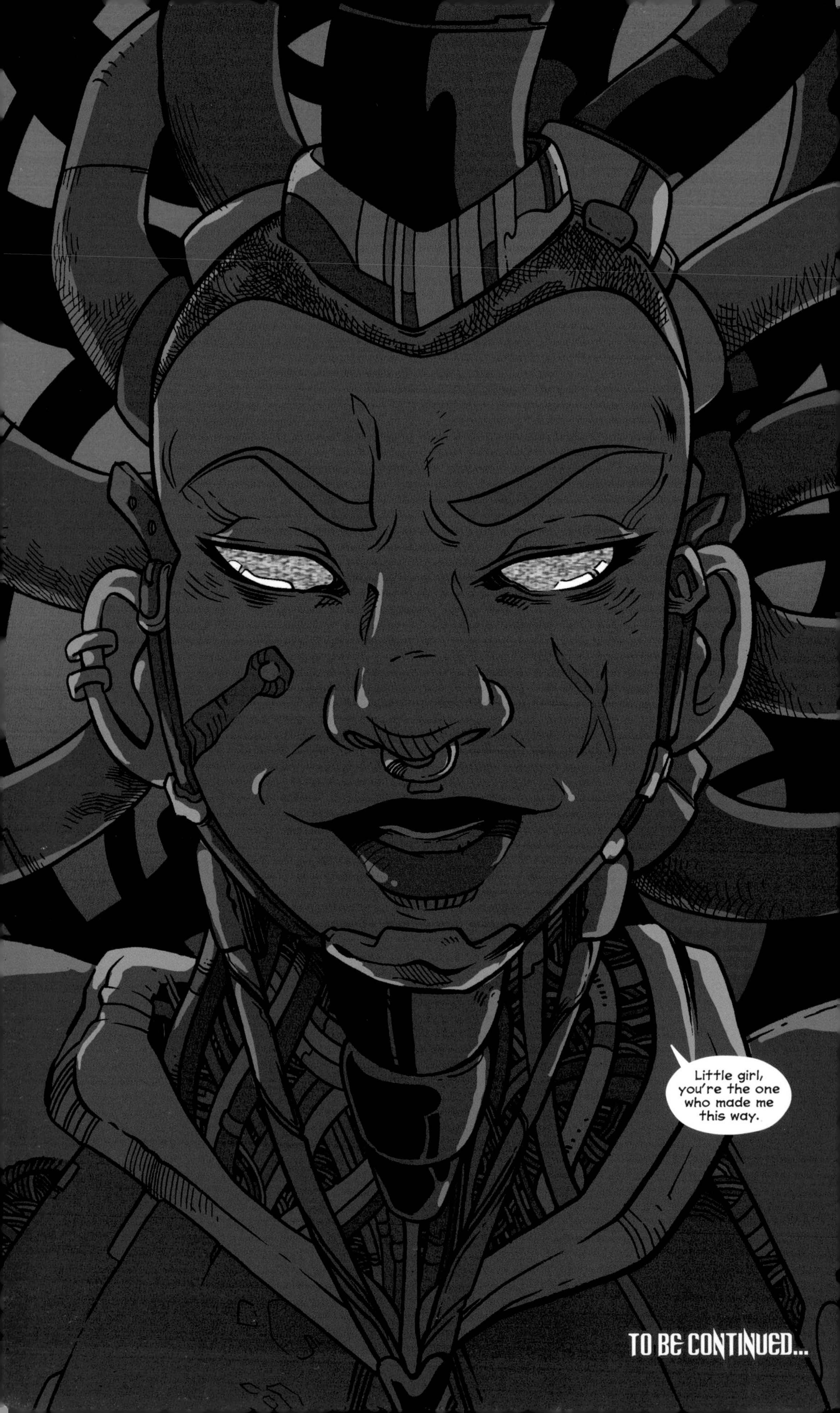
Little girl, you're the one who made me this way.
TO BE CONTINUED...

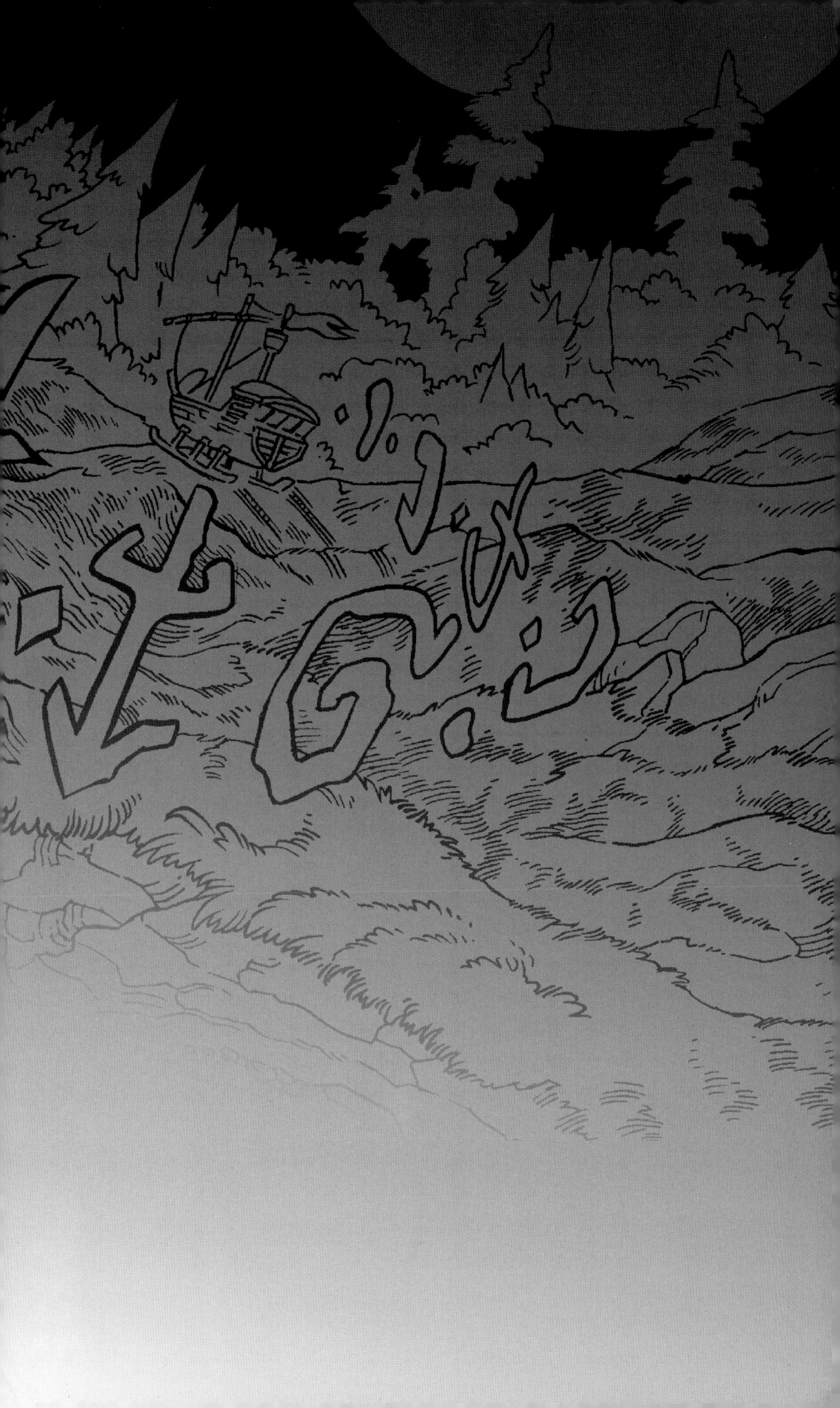

MK REED

is the author of the graphic novels *Americus*, *The Cute Girl Network*, *Palefire*, and *Science Comics: Dinosaurs*. She also writes and draws the web comic *About A Bull*. Her work has appeared in anthologies like *Papercutter*, *Chainmail Bikini*, *The Big Feminist But*, and the Swedish magazine *Galago*. *Americus* was the winner of NAIBA's 2012 Carla Cohen Free Speech Award, and was a 2011 American Booksellers for Children's New Voices title. MK lives in Portland, Oregon, with her very tall husband.

BRIAN "SMITTY" SMITH

is a former Marvel Comics editor, and the co-creator of the *New York Times* bestselling graphic novel *The Stuff of Legend*. He is the writer and artist of the all-ages comic The *Intrepid EscapeGoat*, and the illustrator of *The Adventures of Daniel Boom AKA Loud Boy* series of younger reader graphic novels. He is also the artist of *Madballs* from Roar Comics.

WYETH YATES

is a cartoonist living in Brooklyn, New York. He is the writer and artist of *Hard Luck*, *The Other Gang*, and more. If he gets lucky, he'll be drawing comics for the rest of his life. You can find more of Wyeth's work at www.wyethyates.com.

KENDRA WELLS

lives in Brooklyn, New York, and is an illustrator, colorist, podcaster, and level four half-orc fighter.